Praise for *Brothers and S.*

"From his experience surviving Sadam Hussein's regime and the US-led criminal war against the Iraqi people, to day-to-day humiliations as he negotiated his fractured self as an Iraqi-born teenager in post-9/11 Europe, Junis Sultan's painfully and brilliantly written memoir is a powerful and desperately needed denunciation of enduring orientalism, state delinquency, and war capitalism as much as it is a utopic project for a new humanity."

—Jaime A. Alves, freelance journalist, author of *The Anti-Black City: Police Terror and Black Urban Life in Brazil,* University of Minnesota Press

"Navigating the choppy waters of a mixed heritage background is never easy, but Junis Sultan surmounts his diverse Iraqi, German, Muslim, and Christian roots with a brave and powerful account of how solidarity and empathy can overcome what divides us."

—Robin Cohen, emeritus professor at University of Oxford and co-author, with Olivia Sheringham, of *Encountering Difference* (2016)

"A beautiful story which demonstrates that love and friendship may, and ultimately will, triumph over political propaganda and chauvinistic hatred."

—Fred Dallmayr, professor emeritus, University of Notre Dame

"Any migration is challenging, but the forced migration of refugees from war-torn societies is typically framed by sacrifice and suffering. The result is often one of failed lives. However, Junis Sultan, a child refugee from Iraq to Germany, tells a different story, involving fortitude, survival, and ultimately of personal success. *Brothers and Strangers* offers a counter narrative to racism, rejection, and fear of strangers that has been the typical reactions of receiving societies. By contrast, Sultan's cosmopolitan message of human solidarity has a compelling moral authority from which the citizens of host societies can take instruction and from which the dispossessed may take comfort and encouragement."

—Bryan S. Turner, Australian Catholic University and Potsdam University, Germany

"A deeply moving human story of migration and war, of racism and states, of love and loss, and of families and faith. Nobody, Edward Said reminded us, is only one thing. This beautifully told life story not only attends to the mixing but also shows how the identities that sustain us also pull us apart as societies and as individuals."

—David Roediger, University of Kansas, author of *How Race Survived US History*

"Deeply moving and emotionally honest, this insightful memoir captures the author's personal journey of adaptation to German society as an Iraqi immigrant. Drawing on his uniquely bicultural upbringing, it highlights his hopes, dreams, fears, struggles, trials, and triumphs—universal themes from the immigrant experience. Perceptively crafted, this inspiring story is a portrait of courage amidst despair, resilience amidst adversity, tolerance amidst prejudice, and our shared humanity amidst deep division and animosity."

—Van C. Tran, associate professor of sociology,
The Graduate Center of the City University of New York

"This book is a compelling humanization of a frequent object of study: research, reports, data, and statistics suddenly become one human individual—one with feelings, thoughts, reflections, and unique life experiences. Sultan reminds us that millions have a story like his."

—Elisa Costa-Villaverde, PhD, The University of Hull (UK), lecturer and researcher at the University of Las Palmas de Gran Canaria (Spain); associate editor of *Crossings: Journal of Migration and Culture* (Queen Mary University of London and Intellect Books, Bristol)

"Junis Sultan's memoir is a heartbreaking story of loss, violence, and the quest for identity. Yet, it leaves the reader with a sense of hope. This thoughtful and honest account of the consequences of migration policies, amongst others, on individual lives and families reminds us that we all have a certain responsibility in building a world in which everyone can prosper."

—Lena Hartz, *Routed Magazine*

"The son of an Iraqi father and a German mother who flee Iraq after the first Gulf War, author Junis Sultan adapts to a new environment, learns German as a second language, and begins to notice a climate of anti-immigrant sentiment that creates havoc in his family. This riveting memoir of growing up in both Iraq and Germany depicts a life that has become a universal construct in today's world: that of immigrants or exiles, or people on the move adapting to distant lands and new languages. Mr. Sultan reinvents his life through a solid education but also uncovers conflicts that threaten his family's stability. His own mother develops anti-Muslim attitudes, even though she's married to a Muslim man, one of the more dramatic and heartbreaking developments in the narrative. Mr. Sultan's memoir evokes both the personal triumphs and the struggles of a family caught up in the maelstrom of a world of borders and tense interactions."

—Guillermo Reyes, author of *Madre and I: A Memoir of Our Immigrant Lives*

# BROTHERS
## AND STRANGERS
### A GERMAN-IRAQI MEMOIR

## JUNIS SULTAN

Brandylane
Publishers, Inc.
*Publishing books since 1985*

*Some names, places, and identifying details have been changed
to protect the privacy of individuals.*

ISBN: 978-1-951565-15-2
LCCN: 2021915171

*Designed by Michael Hardison*
*Production managed by Grace Ball*

Printed in the United States of America

Published by
Brandylane Publishers, Inc.
5 S. 1st Street
Richmond, Virginia 23219

Brandylane
Publishers, Inc.
*Publishing books since 1985*

brandylanepublishers.com

*To the faithful who believe unshakably that
we can overcome social division and that we are
better off when we are strongly connected.*

*To the diligent who are eager to fight non-violently against
prejudices, fear of "the others," and discrimination.*

*And last but not least, to all those who struggle to find a place in a
globalized world that seems more demanding. My dear hope is
that this book inspires you to reach out to your neighbors,
regardless of where they come from, and grow stronger together.*

# TABLE OF CONTENTS

## Part IV

## Part V

## Part VI

## Part VII

# PROLOGUE

*And then came the bloody bastard*

Growing up, I often wondered whether my skin looked brown or white. My hair is certainly black, and my eyes are brown. Many Westerners I met probably thought *Middle East* as soon as they laid eyes on me or heard my name—Junis Sultan. "Where are you *originally* from?" I was asked innumerable times. Some were visibly surprised that I spoke their language accent-free. Middle Easterners, however, were oftentimes disappointed that I did not speak Arabic fluently. "Why did your parents not teach you?" For a number of reasons, it was usually impossible for people to label me—and vice versa.

My story is one of unfavorable coincidence and unending re-invention. In the summer of 1991, after surviving the Gulf War, my family fled from Iraq to Germany. I was four years old at the time. One of my early memories is of sitting with my father in our run-down living room and watching the news. He raised his finger and shouted, "The West imposed those bloody sanctions on Iraq, not Saddam.[1]" Intimidated by his anger, I quietly asked him

---

1  Saddam Hussein (Apr. 28, 1937–Dec. 30, 2006): fifth President of Iraq, served from July 16, 1979 to Apr. 9, 2003, sentenced to death after being convicted for crimes against humanity

what he meant. He said, "The West is Europe, North America, and Australia. They've killed millions, and now they are killing us!" His warning scared me. However, when I started attending kindergarten in 1992, I soon realized that his warning had proved wrong. In fact, we would live together happily and in peace with many Westerners for many years.

Since those early days, I've strived to live in harmony with everyone around me, including Middle Easterners *and* Westerners. Even though I've repeatedly failed, I've kept trying to balance both our common need to bond and common need for freedom. During puberty, I was particularly concerned with religious freedom. The divisiveness I experienced, especially in the post 9/11 years, always seemed human-imposed, harmful to our relationships, and therefore self-destructive and wrong. Growing up in Germany, I frequently pondered the purpose of our existence. Were we not all precious social individuals, connected and meant to support each other while realizing our personal dreams?

Despite my strong belief in the need for humans to bond, I often doubted our connectedness when meeting other people. A number of Westerners confronted me with negative stereotypes: "Does your mother wear a hijab or a burka?" "Were your sisters' marriages arranged?" "Do you hate Jews, the United States . . . ?" None of it applied to me. Quite the opposite is true: My mother is Christian, and she has had difficulties accepting my different religion. A number of Middle Easterners have been disappointed by me as well, saying, "Don't drink! Don't wear shorts! Don't . . . ! It's *haram.*[2]"

---

2  Arabic term: "forbidden" or "proscribed" by Islamic law

Interactions like these often left me feeling strange, disconnected, and challenged. How could I ease and strengthen our relationship? Was I overreacting? Were they looking for common ground?

The thousands-of-years-old stories of my name have shaped my complex identity. In 1993, during my first school year, my father told me that Junis derives from Yunus, "a prophet in the Quran who strongly believed in God's rules." In a Catholic religion class, I learned that the Hebrew Bible and the New Testament first told the story of Yunus under the name of Jonah. "Jonah means dove in Hebrew, and a dove is a symbol of peace," my teacher said before she read us his story. "Jonah was ordered by God to go to Nineveh and prophesy against the Ninevites' great wickedness. Afraid, however, that God would simply forgive the sinners, he boarded a ship that sailed in the opposite direction; a serious mistake! God punished him for his disobedience with a heavy storm at sea, and when the sailors found Jonah responsible, they threw him overboard. Jonah was then swallowed by a whale. Inside the belly of the whale, he repented, thanked God for his mercy, and committed himself to God's will, so the whale eventually spewed him out." I looked at my teacher with large eyes. While I had no idea what my life would bring and how I would react—at times quite like an unforgiving, disobedient runaway—I could relate to Jonah's story. I, too, wanted to have a relationship with God and be uplifted when I fell.

My first name mostly caused insecurities among new people. Many Germans called me Jonas after I had introduced myself. Sometimes, when I spelled out J–U–N–I–S, I wondered if my pronunciation was unclear, or whether they ignored my real name out of convenience, or even disrespect. Some asked me to spell it out again, and then wanted to know where the name came from. The problem started when I was naturalized in 1991. "Younes is its international notation, but would complicate matters for Germans. They're not used to Y, which is only used in a few words in German," a public official told my mother. My first name was thus Germanized. I was too young to notice the forced assimilation. Some Middle Easterners did, however. "So are you a *real* Arab?" they asked me after reading my name. "My mother is German, my father Iraqi," I usually told them before I explained how my name was Germanized—which often led to an awkward silence. Growing up, I soon began to understand how much my name defined me.

My last name, Sultan, sometimes amused people, reminding many of a carnival song: "The caravan is moving, the sultan is thirsty . . ." Sometimes, however, it raised fear or false idolization. The word sultan originally meant "strength" in Arabic. Over time, it also became a title for leaders who claimed independence from any higher ruler. According to Wikipedia, one of the most famous sultans, Mehmed II, conquered Constantinople and ended the one-thousand-year-old Byzantine Empire in 1453. I assume his destructive power intimidated the West, which—as Professor Edward Said[3] would say—has continuously strived to invent itself as good in direct contrast to the imagined evil of the Orient. Strangely, my father ascribed the exact opposite value to the Middle East. As if

---

3  Edward Wadie Said (Nov. 1, 1935–Sept. 25, 2003): professor of literature, public intellectual, and founder of the academic field of postcolonial studies

Mehmed II were better than any other murderer, and as if killing four thousand non-Muslims in 1453 was good. I always struggled to understand why some people devalued or even demonized those with different cultural backgrounds while idealizing their own people. Were we not all the same: just people, more or less flawed, and yet all worthy of love?

In my school days in Germany between 1993 and 2006, I mostly learned about the merits of the West. We investigated the European Enlightenment of the seventeenth and eighteenth centuries. Kant's[4] "categorical imperative"—to always act in such a way that one would be willing for his actions to become general law—seemed to me like a precious idea that could bring peace among people. We read the classics of the German literary periods; the eighteenth century Storm and Stress period was my favorite since it allowed the free expression of strong emotions. I excitedly examined the revolutions for freedom and unity: 1776 in America, 1789 in France, and 1848 in Germany.

Above all, I embraced the 1948 Universal Declaration of Human Rights (UDHR), the first document I read at school that was drafted by an international committee with the aim of promoting peace for all people—a dream I wished everybody shared. While our teachers claimed that the unprecedented horrors of World War II led to the UDHR, I learned in 2009 in a rare seminar on "post-colonialism" at Goethe University that Nazi Germany was not a short-term mistake, which killed more than seventy million

---

4   Immanuel Kant (Apr. 22, 1724–Feb. 12, 1804): German philosopher and central figure in modern philosophy, known for his book *Groundwork of the Metaphysics of Morals*

people around the globe, but rather a direct result of the propagan-distic and bloody history of the West. Like Hannah Arendt[5] said, mainstream European nationalism and colonialism blended with post-enlightenment racial theories that proclaimed the natural su-periority of the "white race," paving the way for the pseudo-legit-imized enslavement and killing of non-white and non-Christian people around the globe for almost two centuries before Hitler. Our seminar discussions also revealed the subtle, allegedly colorblind and areligious ways in which millions of non-white and non-Chris-tian people have been killed far beyond the borders of the West since 1945, through economic exploitation, starvation, or military adven-tures that brought chaos, destruction, and even civil war. Still, one burning question remained: how could we stop these processes of dehumanization and these crimes against humanity?

I was eager to find out. After I completed my basic studies at Goethe University, Frankfurt, I studied political science at California State University, Fullerton, from 2010 to 2011. During my politi-cal philosophy course, I learned about Greek, Hebrew, Roman, and Christian societies, which my senior professor called "the founda-tional stories of the West." In particular, I enjoyed our recurring discussions about whether it was possible to establish truths about ethics—right individual conduct—and politics—right collective life. I, like a couple of my fellow students, believed we could.

At the end of the semester, my professor suggested that modern, twenty-first century global liberalism represented the synthesis of

---

5 Johanna "Hannah" Arendt (Oct. 14, 1906–Dec. 4, 1975): German-born Jewish American political theorist

all stories of the West. Skeptical of his Eurocentric perspective, I asked him about the role of the rest of the world. He pondered for a second before he raised his head and said with a raised eyebrow, "Well, there was Mesopotamia, Egypt, Persia, and then came the bloody bastard Mohammed who spread Islam by the sword." Sitting in the last row, I looked at him in disbelief. Did he just really say that? As if the stories of the West were free of bloodshed. I remained silent and waited to hear more about his black-and-white worldview; but he stopped himself. "Oh, shit, is she here? The one with the scarf?" he asked, looking around.

Her name was Manar, which means "guiding light" in Arabic. She was not in class that day, but I was—embodying a vibrant blend of Judeo-Christian-Muslim, German, Arabic, and Ottoman traditions. That day, like so many times before, I wondered: How could we overcome those hostile attitudes against "the others"? How could we connect with one another and appreciate each other? How could we create more happiness and peace among each other and within ourselves?

# PART I

# MOSUL

*August 1986–January 1991*

*Freestyle, chest-high*

*Sunday, August 31, 1986, Around Noon*

A scorching heat penetrated the hospital room from the outside and besieged my parents and me. The air conditioner, necessary during the summer in Iraq, had been sent out for repair. It left a gaping hole in the outside wall of our room. Off and on, a hammering noise broke through the side wall; the hospital was under renovation, which was a rather unusual government measure at the time since the sixth year of the war with Iran had devoured many of our developing country's precious resources. Despite the nationwide shortages of materials, my family was lucky: We belonged to the rich back then. We hardly missed any material things.

My father bent over my mother to kiss her sweaty forehead. She was lying on a metal bed, holding me in her arms. She had lost a lot of blood during the delivery.

Her already light skin was almost as pale as the white strands scattered through her dark, shoulder-length hair. She was forty-two years old and had already lived more than twenty-three years in Iraq when I was born.

"We should give him a name that's easy to pronounce for people in Germany," she said. My father nodded in understanding. He gently kissed my cheek before he walked to the window.

"Look, one can see Nabi Yunus from here!" He pointed outside, looking at the white mosque on the hill of the Nineveh ruins where the Prophet Jonah is believed to be buried. An octagonal minaret ascended into the light-blue sky. From her bed, my mother could see its white spire. She had visited the ancient mosque before and was still impressed by its beauty. "Why don't we call him Younes?" he said. My mother looked over him, thinking over his proposal. My father wore no moustache, which was unusual for Iraqi men. His shirt was damp; the sweat was gleaming on his brown, smooth skin. He was forty-seven years old but looked younger. Finally, she turned to me, smiling. She liked the name.

"From this day on, you are Younes," she said.

Outside, direct sunbeams seared almost every blade of grass, except for those nearest the Tigris River. The turquoise water, calm and shallow, could almost be crossed by foot in some places. From October to May, however, it would swell to two hundred yards across and run majestically through metropolitan space, which was inhabited by more than six hundred thousand people in 1986.

My father's gaze lingered on the riverside miracles. Green palm leaves waved in a breeze. Grapes and pomegranates thrived nearby, as well as apples, pears, figs, and watermelons. Tomatoes, eggplants, okra pods, and cucumbers flourished at the water's edge, where soft-shell turtles jumped into the water from time to time while swarms of black-and-white lapwings perched on tall poplars, calling, full of life.

The Tigris was Mosul's source of life. As a young boy, my father spent many hours playing with his friends from Shifa—a poor district of Mosul—in the Tigris, where black river buffaloes often joined them to cool off, their farmers asleep on deck chairs.

Sometimes, my father and his friends climbed the buffaloes' backs to rest in the water, but the buffaloes would usually resist, occupied with eating aquatic plants, and letting loose their feces in the water. Nature served everyone, including the young boys. When he and his friends were hungry, they would pick a watermelon, eat it, and jump back into the water.

Despite, or maybe because of his simple beginnings, my father reached for the stars from early on in his life. He was born on April 12, 1939. From 1947 to 1956, he attended public school in Mosul. During that time, his family of eight shared a shell of a 250-square-foot studio bungalow. The tiny place barely satisfied their basic needs: food, water, shelter, sleep, and sex. Still, he was privileged in contrast to the rest of the family and given a table for his studies at home. This privilege was a consequence of his parents' will to give the youngest of their six children the chance to study and maybe even see the world one day. In the daytime, his oldest sister helped him prepare for exams while the other family members ran the family bakery. His mother supervised production; his father was responsible for sales. At that time, around fourteen thousand soldiers were stationed in Mosul, and since his father, a World War I veteran, knew some of them, most of their bread was sold to the military base. The family's continuous teamwork eventually paid off: in spring 1956, the family received the joyful news that my father's excellent final grades qualified him for a study abroad scholarship.

My father studied mechanical engineering at the University of Wales from 1957 to 1962. In the winter of 1960, he went to a dance in the Student Union, a plain building with wooden chairs lining a gray wall. He was waiting for a soda at the bar when Monika, a fellow student, approached him with her new friend. While Monika introduced him to the young lady, who had come from Germany as an au pair to improve her English, someone dropped a coin in the jukebox. Shortly, romantic strings filled the room with Maurice Chevalier's "Gigi.[6]" A young man popped up and led Monika to the dance floor, where dozens of couples already danced in a close embrace. Though he was at first quiet and hesitant, my father soon dared to ask the new young lady—who would later become my mother—if she liked to dance. Barely seventeen years old, she blushed but eventually allowed herself to say *yes*. Both felt strongly attracted to each other's courteous and friendly behavior; it made them feel safe although they did not know each other. Smiling, they entered the dance floor holding hands—the beginning of a lifelong bond.

In the next weeks, they met a couple more times on campus and had coffee and long conversations. One day, my father—Adil—wrote an article for the university newspaper about a campus exhibition. He had taken a picture of my mother—Gabriela—and put it on the title page. When she thanked him the next day, half embarrassed and half delighted, he invited her to his apartment for dinner. She accepted the invitation to what would be a casual and pleasant evening together. Soon, she began to visit him more frequently. They would cook together, listen to music, and twist and dance together to their favorite songs. Since she knew how much

---

6  Title song of the 1958 American musical-romance film *Gigi*, which portrayed how love overcomes cynicism

he had to study, she often stayed until the late evening to help him with housework. They enjoyed their get-togethers, and their bond grew stronger every time they met.

In the summer of 1961, Gabriela had to go back to Germany to graduate from high school. At their final meeting at the Cardiff Central railway station, my parents hugged each other and tears began to roll down their cheeks. Suddenly, they felt they were in love, even if they were too conservative and too young to comment on it. Adil's mother used to tell him that having a girlfriend without getting married was a sin, and he listened to her. Gabriela, a cat lover and hobby soccer player, had no experience at all in romantic relationships. Despite everything, both sensed that their separation would be too painful to bear. But what could they do about it?

While Adil stayed in England to continue his studies, he and Gabriela told each other in many letters about their sore unhappiness. "We can't let more days pass by and be separated. We need to find a way to come together again," they agreed. The distance and time between them, however, would only increase. In spring 1962, after he had graduated with a Bachelor of Science degree with honors, Adil returned to Mosul to attend the obligatory twelfth-month military academy. Their love was asking for bold action.

On Tuesday, July 30, 1963, Gabriela made a life-changing decision against the wishes of her parents, who were skeptical about the chances of an intercultural marriage with an Iraqi. This type of union was extremely uncommon then. While the family vacationed in Yugoslavia, Gabriela took a train to Frankfurt, where she boarded a propeller-driven plane that flew 2,700 miles southeast to Baghdad. By late evening, Adil received a telegram from an Iraqi Airways pilot named Stanley. "We've got a young German woman who is asking for you. She can stay the night at our place. Please, pick her up tomorrow."

The very next day at dawn, Adil drove 250 miles south. They met at the airport and hugged each other with tears of joy. The first night, they stayed at his brother Nuri's place in central Baghdad.

On the morning of Thursday, August 1, 1963, they took a bus to the registrar's office in casual clothes to swear their love to a public official, who declared them husband and wife.

Still, it would take some years until things worked out for them. After their civil marriage, Adil and Gabriela drove to Mosul to meet the rest of the family in their new home, which Adil had built with his first salaries. They were welcomed with words and kisses, and although Adil translated everything into English, Gabriela felt quite insecure. She did not know much about the Iraqi culture. She didn't know what to expect from others or how to behave. She wondered if she would be accepted.

Shortly after tea, her uncertainty turned into a personal trauma. Since it quickly got around that "a woman from Europe had joined the family," dozens of relatives came over to see her. Many females looked over her from head to toe. "Why did you pick a European? We have many good women waiting for you here," they told Adil. He did not translate their words to spare Gabriela, but the harm had already been done. She understood their jealous looks and mocking laughter. Adil was trapped in a dilemma. If he had criticized his relatives on this matter or turned his back on them, it would have been considered a betrayal to his people. But exposing his new wife to further humiliation would have been at least as wrong. Not knowing what to do, he stopped the first meeting with his family and led Gabriela to her room upstairs, where she broke down in tears of deep sorrow. She felt betrayed by her own husband, the man she loved, the man for whom she left her family, her friends, her homeland. She also felt completely helpless: she did not have anyone who would defend her, and she could not even protect herself since she did not speak Arabic. How could she cope with the hostilities against her?

In the following weeks, Gabriela spent many hours crying in her room, lying on her bed underneath a running ceiling fan, feeling lonely, being eaten by mosquitoes, and sweating in the face of a heat she had never known before, well above thirty degrees Celsius. Adil, on the other hand, was working long hours in an air conditioning company every day except Friday, the weekly holiday. Gabriela desperately needed at least one person to unconditionally support her, and that would, despite initial personal shortcomings, finally be Adil. He soon managed to create more space, privacy, and safety for his new marriage and his prospective family.

My parents' relationship improved after half a year when Adil started a new job in the field of power generation. Since he earned more money, they could afford to move out and rent their own house. Gabriela started learning Arabic and soon connected with their new neighbors, who were young, open, curious, and friendly. In 1966, Manal, their first child, was born; in 1969 came, Malik, their second child, whose premature death due to a clinically unclear disease in 1977 would forever be too painful for my parents to talk about.

While their new family grew bigger, Adil's professional career developed in unimagined dimensions. In the 1970s, he worked on various projects, including establishing three textile factories in Mosul. When Gabriela was pregnant with their third child, Nour, in 1972, he attended a four-month management course in Sweden. Soon after his return, Adil became the general director of the three Mosul textile factories. His career as an outstanding manager and popular figure of the Ministry of Industry began. In 1979 and in 1982, two more children, Malik, named after my deceased brother, and Alim, were born. In that period, Adil developed plans to expand the Iraqi textile industry. By 1986, businesspersons and ministers from around the world met him in exclusive hotels and government ministries to negotiate contracts. Both directly and indirectly, Adil helped improve the livelihoods of hundreds of thousands of people in Iraq, and far beyond. As fortune had it, I was born into a successful, giving, high society family.

### *Wednesday, September 3, 1986*

Three days after my birth, our private chauffeur, Salim, picked up my mother and me to bring us home. He drove us to a gated community in the Mansur district of south-west Mosul, which bordered the industrial area. Inside the community, we passed several family homes, a kindergarten, a school, and some shops before we stopped at the last right bend across from a huge property, which was a blend of beauty and technology. The two-story, flat-roofed mansion in front of us was clad with hand-chiseled sandstone. Floor-to-ceiling casement windows led to, in total, four large balconies. In the front garden, a prefabricated pathway meandered toward the center of the mansion: a two-story entrance hall that was accessed through an extra-tall, arched front door. To the left and right side, sprinklers watered a neatly cut front lawn and two trimmed palm trees that stretched into the blue sky. Even with the sun high, our house promised to remain cool inside. Two AC condenser units were placed at the rear of our house.

While an electronic gate opened to our left, Salim slowly entered the property. He parked on a long, paved gateway. "We're home," he said peacefully before he opened the passenger door for Gabriela. She thanked him, "Shukran jazilan[7]," and got out of the car.

Carrying me on her arm, she slowly walked behind our house and entered the back yard, where an excited clucking broke out. Dozens of chickens began to run around in the mesh wire enclosure on our left. She grinned at her two-legged friends, who provided our family with fresh eggs every day, before she crossed our manicured, soccer-field-sized lawn, heading toward our multi-colored rose garden. Most flowers in our garden were roses. They blossomed wonderfully. Despite her post-childbirth pain, she bent down to smell the roses' sweet flavor. She smiled again, basking in her love of nature in our large garden.

Sadiq, our private gardener, saw us and approached us from the two-bedroom bungalow that had been built for our employees in the far left corner of our property.

"As-salamu alaykum.[8] Who is it you bring us?" he asked with a smile.

"This is Younes," she said, smiling back.

"Mashallah![9] Ahlan wa sahlan, Younes!" he welcomed me. He

---

7  Arabic term: "Thank you so much"

8  Arabic greeting: "Peace be upon you"

9  Arabic phrase: "God has willed"—expresses appreciate, joy, praise, or thankfulness for an event or person that was just mentioned

turned on the garden hose to refill our turquoise-tiled swimming pool with fresh water.

Behind our pool, a ten-foot sandstone brick wall marked off one of the textile factories Adil managed. The factories improved people's living conditions in many ways. Since the production depended on clean water, Adil had financed the building of new waterworks in Mansur. They also delivered water to other residential areas of Mosul. He enjoyed being helpful and never forgot where he came from. Giving back to the people was a question of justice and of honor for him. From his own experience, Adil knew the limiting effects poverty could have on a family and an entire people. He thus gladly financed the building of two thousand family homes, some schools, kindergartens, and shops in Mosul with the profits he generated over the years.

As the water was running, Gabriela thanked Sadiq for his work and excused herself.

She walked back to our house and entered through an aluminum French door our living hall. Thick, red curtains behind tall, arched windows darkened the cool room. Ornate carpets covered parts of the light, natural stone floor, while two gold chandeliers shone from the extra high ceiling.

Before she could walk to our kitchen, my siblings came running to hug her. "Mama, you are back!" they shouted excitedly. A beaming smile graced her face. She had never imagined living a life blessed with so many children, friends, and riches after her initial struggles in Mosul. Her resiliency, her patience, and her continuous efforts to integrate and thrive in her new environment had paid off.

*Winter 1987*

Saddam Hussein indulged Ba'ath[10] Party members, and especially public officials like Adil, in many ways to keep them quiet and loyal to his authoritarian regime. Almost every year, we were given a piece of land. On a monthly basis, we received plenty of food for free, such as bags of beans, rice, and flour, and boxes with eggs and meat. We also obtained household appliances for a tenth of the market price, such as air-conditioners, hand-knotted carpets, and designer furniture. Given that Iraq had a planned economy, many Iraqis often had to wait months before they could buy these items, whereas certain goods were only reserved for public officials. Gabriela, helpful as she was, always distributed the things we received among our relatives, our neighbors, and our friends, assuming that we would never lack anything.

In winter 1987, a middle-aged man delivered a package four times my height and left it in our kitchen. We waited for my father to come home from work at night to open the box, which contained a modern US refrigerator with an ice maker that would provide cubed filtered ice—one of the things only people like us received. But we did not need it; we already possessed two big refrigerators.

As a result of our material abundance, our basement resembled a warehouse. We possessed another 7,400-square-foot property in the Yarmouk district of western Mosul, and Salim shuttled us

---

10  Arabic term: "Renaissance" or "Resurrection"—political party that mixed ideologies of Arab nationalism, pan-Arabism, Arab socialism, and anti-imperialism; dissolved in 2003

between our houses every day to make sure we did not miss anything. As an infant, I was too young to understand how spoiled we were, or at what cost we maintained our status: Iraqis had to belong to the Ba'ath Party to have a career. There was no freedom of choice.

Adil did not discuss politics to avoid getting in trouble with Saddam Hussein's all-controlling regime. August 1984, however, was an exception. Saddam Hussein invited him for a round of talks because, for the third year in a row, he had been nominated by the Ministry of Industry as "Manager of the Year."

The nomination was based on various categories, such as productivity and labor conditions. The first textile factory of Mosul started with four hundred workers in 1954. When Adil took over as manager, he disposed of all the old machines and bought (with a state loan) expensive, computer-controlled sewing and weaving machines from Europe. Since he increased the productivity and profit rate tremendously, he was able to hire new workers and even build two new factories in the 1980s. By 1987, more than seven thousand people worked in the five textile factories he led. The workers held shares of the company and received regular and advanced training, as well as retirement income and health insurance, all paid by the company—another new concept he introduced. It led to a fair distribution of prosperity.

When he met Saddam Hussein in his palace in Baghdad in 1984, Adil acted quite confident, but this was dangerously naive. Most Iraqis did not dare to look Saddam Hussein in his eyes; it could have been judged as disrespect, which could have unpredictable and even fatal consequences. Still, Adil was positive about creating new opportunities for Iraq's economy and thus did look Saddam Hussein in the eyes. They shook hands in an extremely intense and silent moment telecasted on state television. In the following two-hour interview, which took place at a round table with other key politicians and businessmen, Saddam Hussein talked about Iraq's economy and politics in surprisingly liberal terms, as if he was not a brutal dictator anymore. Moreover, when Adil dared to argue in favor of a market economy, Saddam Hussein, for the first time, publicly advocated it, even though he considered himself an Arab-nationalist socialist. Adil felt extraordinarily proud about his achievements and, like many other Iraqis, looked hopeful toward Iraq's economic development.

It was not the first or the last time Adil appeared on state television. Editors of women's magazines interviewed him frequently since they were interested in the company's progressive, pro-women concept. Six thousand of his workers and three of his seven top managers were women. The televised interviews usually took place in his office. He would sit at his teakwood table, wearing the finest suits, his short, wiry, black hair combed aside, while he listened and answered questions with a focused and determined face, always striving for excellence.

In winter 1987, the picture in his office behind his desk showed him and Saddam Hussein shaking hands. It hung next to the regular portrait of Saddam Hussein in uniform that was present all over the country. It counted as an exceptional social status in Iraq to be in a picture with Saddam Hussein—shaking hands.

Many Iraqis looked up to us. We were almost like celebrities.

*August 1988*

Gabriela left our house in the morning with our new white Toyota Crown to do some last-minute shopping for our upcoming summer vacation. She was wearing oversized black sunglasses and a tailored, black dress, looking a bit like Audrey Hepburn[11], as her friends would sometimes tell her. Rasala, our housemaid, took a picture of her leaving our house and getting in our new car.

Rasala always looked after us with great care when our mother was not at home. For lunch, she sometimes even caught sparrows in our garden with her bare hands to roast for us. Malik and Alim would watch her with large eyes, amazed and appalled by how quick and strong her hands were. She was Gabriela's age and also a Christian. During lunch, Rasala would sit patiently next to us or hold us on her lap and wait until we ate up. Back then, our favorite dish was rice pudding with cinnamon and sugar, which she cooked with love. We enjoyed being with her. She was very sweet to us in many ways.

We obtained our new limousine from the government almost for free in spring 1988. Only a few Toyota Crowns were registered in Iraq, and only public officials drove them. The car came with special equipment: an interior refrigerator, dual-zone climate control, reading lamps, and automatic headlights. The interior was still wrapped in plastic when Salim parked it on our driveway for the

---

11  Born Audrey Kathleen Ruston (May 4, 1929—Jan. 20, 1993); British actress, model, dancer, and humanitarian, recognized as a film and fashion icon

first time.

Since Salim chauffeured Adil in an SUV almost on a daily basis, Gabriela more often drove our new car.

When Gabriela received her driver's license in 1973, she was one of the first women in patriarchal Mosul to drive a car. After Saddam Hussein seized power in 1979, women were given more rights and freedom in different areas of life, such as gaining more access to higher education, work opportunities, and public child-care. He also established the Women's Union, which protected women's rights. Hence, it was normal by 1988 that women drove cars, moved freely, and to a greater extent wore modern clothes that didn't cover their hair and body shape—all major steps forward for women. Iraq had partly become modern by 1988.

These facts, as I'd learn during my studies two decades later, were usually omitted in mainstream Western reports that pictured Saddam Hussein as a cruel, ruthless, and power-hungry dicta-tor. He represented different things to different people. And yet in March 1988, the last year of the Gulf War with Iran, Saddam Hussein ordered a chemical attack in Halabja, a city close to the Iranian border, and killed between three and five thousand civil-ians. Many of those killed were Kurds, some of whom sought au-tonomy. The attack was clearly a crime against humanity.

In August 1988, after Iran accepted the ceasefire, Adil took two weeks off since he wanted to spend time with us during the school holidays. In the past, we had sometimes gone hiking in the moun-tains of northern Iraq (Iraqi Kurdistan) on the weekends; now he planned a trip to Baghdad to show us, among other things, Lake

Habbaniyah, a huge lake near the Euphrates River.

Before we left for our journey, he let me sit on the driver's seat of our Toyota while he took the passenger seat. At an age of almost two years, I could not see through the windshield, but I could reach the steering wheel. Excited, I honked the horn a dozen times. "Fasten your seat belt!" I said.

"Ay, Sir! And you watch the street," he said, beaming with joy as if we were on a real journey. And we were—building our bond as father and son.

My siblings and I appreciated the time with Adil since we did not see him a lot. In addition to long working days in Mosul, his constant business trips took him to forty-three countries by 1988. Each time he went abroad, he received an extra salary per day from the Ministry of Industry. His business trips took between ten and fifteen days. When he returned, the salary he had earned frequently equaled five months' work in Mosul.

We had plenty of money, and it brought material luxuries, and some forms of freedom as well.

### September 1988

Flying was too expensive for most Iraqis and Germans in the 1980s, but we had the money and the freedom to fly to Germany every year to visit my grandmother in Amtal, a small rural village in Lower Saxony. In September 1988, we flew to Germany for an additional, special reason. Gabriela was in her fifth month of pregnancy. Hikmat, our family doctor and friend, recommended that she go to Germany, where the climate was moderate, and give birth there. He was worried the heat in Iraq could lead to complications with her varicose veins and that the local doctors would not be well enough equipped to treat her, although the Iraqi medical facilities ranked as some of the best in the Arabic-speaking world by 1988. This was another fact usually omitted in the mainstream Western narrative about Iraq under Saddam Hussein.

### December 6, 1988

Sophia, my youngest sister and my parents' last child, was born in the hospital of Oslar, a town near Amtal. Gabriela, Sophia, Nour, and I stayed in Amtal afterward, whereas Adil and my other siblings had already flown back in September because of work or school.

### End of August 1989

Back in Mosul, our lives continued as usual, until one morning. The table in our kitchen was not laid for breakfast when Malik, Alim, and I went downstairs. Instead, Adil was standing in front of the table. "We'll go to the hospital today. They'll cut off a small piece of your penis that you don't need," he told us.

"What? Cut off?" I said, terrified. Barely three years old, I tried to escape into the garden, but Adil was faster than I was. He grabbed my arm as I was trying to run away.

"You have to do it. Otherwise, you don't become a real man," he said.

"I'm too small to become a man now. Leave me alone! I won't come," I retorted.

"I got circumcised, your brothers will be, everyone is. It's part of our religion."

"I don't want it!" I screamed.

"But you have to!" he shouted, pulling me outside while Malik and Alim followed quietly.

I was scared to death for the first time, and quite rightly. Malik and Alim both stood the operation well. I, in contrast, died three times on the operating table after numerous respiratory and cardiac arrests. My small body did not tolerate the anesthesia. The doctors needed more than two hours to stabilize me.

Habitually, boys in Muslim families were circumcised between the age of seven and ten, when children were introduced more and more to Islam through their family, institutions like schools and mosques, and the larger society. The circumcision of boys was not required in the Quran, but in the Sunnah[12]. Adil, who had become more religious since the death of Great Malik, as my family would call my deceased brother in the rare and brief moments we talked about him, thought it would be a good opportunity to practice a religious tradition and celebrate his three male descendants with our extended family and friends. Problematically, the circumcision was irreconcilable with what Gabriela and Adil had agreed on before they started a family, namely that their children should have the freedom to choose a religion. Again, Adil bowed to social pressure, and consequently Gabriela and we, the children, were forced to do likewise.

---

12  Traditional Muslim law based on the Prophet Muhammad's words and deeds

## Beginning of September 1989

I was traumatized at the age of three. In my dreams, I saw myself lying on a white operating table, dead still, while doctors jumped around me. I usually woke from these dreams scream-ing. My parents had to calm me down every time. During the day, I imagined I could smell the hospital's sharp disinfectant every-where, even though Rasala soon switched to a new brand of cleaner to spare me.

At the beginning of September, a few days after my third birth-day, I also became aware of the metallic smell of blood. Our three sheep, which Adil had given us a few months earlier as a present, were slaughtered for the celebration of our circumcision. I was see-sawing in the morning when Adil and two other men took our three sheep behind a bush. Shortly after, I heard a hysteric bleat and then saw a stream of blood running onto the lawn. I shouted, "Mama!" as loud as I could. When she came running, she spotted the blood as well. She grabbed me and carried me to the kitchen. "Everything is fine," she said, trying to calm me down, while I could only cry. The sheep had been bought for that day in the first place, but nobody had told us. I felt sorry for our sheep and, even if very young and unaware of many things, felt quite deceived by my parents since I had thought the sheep would stay with us, as they had said.

In the afternoon, about fifty adults and a dozen children visited my family in our Mansur mansion to help us celebrate. We await-ed them in the back yard, where some service people were putting the meat on the grill behind us. I still felt anguish about the loss of our sheep. Like Malik and Alim, I had been dressed in a traditional costume by my mother, who played by the rules. We each wore a white dishdasha[13] and a gold necklace with a Quran pendant. Everyone congratulated us and kissed us on our cheeks. Ammu[14] Nuri took pictures of us standing together on the lawn. My head almost reached Adil's waist. He beamed intensely into the camera. Malik, Alim, and I smiled politely. After the photo shooting, our guests excitedly clapped their hands, while I just felt pain in my penis. I was overwhelmed by the religious ritual, which I neither understood nor accepted. Its compulsive and painful nature even impaired my trust in my parents for some time. Regardless of what Adil had told me, I was no adult yet, but only a very young, mutilated child who was in pain.

While I was traumatized and confused by the religious ritual, I also faced my parents' high expectations regarding our behavior, especially in public. Belonging to high society demanded being perfectly respectable, regardless of whether we liked it or not.

After our circumcision, my brothers and I wore a dishdasha every day. I used to pull the piece of cloth aside so it would not rub on the wound. Adil repeatedly warned me not to do it, especially in front of other people. Before our guests had come that day, he urged me again, "This is bad manners. Don't pull it! Don't say it hurts! You're a man." He also addressed Malik and Alim with a serious face. "Don't put your elbows on the table! Don't eat much! Eat only when older people offer you something! And always listen

---

13  Ankle-length garment with long sleeves

14  Arabic term: "Uncle"—or used as a name for an elder out of respect

to older people! Don't talk much! Talk only when older people ask you something!" They nodded silently. They had heard these types of directions from our parents many times before.

Though I sensed the seriousness of that day, being observed by everyone, my need to protect myself prevailed. I took the freedom of pulling the dishdasha aside as often as I needed, especially after sunset when most adults moved inside to drink chai while the children, including me, stayed outside to play hide and seek. Playing with the other children was pure joy. I hid behind a thick bush and waited to be found. It was unusual for me to be allowed to stay outside at that late, dark hour. Animals rushed by while bushes and trees rustled. The moonlight and uncountable stars illuminated the dark sky. Amazed, I listened to the beautiful whistles, thrills, and gurgles of a bird I had never heard before, accompanied by the chirping of crickets. I knew that the other children would need some time to find me. Leaves covered almost my entire body. I was thrilled: what an exciting night after all!

### Fall 1990

One morning, Salim drove my parents and me to some jewelry shops downtown to buy a necklace for my sister, Manal, who was about to get married. She had met a man, Amir, at Mosul University a few weeks earlier and quickly got engaged to him. She was in love with his honey-colored eyes. Amir studied chemistry. His parents were Bedouins[15] and had thirteen children. Manal

---

15  A grouping of nomadic Arab people of the Middle Eastern deserts, especially of North Africa, the Arabian Peninsula, Egypt, Palestine, Iraq, Syria, and Jordan

studied biology. According to custom, the groom gave jewelry equivalent to ten monthly salaries to his bride on the wedding day, and parents bought practical things for the new household, such as furniture. My parents could afford to buy both.

### *Thursday, November 29, 1990*

About fifty guests gathered in our Mansur mansion to celebrate Manal's and Amir's wedding. Everyone was dressed formally. Manal and Ammu Amir sat on red armchairs at the end of our living hall so everyone could see the bridal couple. My sister wore a white dress. A gold necklace with a Quran pendant, which we had bought, was twinkling on her neck. Ammu Amir wore an anthracite suit. Behind them, hanging above the fireplace, the picture of Adil and Saddam Hussein remained omnipresent. I was sitting on a couch next to my brothers, who were wearing tailored suits. I, in contrast, was wearing a green pullover with a biker logo and "FREESTYLE" printed in white letters, chest-high, over a white shirt. Gabriela had dressed me. She knew I did not like to wear tight suits, and she knew about my strong will to go my way, free of limiting regulations—a behavior that was typical for a small child and yet somehow still desirable for an adult who had to abide by many rules that didn't always make sense.

Three dining tables were arranged behind each other in the middle of our living hall. On the middle table, a three-tiered butter cream cake was waiting to be cut. "Let's first take a picture of the family and the bridal couple before we eat," Adil told us. As we went to the front, I looked at Ammu Amir. He looked like Saddam

Hussein with his black mustache, his stern expression, and his wiry hair combed back. I was worried that he would take away my dear sister and not treat her well.

"Watch out! Don't you treat Manal badly!" I told him with a raised finger.

"Careful!" Adil rapidly grabbed my arm. "What did I tell you? Don't talk!" he said. I looked at Adil with lowered eyebrows, as I often did when I was muzzled. I did not like to be silenced, and yet I felt guilty about not being the good boy he wanted me to be. I also sensed—to the little extent a four-year-old could—that respecting this special moment together and celebrating this new bond was more important, so I kept silent.

In the course of the next weeks, I learned that Manal's wedding did not mean that she would leave us for good. In fact, she still visited us on a regular basis. She also celebrated with the entire family the next Christmas, like every year before. As usual, our Muslim neighbors celebrated with us as well. I did not know what Christmas was about back then; I only sensed that it was an exceptional, colorful, and heartwarming day—a celebration of family, friendship, and love.

### Thursday, January 10, 1991

Six weeks after Manal's wedding, Nour got married as well. She had met Serhat for the first time in fall 1990 when she visited Manal at Mosul University. Serhat studied physics. He was a proud Kurd[16]. With his long, full brown hair, he reminded Nour of George Michael[17], her favorite singer. Even though Nour was only seventeen years old, and even though she had not yet graduated from high school, the wedding followed quickly. My parents barely had any time to comment on it.

On the wedding day, January 10, we hosted about a hundred and fifty guests. Our Mansur mansion was action-packed with chatting, laughing, and singing adults and children. Since my parents were busy attending to all our guests, I had more freedom to do what I liked. I flitted from person to person, listening, laughing, talking, and running. Another exciting night!

I enjoyed my early childhood. Despite my parents' strict education, especially in regard to our behavior in public, I felt loved and free most of the time. I felt loved by my family, our employees, our neighbors, and our friends. I felt connected to everyone around me, as well as to my thoughts, emotions, actions, and myself— even if I wasn't fully aware at this young age. I had everything a small child could need and much more. I lived in security, comfort, even luxury, and I took everything for granted; until I faced the other side of life. What happened next, in January 1991, changed my family's lives forever.

---

16  Ethnic group in the Middle East, mostly inhabiting an area spanning adjacent parts of southeastern Turkey, northwestern Iran, northern Iraq, and northern Syria

17  English singer, songwriter, record producer, and philanthropist; known for his work in the 1980s and 1990s

# PART II

# IN THE AIR
# AND ON THE ROAD

*January–October 1991*

*Fear and love need no language*

*Thursday, January 17, 1991, 3:00 a.m.*

I was sleeping soundly when the siren behind our back yard started howling. I woke up and squinted out the window. Everything was dark, a total blackout. Alarmed, I started to get up to find my parents, but Gabriela was already there. She tore open my door with Sophia on her arm. "Go downstairs, now!" she shouted. Something was seriously wrong, I knew by the tone of her voice. I followed her to the hallway, where the whole family was gathering—apart from Nour, who was staying with Ammu Serhat in Duhok (Iraqi Kurdistan).

We rushed down to the first floor, the sirens wailing. Adil kept shouting "Yallah![18]" I was frightened and confused. Downstairs, Abu Rabi, our personal bodyguard who lived across the street and who worked for the secret service, hastily opened our front door. "I'm obliged to tell you that you need to get out, now!" he shouted. "Every big city is a death trap now. You'll be brought to a safer place."

Adil hugged us in a hurry. "Get in the car! Do exactly what you are told!"

We ran to our white Mitsubishi Pajero. Salim already waited behind the steering wheel. Only after we had fastened our seatbelts did I notice that Adil did not come.

---

18  Arabic phrase: "Hurry up"

"Wait! What about Baba?" I asked, grabbing Gabriela's shoulder from the rear seat.

But she remained silent.

"I'll bring you to a village, away from the targets. I know the people out there," Salim said. "Your father needs to stay close to the factory."

Gabriela looked at Adil with tears in her eyes.

I banged my hands on the window. "Baba, come with us! Come with us!" I shouted, but he stayed behind at the front door, looking at us like a statue with a terrified face.

"Abu Rabi will take care of him," Salim said.

Sophia started crying, "Baba! Baba!"

But our protests were in vain. Salim switched on the engine. Before he found his way out, he bumped into our metal gate. He did not turn on the front lights so no one could spot us as we sped away.

The US-led "Operation Desert Storm" had targeted Mosul, the ancient metropolis, with tens of thousands of deadly weapons. We had just entered the road when we heard a howling sound coming from high in the sky. Shortly thereafter, an explosion went off behind our back yard. It was the loudest bang I had ever heard, as if a massive avalanche struck instantly and with full force in the immediate vicinity. Our car was shaking violently. My bones rattled. I felt a piercing pain in my chest. Once again, I was terrified.

Salim drove down the main street at maximum speed. He drove through the barrier at the gate, turned onto another street, crossed a ditch, the freeway, and another ditch before he hit bumpy desert soil. "The village is thirty miles west of Mosul," he said, while we sat in the back of the car, struck dumb with horror.

As we stole away into the desert, Manal constantly tried to cover my eyes since I could not stop looking outside the window. Warplanes continuously approached Mosul like gigantic buzz saws from above. Even though I could not detect them, their attacks were unmistakable. Every time they got closer, an aerial shrieking turned into an ear-splitting thunder as wailing lights incessantly rose from the ground into the sky, trying to stop the warplanes, but most of the time in vain. Intense lights, one after another, illuminated the ground. Every time a bomb was dropped, an abyssal bang and a following shock wave haunted us. We felt the vibrations at the car door. The more bombs were dropped, the less we could see of Mosul. Mosul was sinking in dust and fire. I clung to Manal, speechless.

We drove one hour into the dark desert under lethal warplanes. After we had crossed a short bridge, we finally arrived at a walled-in village—Sheikh Ibrahim. Several men stood in front of the gate, covering their mouths with rags. I wondered why but remained silent, weighed down by all the destruction I had seen. My body shook with fear.

Salim got out of the car and talked to an old man who wore a full beard and a dishdasha. After a minute, Salim came back and opened our doors. "You can get out now. My uncle will take care of you. I'll go back to Mosul now. Inshallah[19], I'll come back tomorrow with your father and some supplies," he said.

---

19  Arabic expression: "God willing" or "If God wills"

It was hard to understand what was happening to us. When we got out of the car, another unit of bombers approached Mosul. I looked up to the red, cloudy sky, illuminated by the fires of Mosul. Warplanes flew over us with a terrible roar, one after another in rapid succession. The ground was shaking. Manal grabbed my arm. We quickly followed the old man through the gate.

"You'll live with us. The farm is my home," the old man told us in a chesty voice. Sheep, donkeys, and chickens were running around, kicking up dirt in panic. "If you need the backhouse, find your way amidst the animals," he said, pointing to the left while guiding us across the yard.

We stopped in front of a small wooden barn door. "There are blankets in the closet," he said. Gabriela bent down and entered the chamber. We followed, one after another. A brown carpet covered the cold floor. Two mattresses lay in the corner. The small chamber had no window. "Push the lock bar so you don't freeze. It might freeze tonight," he said. Next to the mattresses, we spotted a small metal stove. "Let me bring you some paraffin," he said, and left.

We looked at each other in disbelief. The entire situation seemed unreal. After a few minutes, the old man came back with a bottle of paraffin and his wife. "The Sultans, ahlan wa sahlan! Please sit down," his wife said. As we all sat down, a smile appeared on her round face, framed by the white scarf she was wearing. "I've heard good things about you." She looked at each of us. "Masha'Allah! Lovely children."

"One is missing. We don't know where she is now. Maybe she's with her husband somewhere in Kurdistan," Gabriela said.

"I'm sure her husband takes care of her. I'll pray for them," the woman said, looking into Gabriela's glazed blue eyes before she said, "Tell me, how bad is it?"

That moment, Gabriela started whimpering.

I was completely overwhelmed. I felt very sorry for my mother and wanted to comfort her, but I was paralyzed from shock. I was four years old, and still dependent on her. I had thought my mother would always be strong. But my whole world had changed in the last two hours. Nearly everything I thought that was certain and safe was gone. Fortunately, the old woman hugged her and calmed her down. I slowly pulled my knees up tight against my chest and remained quiet for the rest of the night while Mosul sank beneath rounds of fatal bombs, my dear father still in the city.

At dawn, I followed Malik and Alim to the backhouse. We slowly crossed the inner courtyard. My feet were cold and my legs felt heavy as we walked among the animals. The smell of hay, feces, and sheep lay in the air. "Wash your face, especially the salty traces from last night," Gabriela called behind me. She did not know that there was only a hole in a wooden, piddled board in the backhouse. I urinated and quickly left the stinky room. Malik and Alim needed more time.

Outside, I looked around and gradually awakened to our new reality. There were no sweet scented roses. There was no washbowl, no tub, no hot water, no power, no refrigerator, and no personnel. We were trapped with a few villagers in loam huts that did not differ very much from the sandy desert behind the yellow village wall. Nothing of my former life existed in Sheikh Ibrahim, except that I was with part of my family.

Half-desperate, half-curious about how we could live in Sheikh Ibrahim, I left the courtyard to explore my surroundings. A strip of green grass had grown along a little stream in front of the village gate. It revitalized the desolate area. Comforted by the only fresh colors in sight, I smiled.

Gabriela observed me carefully from our chamber while I kept myself busy, picking up pebbles from the ground. She let me stay outside. She knew that sitting inside our chamber, inactive and facing raw uncertainty, would be too discouraging, too disturbing for a young child.

As I was collecting stones, a distant sound of an engine suddenly reached my ears. I turned around and detected a car on the horizon, driving toward Sheikh Ibrahim. The car was white. The shape looked familiar. I ran to our barn door and shouted, "Everybody, come here! Salim is coming." My family came immediately. We waited in front of the village wall, impatient and hopeful. "Your father is coming too!" Gabriela said excitedly, the first to notice him.

When Salim parked in front of us, Adil jumped out of the car. We all hugged each other for a long moment. I felt safe again. *We are together again*, I thought. Almost.

"Any news from our daughter?" Gabriela asked.

"No, but I'll look for her," Adil said, visibly worried. "How have you been?"

"We had no sleep. Malik and Alim have diarrhea. We need medicine," she said.

"I'll take care of that," he said. His legs began to shake. "They destroyed the factory."

Gabriela stared at him, bewildered and, at the same time, trying to keep her nerves. "Let me come with you. I will get the things we need here."

"I'll come too!" I said, trying to stay with my parents. But they wouldn't take any of us to Mosul since another strike was possible anytime and anywhere. Manal knew and held me back. Existential fears overcame me. Would I lose my parents, the most important people in my young life, in the next strike? Would my siblings and I die instead? I began to cry. Manal calmed me down.

In the late afternoon, Salim came back with my mother. I felt a great relief to see her again, but also a crushing fear for my father, who stayed in the city of death. Still, he sent a few material items to satisfy some of our basic needs. When Salim opened the trunk, we spotted plastic bags with salt, meat, and medicine, bottles with petroleum and water, and the blankets and pillows—which Gabriela had embroidered—we had slept with the night before the war began. They gave us some feeling of home and shelter.

### End of January 1991

Despite Salim's regular deliveries of supplies from Mosul, clean water remained scarce in Sheikh Ibrahim. It had to be collected from an olive grove three hundred yards away from the village. Since we had barely enough drinking water, Gabriela used our water sparingly. Only at night, when we gathered in our chamber, would she put a bowl on the stove to wash our faces and hands with warm water before we would lie down.

Sleep, however, was also scarce. After the first week, the bombardments decreased for a few days but then increased again. The heaviest strikes took place at 2:00 a.m. and 4:00 a.m. Every night I would lie close to my siblings and listen to the heavy warplanes that raged around us and dropped bombs everywhere. The unending echoes of explosions pierced the night air. Sometimes, when the bombs were dropped on neighboring villages, we felt the vibrations in the ground. It was impossible to fall asleep in the face of death. Would they also throw bombs on our heads?

On most nights, it took me more than an hour after the last strike to surrender to my fatigue and fall asleep for a few hours. There was one routine that calmed me down little by little—the soothing conversations of Gabriela and Umm Shihab, the old man's wife. Despite the coldness, our barn door always remained a slit open since Gabriela could not fall asleep either. She would sit on the doorsill with Umm Shihab, who came after the last strike with chai and kleicha[20]. Umm Shihab would tell stories about the city people she had met. The even rhythm of her husky voice seemed to make Gabriela forget about the war and the cold. Sometimes they even laughed together, as if everything was well. Listening to them and watching them have a good time together made me forget about our hardships.

Still, staying in Sheikh Ibrahim during winter increasingly

---

20   Yeast cookies filled with nuts or dates

drained our strength. After breakfast, which normally consisted of tea and flatbread with sesame paste or dates, my siblings and I would leave our chamber to play with the children of the other five families from Mosul who were also staying at Sheikh Ibrahim. Even when the mornings were so cold that we could see our breath, we kept our habit of playing outside; it was a good distraction. We usually played among the donkeys, geese, and chickens by the stream. Sometimes we drew pictures in the mud with sticks. In the course of time, my skin cracked in places from the dry cold. Dirt got into my wounds. Soon, green pus-filled blisters grew between my fingers. They hurt terribly, but I wanted and needed to keep playing with the other children, even if we never talked much. We were traumatized, but I felt better being with peers who shared the same blow of fate. Company made our burden more bearable. We kept the habit of playing together, yet we couldn't escape reality: the longer we stayed in Sheikh Ibrahim, the weaker we became—physically and mentally—witnessing how Mosul was being destroyed more and more.

One day, we stayed in our chamber after breakfast since it was raining. For the first time, I realized, to the tiny degree a small child could, that a foreign power could have a direct impact on our lives. Gabriela and Manal asked themselves what would happen to us now that Saddam Hussein had put the world against Iraq by illegally invading and annexing Kuwait. I was suddenly deeply worried. The picture of Adil and Saddam Hussein appeared before my eyes. "Will they punish Baba? Is Baba bad? Like Saddam?" I asked.

"No, Baba is good. And don't mention the other name! People

are not supposed to speak about him," Gabriela said urgently.

Saddam Hussein's oppressive regime proved to be brutally vindictive. Whoever spoke against him was then afraid of facing fatal consequences. Surveillance, abduction, torture, and political murders were almost a daily occurrence; a widespread fear of expressing one's opinion set in. I did not know about it at the age of four. Twenty years later, during my studies, I could come to understand the repercussions of this, and to see why social and political progress was so difficult in Iraq. After having lived under Saddam Hussein's dictatorship for twenty-four years, Iraqis struggled to establish democracy. Freedom of expression and the ability to resolve conflicts non-violently had been almost eradicated from the public consciousness. They basically had to be re-introduced, consistently re-affirmed, and defended to establish democracy.

### Beginning of February 1991

One afternoon, Gabriela, Sophia, and I accompanied Umm Shihab to the olive grove to collect water. On our way back, Umm Shihab walked far ahead of us. I was walking behind Gabriela, who had Sophia on her arm, when I heard a sound suddenly breaking the sky behind us. I quickly looked over my shoulder. For the first time, I spotted the gigantic buzz saw by daylight—a gray warplane, like a huge bird. Gabriela had watched out for it every time we played at the stream. Now, our time was up.

"Mama, wait! Carry me so that they don't see me!" I shouted in panic, thinking that my mother could protect me from all the evil of this world. She turned around and saw it coming too. Terrified, she ran to me, grabbed me, and began to run with Sophia and me on her arms as fast as her legs could carry all three of us.

We were a hundred and fifty yards away from the village when the warplane began to hunt us with constant machine gun fire. The bullets exploded on the ground close to Gabriela's heels. Sand blasted into the sky. It almost threw her off balance, but she kept running and running. I held my breath. My heart cramped. Once again, I was scared to death.

Umm Shihab held the village gate open, screaming hysterically, "Allahu Akbar![21]"

When we finally reached the gate, the warplane veered toward Mosul. It did not come back. The pilot spared us strangers. We had escaped death by a heel.

Stories like ours generally remained untold in the West. Instead, people were told that "smart weapons" would ensure the victory for the coalition forces, while in fact thousands of civilians were killed—people who had lives.

## Mid-February 1991

After the incident with the warplane—an F-16, as Gabriela told me later—I was only allowed to go to the stream and no further. I understood the precaution. The next warplane could come anytime, and I started to examine the sky even more carefully whenever I left our chamber.

Staying in Sheikh Ibrahim—to a certain extent in the wild,

---

21  Islamic Arabic expression: usually translated as "God is [the] greatest," used in various contexts by Muslims—in formal prayer, in the call for prayer, as an informal expression of faith, in times of distress, or to express resolute determination or defiance

away from the densely populated city, and yet in the face of death all the time—sharpened my senses in unusual ways. I did not know how long we had already stayed, but I developed a feeling for the time of day. I had begun to observe the location of the sun and the adhan[22]. It gave me something to hold onto.

Nevertheless, neither playing with the other children nor observing the environment could take away my constant fear. My family was still separated from each other by the chaos of a war that could easily delete us. We did not know where Nour was or whether she was still alive. We lacked sufficient nutrition and a bombproof shelter. The medicine we had brought was supposed to last six weeks, yet we had used it up within two. We needed a new spark of hope—hope for the end of terror.

### Sunday, March 3, 1991

Salim arrived in Sheikh Ibrahim around noon with international news. "The ceasefire conditions are set up. Iraqi troops are out of Kuwait. The US and other forces will soon move out as well. I'll bring you back home today," he said.

Manal called out "Alhamdulillah![23]" and hugged each of us.

"We go back to Baba, right?" Malik asked. Gabriela nodded with a thoughtful smile. We collected our things within a few minutes and hugged everyone in the village to say goodbye. I was glad we could finally go back home. Somehow, despite the war, I still believed that everything would still be beautiful and enjoyable there.

---

22  Islamic call to worship—recited by the muezzin at prescribed times of the day

23  Arabic phrase: "Praise be to God"

But my childlike anticipation soon turned into distress. Entering Mosul, I felt the rubble from the destroyed city rumbling under our wheels. No one was able say a word. We stared outside the window in disbelief. An endless picture of total destruction opened up in front of us. Streets were torn open. Buildings and bridges lay in ruins. Power poles were lying on the streets. We zigzagged through the city that we had always called home, a city we hardly recognized now.

Mosul was strangely desolate. The small cabin next to our gated community was not manned. The barrier, which had secured the gate, lay on the street, broken. We drove over it with a knocking sound. "Where are all the people?" Alim asked. He did not receive any answer.

After a moment, Manal said, "Mosul is not only destroyed. It's dead." She broke out in tears while I sat on her lap.

When we stopped at our house and got out of the car, we spotted blood spots on the sidewalk, leading to our neighbors' car. Their car was burnt out. I was horrified. Did the death from above kill them?

Suddenly, Adil spoke to us from behind. We turned around. "Don't be shocked. Nothing is cleaned up. I told our personnel to go home," he said. I felt a great relief to see him again—alive. We hugged him at the front door and followed him inside the house. He showed us around so that we could see what damage the war had caused. Some interior doors were lying on the floor, blasted out. The windows were gone too. Shards of glass covered the ground. Our Christmas tree lay on the floor. The ornaments were broken, the curtains and couches tattered; the picture of Adil and Saddam Hussein lay on the floor under shards of glass. The bombs had destroyed our beautiful home. I was shaken.

Speechless, I followed my family outside. We crossed the lawn and headed to the mesh wire enclosure. All the chickens were lying on the soil, dead. "They must have had a heart attack," Gabriela said. Tears filled her eyes.

"There were too many targets next to Mansur: the power plant, the military base, and the airport," Adil said with a gloomy face. We slowly continued our walk across the lawn, which was partly covered with broken bricks from our backyard wall. Some orange and fig trees close to that wall were uprooted. Cartridge cases were swimming in our pool. I couldn't grasp the level of destruction until I grabbed some cartridge cases and looked at them. Adil took a slow breath and said tiredly, "Leave them; they're not toys." I threw them back to the water. We looked at the factory behind our rose garden. The power and the storage building had been reduced to ruins.

"What will happen now?" Gabriela asked with quiet despair.

"I don't know." Adil paused. "The bombs were just the beginning. The Iraqi Dinar has become almost worthless. The UN[24] sanctions will hit us now even more," he said.

I didn't understand what he meant, but I understood that the beautiful and enjoyable times were over.

"What about Yarmouk?" she asked.

---

24 United Nations: intergovernmental organization to promote international cooperation

"We'll go and stay there for now. It's not as damaged as our house here."

"Can we go to school again?" Malik asked.

"There's no school, habibi[25]. You just stay at home for the time being," Adil said.

Shattered and heavy-hearted, we walked back to our house to collect some things for Yarmouk.

### End of April 1991

In Yarmouk, Adil repeatedly told us that the UN sanctions regime in Iraq had banned the manufacture of chlorine and radically restricted its import. I didn't understand what that meant, but I soon faced the consequences of contaminated water that could not be treated with chlorine. Although Gabriela always boiled the tap water before she gave it to us, I woke up with severe diarrhea one day. I was unable to digest any nutrition. After two days, I was too weak to move.

I was lying on the sofa in our living room when I fainted as my mother was washing my face. Hikmat, who had joined us, came within minutes. He gave me an injection. Slowly, I became conscious again.

"We've got twenty-four hours, maybe less. He's too weak," Hikmat said.

Adil spoke straight into his face, "Do something!"

"I've used up all my medicine. The local hospitals don't have any, either. I've had hundreds of such cases in the last few weeks. It

---

25  Arabic term: "My darling"

always first hits the young, under the age of five," he said.

Gabriela turned her back to us. "Ya Allah![26] Don't take another son from me!" she cried.

"I know a doctor in Samarra. He's a good friend of mine. It's three hundred and fifty miles round-trip. Maybe he has got the shot. I'll drive there and check now," Hikmat said.

Adil nodded, staring at him. "What can we do?"

"Take him to the hospital. They might take away his pain at least. I'll meet you there."

Late that night, Hikmat came with the shot I needed. I was lucky.

Too many children my age who had not been born into a high society family and who did not have special connections to influential people died from drinking contaminated water, which large parts of the world community either did not care about or blamed on Saddam Hussein—both fatal errors in reasoning. The sanctions always punished the wrong, innocent Iraqi families, and mainly killed the most vulnerable—children and the poor. As a result, a growing number of Middle Easterners blamed the international community, led by the USA, for the dramatic emergency in Iraq, and not Saddam Hussein, who remained an anti-Western dictator. The sanctions led to a lose-lose situation. Not only did they prevent positive development and peace inside Iraq, but also between the Middle East and the West, a relationship that was now burdened even more with contempt and the desire for revenge.

---

26 Arabic term: "My dear God"

*Mid-May 1991*

Adil regularly left the house during the day to meet with public officials and inquire about Iraq's future. Usually, he came back for dinner. One evening, he made a crucial announcement as we were sitting at the oak corner booth in our kitchen.

"Tomorrow, we go to Amman. We will stay there until things improve here," he said.

Gabriela looked at him with big eyes. "What about school? It starts soon."

"Nothing will be like it used to be. They won't order new books. There'll be even more fatal shortages of food, medicine, and all kind of services. We need to get out now while it's still possible."

"And leave everything behind?" she asked.

He looked at her with a rigid face and nodded.

She put down her fork, visibly concerned, and nodded slowly. It seemed as if escape was our only option. I felt anxious. My parents, my guardians, were forced to take us away from our beloved home.

We did not leave voluntarily. We had no freedom of choice. Our options were to leave, or die. If the war and the sanctions had not happened, we would have very likely stayed in Iraq forever.

After dinner, we packed thirteen suitcases. It was not the first time we would travel to Amman, Jordan. We had vacationed there before. Yet it was the first time we left without knowing whether we would ever come back home. The complete uncertainty about our future almost crushed the last remains of our basic feeling of security.

## *Mid-May 1991*

Apart from Manal and Nour, who stayed with their husbands, we escaped from Mosul in an old taxi at night. My siblings and I slept until sunrise, when Adil announced from the passenger seat, "We're close to the Jordanian border. I've been told it's almost impossible to cross, but they might make an exception for us. Just let me talk. If anyone asks you, we're vacationing in Amman. Period!" Everyone nodded. We knew that the situation was dead serious.

Our driver stopped twenty yards in front of the border checkpoint, which was patrolled by a dozen soldiers. Some were pointing their machine guns at us. My heart began to race. Would they shoot us?

Two soldiers approached us. While one asked our driver to lower the window, the other kept pointing his machine gun at us. At the soldier's request, Adil handed over our documents. The soldier looked at them with narrow lips before he called for reinforcements.

Next, he asked us to get out of the car. Two additional officers opened the trunk. They rummaged our suitcases while the other two soldiers interrogated Adil. The procedure took almost an hour, but Adil stayed calm the entire time. Somehow, he convinced them with his peaceful persistence to open the border. Once again, he proved to be my hero. I was thankful for having him, thankful we stayed alive, thankful that they let us pass, and yet I wondered: what was waiting for us in Amman?

In Amman, our driver dropped us off at a tall, white building with five stars—the Amman Marriott Hotel. As we walked in the foyer, Oventin, Adil's Taiwanese business partner and friend, walked up to us, smiling, along with a dozen other people I did not know. Most of them hugged and kissed us. One man introduced himself with a handshake as the cousin of a Jordanian Minister.

"The Sultan family is alive! Let's celebrate!" Oventin said.

His big smile made us smile as well.

"I'm so glad to see you, my friend!" Adil said. "Just let me quickly check in." He looked at Oventin, astounded, and added, "How did you know we were coming to Amman?"

"Are you kidding? I thought the next time I'd see you would be at your funeral. No way! Your family is my guest the entire time you're in Amman, anything you want! I checked you in already." He paused. "I was looking for you and asked around!"

An excited, middle-aged couple came up to us, saying, "We reserved a room in the restaurant. You must be hungry and thirsty. We'll wait for you there." We felt warmly welcomed and appreciated. My parents thanked everyone and excused us before we took the elevator to our suite. A bouquet of roses and a basket of fruit awaited us on a table. Gabriela bent down to smell the fragrance. We could see from her smile that the roses smelled as good as the ones from our garden in Mosul. Finally, we regained some feeling of security.

After we had freshened ourselves up, we went downstairs to the restaurant. Oventin had already ordered plenty of food. We sat down at a long table. As we started to eat, the adults began to talk about the good old times together. Time and again, they laughed out loud. I was full after two plates and got up with Malik and Alim to collect the empty Pepsi cans. We piled them up on the red carpet. One tower held my height at nine cans. While Gabriela took some pictures of us all, Adil and the Taiwanese ambassador, who had also dined with us, were interviewed for what would become the headline of a newspaper article: "Taiwan Rescues the Sultan Family." Oventin would feel pleased about the successful escape story. We were indeed lucky, in contrast to hundreds of thousands of Iraqis who were internally displaced because of the war and had no opportunity to leave the country.

### Tuesday, June 25, 1991

We stayed in Amman for six weeks. Almost every night, we were invited by Oventin or other business partners and friends to dine and celebrate in an exclusive restaurant. Grilled meat, tabbouleh[27], lentil soup, fruits, and much more were served on porcelain dishes on extended tables while waitresses poured drinks under shining chandeliers. At times, it seemed as if the war and the sanctions had never happened.

But they had, and thus one question came up again and again: what are we going to do now? My parents considered our options. One evening, the German Consulate General dined with us. She told Adil she would try to get us six-month visas to Germany—the beginning of a plan that would soon take shape.

A few days later, on June 25, Adil called us into our suite early

---

27  Arabic and Levantine vegetarian dish—bulgur with parsley, tomatoes, and lemon

in the morning to make another announcement that would change our lives forever. He asked us to sit at the round table in the living room.

"Today, our vacation ends. Your flight is tonight," he said in a serious voice.

"Do we go home?" Malik asked, expectant.

"No. You'll go stay with your grandmother in Amtal, Germany," Adil told us.

Gabriela asked with raised eyebrows, "What about our daughters?"

"They're married now. Their husbands will take care of them; and I will, too," he said.

"And you? Why don't you come with us?" Malik asked.

"Because it's complicated for me to leave now. But you can go to Germany, where it's safe," Adil said.

I was scared for my father and yet too young to understand the pressure he faced in Iraq. It was more than difficult for a prominent person like him to get a visa, leave the country, and not return.

Gabriela probably knew this. Still, she stared at him, shaking her head. "I can't manage that. My nerves are already raw because of the war. I can't start from zero with four small children and a husband somewhere abroad. I am forty-seven years old. What are you thinking?"

"If we go back to Iraq, the boys will be drafted soon, if they don't die beforehand from a simple, curable illness. Our young children can't live in Iraq, you know that." He raised his voice.

"Iraq is done for the next twenty-five, if not fifty years! Even the public officials admit that."

Once again, I felt troubled. My parents were forced to remove us ever farther from our beloved home. They got up without another word and went to their bedroom to pack our bags.

I followed them. "Baba, I'll come with you," I said with tears in my eyes.

"No, habibi. Go back to the living room and let us pack your things," he said.

He let the air out of the red swimming tube that was lying on their bed. The corners of my mouth turned down. Tears began to roll, but he did not dare to look at me. "Please, go, habibi," he said.

I obeyed, went to the living room, threw myself on the couch, and cried my eyes out. Despite being too young to articulate the complex break in my family, I sensed that it was severe.

In the evening, a taxi drove us to Queen Alia International Airport. Our friends followed us in another taxi. They checked in our baggage and walked us to the gate.

"Be careful. Ba'ath Party members can get into trouble now," Oventin told Adil, anticipating that the international pressure on the Iraqi government would continue in unforeseen ways.

"Baba, don't go back to Iraq! They'll kill you there," I said.

"Don't speak like that! Abu Rabi takes care of me. Don't worry," he said.

Gabriela looked at him with big tears in her eyes.

He sighed. "It's still possible to escape now. The minister recommended it and our mayor as well. I dearly hope that we, inshallah, will live together again soon." He turned to Alim and Malik. "You're smart boys; you just finished primary school with excellent grades. You'll manage in Germany. And always listen to your mother!"

"Yes, Baba," they chorused.

Next, he turned to me. "I know you're strong. But always listen to your mother!"

"Yes, and you come to Germany soon!" I said.

He hugged each of us, and I, grief-stricken and shaking from fear, felt as if I had just seen and touched my father for the last time. The separation was almost unbearable for me as a four-year-old.

That night, we took off with Royal Jordanian Airlines. My father, my elder sisters, our beloved, caring relatives, our faithful employees, our good friends, our ample, sweet-scented gardens, the far-reaching metropolis, the majestic Tigris River, and all the people who appreciated us—Mosul, the place I thought of as my home, where I felt loved, where I could just be . . . we left everything behind. Mosul would become a painfully pinched-off place in my heart, even if I was not fully aware of it yet.

### *Wednesday, June 26, 1991*

We landed in Frankfurt in the early morning. Inside the airport building, we faced hordes of people rushing in different directions. Some talked in Arabic, but most spoke unfamiliar languages. I stopped walking and looked around; so many new impressions! So many signs, so many lights . . . Malik looked over his shoulder for me. "Yallah, follow us!" he said. Abu Rabi and Salim were missing.

Feeling strange, small, and vulnerable, I caught up with my family.

Gabriela and Malik each got a baggage cart. After we had loaded the carts at baggage claim, we rushed customs. When it was our turn, an officer in a green uniform began to ransack our luggage. Gabriela had neatly packed our clothes, but after the search, our suitcases could not close anymore. With a wrinkled forehead, she swiftly refolded our clothes and replaced them. Some passengers behind us groaned impatiently. "Hurry up Mummy," a man in a suit said, annoyed. I wanted to help her, but I was too little to reach the desk. I stayed close to her, hoping she would stand up to the pressure even without much help from our side. Fortunately, she did.

"Follow me to the arrival hall!" she said. We walked on gray granite flooring to a large hall. Countless people were standing around, some sitting and chatting, some sleeping. Suddenly, someone waved his hand. "Onkel Walter!" Gabriela said and smiled. I did not remember him from our previous visits since we always stayed with my grandmother. Onkel Walter had short brown hair, and was one head taller than Gabriela. After he had hugged her and exchanged some words with her in German, which I did not understand, he gave each of us a firm handshake. I felt tense and nervous, wondering what would happen next. I knew that this stay would be much different from our short visits in the past.

We followed him to the underground garage, where we got into an old, smoky station wagon. As we left the airport area, I looked outside the rear window. The freeway was clean. The trees at the roadside were full of leaves. Fields were systematically arranged and cultivated. I was impressed. Germany, in contrast to war-torn Iraq, seemed in perfect order, and so green.

After a fifteen-minute drive, we exited the freeway at a large blue sign. Even though I could not read, I became aware that the letters on the signs were not Arabic anymore. "We're in Kastel," Gabriela announced. The name sounded unfamiliar to me. Soon we stopped next to a property hidden by green cypresses. The place looked unfamiliar to me as well. I felt tense again. Onkel Walter led the way.

We entered the property on a pebble walkway. Compared to the smooth, pre-fabricated pathway at our house in Mosul, it felt almost unsafe to walk on that uneven path. I spotted a lush lawn on our right. The grass was greener and thinner than in Iraq. Several trees that I had never seen before grew and thrived in the garden. The vivid shades of green made me hold my breath. Behind the trees, I spotted a sailboat on a terrace, laid upside-down on red bricks. The house behind the terrace was built with the same bricks and had a pitched roof that rose into the sky. I had never seen such a steep roof before, and it looked somewhat dangerous to me. As we walked around the house, a row of fir trees cast a dark shadow on us. The temperature was mild in contrast to Iraq although it was mid-summer here.

After we arrived in Germany, I became a stranger to myself, constantly confronted with new impressions, unfamiliar thoughts, and mixed feelings. I felt as if I had lost control of my life. In Iraq, I was just a four-year-old boy who hardly thought about "losing control." Fleeing from our home and adjusting to a new, very different environment was extremely demanding.

Through a back door, we entered a small, smoky hallway. Gabriela turned to us and announced, "Your uncle flies to Mallorca with his family today. We can stay here for some time. Follow him to the living room. I'll call grandmother now." Bashfully looking at each other, we did as we were told. We sat down at a wooden dining table. Sometimes, I dared to look at Onkel Walter. He was smiling, but he avoided eye contact; I wondered if he enjoyed having us in his home.

After a few minutes, Gabriela joined us. With tears in her eyes, she said, "Nour will fly to Frankfurt Thursday night." It took me a moment to understand what she had said. Nour was alive! Moreover, she would be back in our life! Malik, Alim, Sophia, and I got up from the table and our family shared a moment of pure joy.

### Friday, June 28, 1991

When the morning sun sneaked through the shutters, I woke up with only one thing on my mind: Nour. I walked upstairs with a smile and carefully opened the room door. Nour was lying on a king-sized bed. Slowly, she turned her face toward me. She had dark circles around her eyes, and her face was sallow and bony. I was shocked.

"Habibi, Junis. Come to me. Don't be afraid," she whispered in a weak voice.

I slowly walked to her and sat down at the edge of her bed. She sat up. Her skeleton body was covered with white, shapeless clothes. She looked like a ghost.

"We survived," she whispered.

"How are you?" I dared to ask.

"I'm good now. Ammu Serhat and I fled by foot to Turkey." She paused. "Oventin found me in a refugee camp with the help of the Turkish embassy." She took a deep breath, in and out, as if she had to recover from the words she had said and collect new strength to continue. "After Baba had initiated my visa application from Mosul, I was driven to Istanbul. I stayed in a Catholic church until I was allowed to fly to Frankfurt," she said.

Her flight, I sensed, was at least as traumatizing as ours had been. With tears in our eyes, we hugged each other. I was thankful to know that she was safe and that we were together again.

### End of July 1991

Four weeks passed by quickly. While Gabriela went to administrative offices during the day, Nour looked after us as much as she was able to. She was six months pregnant and weighed only eighty-eight pounds when she arrived in Kastel. We were glad to see that she soon regained some weight and strength. When she felt strong enough, she came downstairs and joined us in the living room. We occasionally watched Sesame Street together. I asked my siblings time and again what the series was about, but of course, they did not understand German either. The program was still appealing and fun to us. Gabriela told us not to raise Onkel Walter's electricity bill, so we did not watch television every day. Most of the time, we just stayed at home, rested, and waited for Gabriela to come back.

When Nour felt particularly well, she sometimes took us to the playground close by and bought us chocolate at the kiosk. I appreciated these small gifts. I had no sense of how much money we had, but I knew it wasn't much anymore. Gabriela told us, in Arabic, that we now had to spend our money very carefully. She didn't start teaching us German. She knew it would have almost certainly overwhelmed us because Arabic was one of the few familiarities we had left. We were trying to find ourselves again after all the loss we had experienced, which was enough of a challenge. We hardly recognized our lives or ourselves. Moreover, this estrangement we had experienced since the war was just the beginning of what would be a long and challenging journey to find some normalcy again.

When Onkel Walter and his family returned from their vacation, we had to leave the same day. "The house does not have enough space for two families," he told Gabriela. I was perplexed: in Mosul, our relatives often slept over on mattresses in our houses, unannounced, even in our smaller house in Yarmouk. But in Kastel, I learned that things worked differently.

After we had packed and brought our suitcases to the living room, Onkel Walter confronted Gabriela, "A six hundred and fifty DM[28] telephone bill? What did you do when I was away?"

She went red in the face and turned to us. "Did you use the phone?"

"Sometimes. I had to call my husband. He's stuck in the camp," Nour said.

Gabriela raised her voice. "This is our entire welfare income I

---

28  Deutsche Mark: the official currency of Germany until the adoption of the Euro in 2002

have to pay back to your uncle now. How could you do that? Have
you lost—"

Onkel Walter interrupted with a loud and clear voice: "Stop it!
I don't want any trouble in my house. Get to the car now! All of
you."

Everyone went quiet at once.

After a tense moment, Alim broke the silence: "Where are we
going now?"

"To your grandmother," Gabriela said in a low voice.

I felt desperate. How long could we stay there? And what would
happen thereafter?

On our three-hour trip north, I mostly stared out the window,
pondering. I was almost five years old when I started to understand
that our previous life was lost. I missed my father, Manal, our relatives, and our friends. I did not speak the language other people
spoke. We had no permanent place to stay, and I did not feel safe
and secure in this country that seemed so strange. Money, food,
and medicine were scarce too. My teeth were rotting due to malnu-
trition. I felt displaced. I didn't miss high society life; all I wanted
was to have our whole family united again, to have a home again,
to feel appreciated and stable again.

Despite how I felt, we were lucky. Oma Erika, my grandmother, awaited us in Amtal, a rural village with a few hundred
inhabitants. She was seventy-five years old. Twenty-five hundred
miles and thirty years had separated us, but her love did not dwin-
dle away. In the late afternoon, we parked in front of her trelliswork fence. Oma Erika opened the front door, clung to the stair

railing, and made her way down the stairs. Her hair, tinged in gray, was proudly pinned up. We got out of the car and met her. She smiled, gave each of us a warm hug, and announced, "Ihr seid hier immer willkommen, egal was passiert. Hier seid ihr in Sicherheit." I did not understand what she said, but when she took me by the hand, I instantly connected with her. She seemed to be a very caring person, and I quickly learned that love needs no language.

She led us inside the house. First, we went to the kitchen, where she opened a fridge filled with food. "Guckt, meine Lieben, wir haben Wurstsalat, Schillerlocken, frischen Käseaufschnitt, Butter und noch viel mehr. Und frisches Brot ist auch da," she said with a smile. Next, she grabbed her walking stick and led us to a clean and spacious living room that had a shiny, oak parquet floor and antique furniture. Golden embroidery decorated a green corner sofa. Thick, red curtains were draped around the room. Delighted by the beautiful sight, my siblings and I smiled. When Onkel Walter entered the living room with two suitcases in his hands, Gabriela asked us to collect the rest from the car and bring it to the second floor. Upstairs, more pleasant surprises awaited us. The rooms were cozy and colorful. One bedroom was painted sun yellow, another rose, and one turquoise. There was a bed for each of us with thick blankets and cushions. New coloring books and pencils were waiting on the desks. The bathroom had toothbrushes, towels, and two washbowls. The kitchen had a fridge with more fresh food. From the kitchen, we could access a large, sunny balcony. The house was even bigger than ours in Yarmouk!

With bright smiles on our faces, we walked back down to the

kitchen. Oma Erika announced, "Am Montag haben wir einen Doktortermin. Ihr werdet dann komplett untersucht. Aber jetzt feiern und essen wir erst einmal." I understood the word "doctor" and knew that Oma Erika was going to take great care of us. Next, she led us through a French door to her veranda. The table had already been set for lunch. We sat down. Oma Erika smiled and so did we. I felt warmly welcomed, appreciated, and secure again. Being with her felt like true family, like maybe this could become our new home.

### Thursday, August 15, 1991

Oma Erika used to be a teacher and thus began to teach us German every day. When we went grocery shopping, when we set the table, when we prepared lunch, she taught us the essential German words and let us repeat them again and again. Since she had a vegetable patch in her back yard, she taught us all those names as well: rotkohl (red cabbage), karotten (carrots), kopfsalat (lettuce), rhabarbar (rhubarb), and zwiebeln (onions) all grew in front of the veranda. She also taught us the names of the fruits that grew along the trelliswork fence: äpfel (apples), birnen (pears), himbeeren (raspberries), and brombeeren (blackberries). It was a natural, progressive learning process.

My siblings and I loved spending time with Oma Erika in Amtal. From the back yard, we could look out over a valley with green meadows, cows, and sheep. The meadows were surrounded by a beautiful dark forest. Amtal was joyful and peaceful—like the time we spent with Oma Erika—and sometimes I almost forgot about everything we had lost in Mosul.

In addition to teaching us German words in day-to-day life, Oma Erika started giving Malik and Alim writing lessons to prepare them for school. Every day, they sat down at the small kitchen table, where she dictated letters to them, and eventually words and small sentences. I always watched them and listened carefully.

On August 15, Malik and Alim had their first school day at the comprehensive school in Oslar. We all got up at 5:00 a.m., excited and happy for them to finally go to school again. In Mosul, they had always attended school with joy and pride, and we hoped it would be the same for them in Oslar. When they were ready this morning to go catch the school bus nearby, we all kissed them goodbye and wished them well.

We waited for them on the driveway in the afternoon. As they approached the trelliswork fence, Malik suddenly started to wail. I had never seen him so desperate. I was appalled.

"Malik, habibi, what happened?" Gabriela asked, rushing toward him. He could not answer, though. He lost himself in uncontrollable sobbing. She hugged him for a long moment while Oma Erika walked to him with her cane. Too embarrassed to look anyone in the eyes, he said, "The children peed in my water bottle and laughed at me throughout the day because I, unknowing, almost drank from it."

I felt so sorry for him. He always tried to be like our parents wanted us to be, but now he was not perfect anymore. He could not speak German fluently, and he looked different with his curly brown hair and relatively brown skin. His recognizable difference was considered inherently negative. As a result, he was bullied by the other children at school.

Oma Erika took him by the hand and walked with him to the kitchen. "I know the principal. I'll call him right now and make sure you will never be treated like that again!"

Before she dialed the number, Gabriela asked Alim about his day.

"I felt like an alien," Alim said.

I was alarmed. Alim had straight hair like me, lighter skin, and was more outgoing than any of us was, and even he struggled to find a friend at school. In that moment, I developed a new fear. If my big brothers weren't so big anymore, what would the other children do to me?

### End of August 1991

We made a few friends in Amtal. Some children, especially the older ones, ignored us on the playground. Some of the younger ones were told by their parents to leave us alone. The ostracization hurt us of course, but some children were allowed to play with us since their parents knew and trusted my grandmother. Even if I was not fully aware of it then, it taught me an important lesson: human connections can easily multiply.

Oma Erika helped us make friends by also inviting other children and their parents over. Sometimes, we played in the driveway with the toys she gave us. Malik and Alim tried to speak German every now and then, whereas I avoided it. Despite trusting Oma Erika and her circle of friends, I was too afraid of making mistakes and possibly being bullied. But I also learned that, fortunately, playing with other children did not always depend on the German language.

### Saturday, August 31, 1991

Despite my new fear of being rejected, I knew I could count on Oma Erika. She was one of the most caring and giving people I knew. She was sensitive to our feelings and met our needs as best as she could. She hugged and praised us every morning and spent a lot of time with us every day. She taught us how to do the housework efficiently. She paid for all our spare time activities without hesitating: outdoor clothes, books, and tickets. Sometimes, she even spoiled us. When the mobile shop rang its bell, she would go with us outside and not only buy fresh, expensive food, but also give each of us a one DM coin so we could buy what we liked. I liked

Kinder Surprise (a chocolate egg with a toy inside) best. The chocolate tasted sweeter than in Iraq and melted so gently in the mouth.

On my fifth birthday, Oma Erika gave me twenty matchbox sized cars. I grinned when I opened the present on the veranda. Soon, my siblings and I sat down on the carpet and began to excitedly fire the cars at each other. Nour watched us with a glowing, smiling face, wearing her maternity dress. She was healthy and well. Everybody was full of joy.

That afternoon, we all sat down at the corner bench to celebrate with tea and cake. After everyone had sung Happy Birthday to me in German, English, and Arabic, we tried Gabriela's butter cream cake and the pastries Oma Erika had bought: streuselkuchen, elephant ears, and vanilla pudding cake with a thick chocolate icing on top, which was my favorite.

When Oma Erika's elderly neighbor came over to take a picture of our family, the full force of our loss and the subsequent emotional stress overwhelmed me yet again. It was such a bittersweet moment. Painful questions suddenly stormed my mind. Where were my father and Manal? Were they still alive? Why did all this happen to us? Could we ever go back to Mosul? I broke out in tears and could not say a word. No one could calm me. I could not grasp the complex emotions that pulled me down.

*Beginning of September 1991*

The longer we stayed in Amtal, the more telephone calls we received from Turkey during the nights. Since we slept upstairs, we rarely heard the ringing. Oma Erika, who slept on the first floor, picked up the telephone in the living room most of the time. "Hier ist Linde," she would say, and the person on the other line would respond in Arabic. She would walk to the hallway and shout, "Phone call from Turkey." And the yelling would start all over again.

"Why can't they call in the daytime, for God's sake!" Gabriela would shout at Nour. It was usually Ammu Serhat on the phone, asking if we could help him and his family get from the Turkish refugee camp to Germany. Nour would beg Gabriela, who would respond angrily, "They can't come, period! It'll get too crowded. Oma Erika will kick us out." Nour would begin to cry, while my siblings and I listened to the commotion from our beds. The longer we stayed in Amtal, the more the nightly yelling and crying robbed our sleep and shredded our nerves.

Gradually, my halfway recovered life was unsettled again: not by war, but by the fighting between those nearest to me. The increasing suffering and inaccessibility of my mother affected me most. She knew she was putting a big burden on Oma Erika because of Nour's relatives, and yet she didn't know how to solve the problem. As a result, she became easily irritable. Sometimes, she shouted at us for no reason. Sometimes, she cried. She hardly ate or drank and rapidly lost weight. Nour and Oma Erika stayed quiet and tense most of the time, while my siblings and I wandered around in an emotional minefield, trying, often in vain, to find a sense of emotional security in our family.

But there was hope. One evening, Onkel Walter called to inform Gabriela that he had purchased a house in Kastel that he would rent to us if we decided to move back. He earned well as a chemical doctor and department manager in a chemical and pharmaceutical facility in Frankfurt.

Gabriela informed us about the house right after their talk. I was happily surprised! I would have liked to stay with Oma Erika, but I knew that my mother wanted to minimize our burden on her. Oma Erika was divorced and had lived alone for many years. She had a strictly organized daily routine: getting up at 5:00 a.m., washing her hair, preparing the kitchen, having breakfast at 7:00 a.m., lunch at noon, a one hour rest at 1:00 p.m., coffee at 3:00 p.m., dinner at 7:00 p.m., and going to bed at 9:00 p.m. Including six traumatized refugees in her routines was not easy. Keeping her routines and taking care of at least twice the number of refugees would have almost certainly been impossible.

*Tuesday, September 17, 1991*

Despite the difficulties in our family, we kept our routines of spending time together.

One evening, we were all sitting at the round table in the living room as usual, watching the eight o'clock news on ARD[29]. The news anchor announced, "In Hoyerswerda, Saxony, an eleven-story residential home of guest workers was attacked by thirty to forty neo-Nazis. Stones, bottles, and Molotov cocktails were thrown. The building was set on fire. Hundreds of German residents joined the mob and applauded. The police retreated. Shortly after, a house of asylum seekers was attacked. Thirty-two people were injured. The victims were beaten, cut, or burned."

---

29 Arbeitsgemeinschaft der öffentlich-rechtlichen Rundfunkanstalten der Bundesrepublik Deutschland: consortium of public broadcasters in Germany

I did not understand most of the words, but I understood the violent pictures. I was scared.

After a politician commented on the problem that a large number of asylum seekers had come to Germany from Eastern Europe, Africa, and the Middle East, Malik asked Gabriela in Arabic about the meaning of the term "asylum seekers."

Gabriela answered, gazing at the television screen with an upset face, "People who flee to another country because of war or because they're treated badly in their home country."

"Like us?" I asked.

"No," she promptly said. "I'm German, and soon you will be too."

"Will they beat us?" I asked.

"No." She turned to me and shook her head. "You live with your grandmother and not in such a building, and your grandmother is German too."

Still, I felt alarmed. If we were welcome here, then why did Malik's classmates pee in his water bottle? And why did some parents not allow their children to play with us?

*Friday, September 20, 1991*

One morning, the doorbell rang. Oma Erika opened the front door, and there he stood, unannounced—Ammu Serhat. We met in the living room. We hardly recognized him. His bones stuck out of his face, and he had a full beard. No one dared to say a word. Suddenly, the telephone rang. Nour picked it up. His relatives were calling, again. She looked at Oma Erika and said, "Please, help us."

But Oma Erika raised her voice: "I can't take more. If it doesn't stop, you'll all have to leave!" Nour ran out of the house. Ammu Serhat followed her.

Gabriela started to cry. She sat down at the desk and sent a text message to Adil: "If you don't come now, you'll visit me at my grave. Serhat and his relatives cause a lot of problems. If they don't leave us in peace, my mother will kick us out." Shortly after, she fainted. Oma Erika rushed to the phone, but Gabriela regained consciousness as she was dialing the emergency number. I was watching everything, transfixed and aware that my family urgently needed help.

### October 1991

Fortunately, Adil got a short-term visa for Germany and managed to come. He called Gabriela right after he had landed in Frankfurt. We were sitting in the living room, eagerly listening to their talk. He told her that he would first get a car, a small Volkswagen, from a colleague and then drive to Amtal. We all looked at each other and smiled. I was looking so forward to finally seeing him again for the first time since Amman. I missed him more than words could say.

He arrived the next afternoon. I hugged him in the driveway for a long moment, relieved to see him alive and overjoyed to be with him again. Our family felt almost whole again. Only Manal was missing.

### *Thursday, October 31, 1991*

Malik, Alim, Sophia and I woke in the middle of the night, alarmed. Nour was screaming in pain as she was walking down the stairs with Ammu Serhat. Oma Erika and my parents were waiting in the hallway on the first floor. When Nour arrived downstairs, two first aiders came in and carried her outside on a stretcher. Ammu Serhat followed them. She was about to give birth! I was worried about her suffering from birthing pain, but excited for her to become a mother and for our family to grow!

Before my parents could go to their car, Oma Erika grabbed Adil's arm. She told him, with a serious face, something I could not understand. Gabriela translated into Arabic and nodded. "Nour and Serhat can't come back to this house anymore!" Adil glared at Gabriela for a moment before they silently left the house. I did not understand what was going on, and was shocked by the cold manner of the discarding. Why could Nour not return to us? What would happen with her now? Would we see each other again?

### *Beginning of November 1991*

On the day of Nour's release, Gabriela went to Oslar hospital with Onkel Walter, who had come with a transporter that was loaded with used furniture for Nour's new apartment.

Out on the veranda at Oma Erika's, Malik and Alim explained to me what was going on. They informed me about her move. They also said that my parents were still disappointed with Nour's

76

decision. "She was only seventeen years old when she secretly met with Ammu Serhat in a hotel in Mosul," Alim said. Malik added, "And when our parents heard the rumors from other people, Nour and Ammu Serhat had to marry to safeguard our reputation, even though Ammu Serhat didn't have the high standing we had." I could not understand my parents' attitude. How could these be good reasons to condemn her and her new family?

Still, Nour, Ammu Serhat, and Rahila, my newborn niece, moved into an apartment in Oslar, while my parents and Oma Erika forbade us from visiting them. I felt confused and upset. As a young child, I had taken it for granted that my family would always try to stay together. Reality, however, taught me that family could not be taken for granted. In our case, the elders voluntarily decided to break close contact with Nour and her new family. I felt guilty that we had abandoned them; my siblings and I protested against our parents' decision, but in vain. For the first time, I doubted if I could always count on my family. Would they abandon me, too, if I broke their rules?

A few days after Nour moved in her apartment, Adil had to fly back to Mosul. Once again, I was afflicted. Would my family ever be united again?

# PART III

# KASTEL

*November 1991–March 1992*

*Application for negative certification*

*Thursday, November 21, 1991*

*Tap tap tap ding zip tap tap* . . . Onkel Walter was sitting at his desk under a yellow table lamp. His face was tense. Dozens of cigarette butts filled the ashtray next to his typewriter. Between piles of folders, he was typing a letter to the Society of St. Pius[30], which had put up a house in Kastel for sale. He signed the purchase contract at the end of August, intending to rent out the house to us and help us settle in Kastel. He and my parents favored Kastel over Amtal since its infrastructure was much more developed. Kastel had doctors, schools, kindergartens, shops, job opportunities, public transport, clubs, and much more.

However, when the Kasteler town council found out that my family was planning to move in Paul-Ehrlich-Straße[31] four, it decided to block our efforts.

*I would like to inform you that the Kasteler town council made use of their right of preemption, which means they aim to buy your property for "infrastructural reasons" even though a private person, me, already signed a purchase contract.*

*The case was already discussed at two town council meetings. Prior to the first meeting, my lawyer, the vice mayor, and I met in the town hall to a) let the town council know about the reasons for*

---

30   A Roman-Catholic priestly fraternity

31   Name of a street (*Straße*)

*my purchase, hoping they would give up the right of preemption, and b) explain the urgency of the case and its legal uncertainty.*

*After the first town council meeting, I was informed by a letter to abide by the deadline in case I wanted to object to the town council's decision. My lawyer thus sent a request for a negative certification to the town on October 28, 1991. Consequently, the case was discussed on another town council meeting on November 6, 1991. Before the second meeting was held, the Catholic pastor of Kastel called the vice mayor, at my request, and recommended selling the house to me.*

*When I called the mayor after the second meeting, he told me that the town council decided to let the Mühlheimer State Association of Towns and Municipalities investigate the case "due to the problem of asylum seekers." I told him that I could not understand the town council's determination to only give up the right of preemption if it was legally enforced. Moreover, I told him that my sister was not an asylum seeker, anyway, but a German citizen in urgent need to find a place for her four children who would soon be naturalized. He told me, once again, that her social situation was irrelevant.*

*I assume that the town council, knowing that they are in an indefensible legal position, engages the higher authority in Mühlheim to receive a superior affirmation that they cannot create any housing space for asylum seekers, which they claim they do not have. This way, they almost certainly also intend to counter future allocation of asylum seekers by higher government agencies.*

*Two years ago, the town council a) sold a house that was inhabited by a Turkish family to a company that tore it down to build owner-occupied flats. The company owner's wife is a party member of the Christian Democratic Union (CDU) and of the town council, and b) sold a house that was inhabited by asylum seekers to a third person who forced the residents, per lawsuit, to leave the house for personal use. There might be even more current, similar cases.*

*With this knowledge, one needs to try hard not to lose one's self-control. I thus intend to continue in the legal way. My sister and her four children will move into Paul-Ehrlich-Straße four tomorrow, November 22, 1991, as we agreed upon on the telephone.*

*The commitment for a mortgage loan has already been issued. Due to the delay, which has been caused by the Kasteler town council, the transfer of property could not take place yet. This, however, is the condition for the payout. Based on our purchase contract of August 28, 1991, the right of withdrawal can be exercised if the purchase price (150,000 DM) is not paid by December 2, 1991. I assume that the legal inquiry will lead to a verdict in our favor, so that the payout can follow soon. In the meantime, I will pay the interest on which we agreed. I hope for your understanding. Respectfully . . .*

### Friday, November 22, 1991

We left Amtal after lunch under a blue sky. When we arrived in Kastel, the sky was covered with gray clouds. We got out of the car and stepped on a narrow sidewalk. A cold wind was blowing down the street. I was freezing even though I was wearing Alim's old pullover.

"That is it!" Gabriela said, pointing at a dirty, yellowed house. Moss beset much of the pitched roof. The front garden hedge was wild and untrimmed. I was skeptical. That condemned house was our new home?

Wary, I followed my family. We entered the property through a corroded metal door on concrete slabs that were largely covered with soil. The front garden mostly consisted of dirt. "Your uncle cleared out all the rotten trees," Gabriela said before she led us around the house under barren grape vines, which hung down from a corroded metal frame. Two tall trees had grown in the back yard, one in front of a garage, the other one next to it. "A cherry and a plum tree," Gabriela said. It was the first plum tree I had seen, and it was huge. Its thick, dark brown trunk covered the gray light post of the street behind our back yard. Looking around, I noticed that neither tree held a single leaf. Our garden looked like the dead place around Sheikh Ibrahim, only in darker tones. I had flashbacks of the war.

"Yallah, we go inside," Malik told me. We followed Gabriela back to the entrance. As she was looking for the keys in her purse, cars passed by behind us. Beyond, we heard the horn of a train. The railway station was only one hundred yards away from our house. Kastel was much louder than Amtal. Would the inside of the house also be so different from Oma Erika's place? I wondered.

We entered a narrow, shady place. "The house was built in 1954 and has 775 square feet," Gabriela informed us. The hallway had brown linoleum flooring; the surrounding walls were covered with dark brown wood panels. A filthy olive carpet was glued on the stairs that led to the second floor. The living room in front of us had the same carpeting. On our left, we passed a tiny, foul guest bathroom before we entered through a rusty doorframe to a small kitchen. White, wooden cupboards stood around, unarranged. "I painted them when your father looked after you," Gabriela said. "The windows are only single-glazed, but they have shutters," she continued uneasily. We followed her to the living room, which was relatively spacious. She opened a squeaky glass door to the veranda. Once more, I looked at the fallow garden—disappointed. This house was not at all like Oma Erika's house, or Onkel Walter's! Moreover, it was even further away from what we used to have in Mosul—a home.

"Let me show you your bedrooms and the bathroom upstairs," Gabriela said. Only after she had said these words did I realize that we did not have to flee anymore. We finally had our own house again. Suddenly, I felt relieved, even curious and excited to inspect our rooms.

Sophia and I went ahead to the second floor on squeaky stairs. Each of the three bedrooms contained a gray carpet, yellowed wallpaper, and an old gas heater. The bathroom had gray tiles. Some tiles were broken. The bathtub was yellowed and scratched, and the silicone joints mildewed; but I accepted everything and smiled, thankful that the toilet did not stink as much as the one downstairs. I was not aware of it then, but thankfulness made a lot of things easier. In our case, it was like a shortcut to a feeling of success on our long journey to find a new place we could call home.

When we walked back to the living room, I noticed a strange smell. "What's that?" I covered my nose.

"It's the gas heater. It leaks. I turned it on before we went upstairs," Gabriela said. I learned that gas smelled like rotten eggs. "Go collect our bags from the car, and the two mattresses. We'll sleep in the living room tonight. We can't afford to heat all of the rooms," she said. We did what we were told.

That night, I slept soundly, thankful that we finally settled somewhere even though I knew that much had to be done to transform this house into a home.

### *The last week of November 1991*

After the question of Paul-Ehrlich-Straße four had been discussed in a third town council meeting, the mayor called Onkel Walter. He told him that the town council decided to give up the right of preemption and issue the negative certification in the course of the week.

### *Monday, December 2, 1991*

Since the negative certification was not issued as had been promised, Onkel Walter called the mayor, who promised that a messenger would deliver the document by December 6. When Onkel Walter complained that the seller would now gain the right to withdraw from the contract due to this delay, the mayor hung up without a word.

The town of Kastel tried every trick to prevent our family's housing arrangement.

*Mid-December 1991*

Kastel was a conservative town, led by the CDU. It counted about ten thousand inhabitants who predominantly belonged to the white middle class. About a hundred and thirty asylum seekers, largely coming from North Africa and the Middle East, lived in small metal trailer homes at the town border. Not only were they physically segregated like in most German towns, they were also put in emotional distress, since many were denied a working permit, and some were only given a temporary suspension of deportation.

Around Paul-Ehrlich-Straße, my siblings and I stuck out with our darker skin and black hair. I did not notice the difference—until we were treated differently. Our neighbors greeted each other every day when they collected their mail. When we greeted them, they stared at us or turned around as if we did not exist. It bothered me with questions and feelings of inadequacy. Why did they reject us?

The Hoyerswerda riots of September 1991 marked the beginning of small, but violent acts of civil unrest against immigrants in Germany. The country was not only struggling with increasing numbers of asylum seekers but also with the political challenges and economic costs of its recent reunification. After we had collected a television from someone's bulky garbage left out on a sidewalk one night, we watched over and over again as the homes of asylum seeker were burned down and non-white people were injured by white mobs. The people that were harmed often looked like us. The situation frightened me, and I worried that we would soon be attacked as well.

One afternoon, as my siblings and I walked to the town center, a middle-aged couple walked toward us on the same sidewalk. They were coming closer, they crossed the street to the other sidewalk. The woman whispered something to the man, and both glared at us with judging eyes. Suddenly, three-year-old Sophia started shouting, "Ausländer raus!"[32] the first slogan she had adopted from television since we moved to Kastel. Malik quickly held his hands over her mouth while the couple kept glaring. I was scared they would come over and harm us. Fortunately, they let us walk away.

Still, the covert and overt hostilities our family faced again and again made me feel alienated and unsure of myself. Soon I began to wonder: What was suddenly so wrong with us? Were we monsters in the eyes of the Germans who so disliked us? The more I questioned, the more I began to believe that something could indeed be wrong with us.

### *End of January 1992*

While I spent most of my time with my siblings at home, the legal battle against the town continued. Onkel Walter's lawyer sent a letter to the town council, requesting they issue the negative certification by February 4, 1992. He also threatened to make an administrative claim against the town in case of further delay. The town council kept us in limbo the entire time.

---

32  German: "Foreigners out of here!"

*February 1992*

Gabriela did not talk with us about our problematic social situation. She was hardly ever at home anyway since she worked three jobs to feed us and pay the rent. Still, we felt her growing sadness and anger.

She would leave in the early morning to work as a cashier in a bakery, and come back home around noon to cook for us. When she entered the house, she usually looked exhausted. Little incidents often irritated her. My and my siblings' biggest challenge was to keep our house tidy and clean. But even when we left only a coloring book or a glass on the table, for instance, Gabriela increasingly lost self-control. Sometimes she even chased us through the house, shouting, "You're nothing but a catastrophe! What have I done to deserve you?" Or, "I can't expect anything from you because you have your father in you! You have no manners, no culture, no religion, nothing!" The more often she said such things, the more I felt like a useless burden on her, and the more I tried to satisfy her. But even when we had cleaned the house and had done all the chores she had given us, she frequently looked at us as if all our work was not good enough. Stressed, she would run to the basement, cook, and call us to collect our food. She rarely sat down with us to eat together, and soon we gave up asking her if she would. Maybe she was afraid of losing control over us. Maybe she was too tired from work to show a lot of interest in us. Maybe she felt ashamed of who we were in Kastel: strangers. Maybe she was utterly overwhelmed. We didn't know and didn't ask why she had changed so radically. We only knew that something was wrong, and that we had to do what she expected to help her and take some pressure off her.

After lunch, Gabriela normally went to the bakery again. Around 7:00 p.m., she would come back home, often too exhausted to speak much and pressed for time. She would quickly eat a piece of bread with spread and leave again to clean a medical office. Sometimes, she went to the medical office directly from the bakery. Twice a week, she also did a paper route from 9:00 to 11:00 p.m. We therefore went to bed alone. Even when she was at home in the evening, Gabriela would not sing us goodnight songs like in Mosul, or hug and kiss us. Instead, she would send us to bed by a tired command. Our new life in Kastel left deep marks. We missed her affection. I gradually began to feel abandoned and wondered if she still loved us. What did we do wrong? What *was* wrong with us? Being a six-year-old child who naturally depended on his mother's affection, I began to blame myself—which fed a feeling of shame inside of me.

One day in February, around noon, we were watching television when Gabriela suddenly entered the living room. We did not hear her open the front door. "I work day and night and you useless guys watch television?" she shouted. Malik switched off the television at once. Gabriela ran to the hallway, where she saw my shoes in front of the shoe rack, came back, grabbed my arm, and dragged me along.

"Please, what have I done?" I dared to ask, anticipating what was going to happen.

She threw me in front of the rack and said, "I told you to put your shoes inside the rack!" Next, she reached out and slapped my cheek full force with her flat hands: left, right, left. When I tried to protect my face, she began to hit my shoulders, my back, the back of my head—again and again—until she finally stopped. I curled up next to the shoe rack. She looked at me for a moment, apathetically, before she disappeared into the kitchen. The pain I felt was immeasurable; I had never been beaten in Iraq. My body was shaking from terror. Tears rolled down my cheeks as I stared at the brown linoleum, inconsolable, wondering, *Why?*

From the time we moved to Kastel, Gabriela started attacking us more and more often. We were soon alert to when she was at home. Still, none of my siblings were targeted as often or as violently as I was. Malik and Alim remained an allied pair like they had in Iraq. They went to school together and after school did almost everything together. They also grew stronger physically as they hit puberty. Malik was never physically targeted especially since he was assigned to look after us. He relieved Gabriela by taking responsibility for us. Alim was slapped a few times, but he knew how to comfort Gabriela. He learned to play the flute at school and played it at home every time she asked for it. Sophia was beaten more often than Alim, but not as often as I was. She seemed to be something like Gabriela's last hope—her only child who carried a German given name and looked "German." Still, Sophia's skin was also somewhat brown, and I assumed that she would face difficulties being accepted in Kastel.

### *Spring 1992*

The telephone rang one evening. I picked it up. "Sultan."

"Habibi, how are you? I miss you!" Adil said.

It was almost a miracle when the telephone lines to Iraq were open.

My heart began to race. "Baba! When do you come to Germany?"

"Inshallah, soon. Your mother told me she has been looking for a kindergarten place for you for four months, but no one wants to take you. I hope she finds a place soon."

"I don't need any kindergarten. When you come, we can just go for a walk," I said, unaware of Gabriela's setbacks until then.

"Habibi, we'll do that," he paused. "Do you listen to your mother?"

I wanted to tell him what was going on in our new home, but I just said yes. I had promised him that I would listen to her, and I wanted to keep my word and be a good son. Also, I believed, for some reasons I was not aware of then, that everything would become better again. Maybe this belief was just childlike thinking. Maybe it derived from happy memories of our family life in Iraq. Maybe it came from deep within, from an almost indestructible human confidence or hope that we could make our lives better than this.

### *Rose Monday, March 2, 1992*

Gabriela introduced us to Carnival. Since we did not celebrate this festival in Iraq, she explained the tradition to us and made us curious: "People dress up in costumes and have fun together." At my aunt's, we borrowed costumes and used make-up. Malik and Alim painted their faces white; Sophia put on a pink princess dress while Gabriela made a clown of me. She painted my face white, my nose red, and drew three red teardrops on my cheek. A red hat almost covered my black hair. We were ready to go.

The local gym was already packed with people when we arrived. Gabriela led us to the last free table next to the stage. As we sat down, we looked around with large eyes, impressed by the colorful costumes. Almost everyone was dressed up. Some had dyed their hair in neon colors. Some families were sitting at tables, eating sausages and drinking soft drinks. People were chatting and laughing. Some gazed at us. I noticed the strange silence at our table and felt somewhat out of place. Did I look stupid? Did we look stupid?

"You can eat or drink something over there," Gabriela told us. Knowing that we could not afford the expensive food outside, we politely thanked her and said no. As we kept looking around with big eyes, she gave me a two DM coin. "Just go like the other kids and get something to eat," she said. I got up and walked to the food counter, wearing my red silk clown costume. When it was my turn, I put the two DM coin on the counter and pointed at the French fries. The people close by eyed me from head to toe. No one was so perfectly dressed up. I felt like a real clown—like I was alone, there for people to laugh at. No one talked to me, and I did not dare to approach anyone either since I knew that my German was insufficient. Fear of rejection or even humiliation by others made me walk back to my family. They were everything I had. Despite the turbulent times we had to manage, I was glad to have them and not to be completely alone.

*Friday, March 6, 1992*

In the end, our ongoing struggles in the aftermath of the war led to some successes. My family, except Adil and Manal, had escaped to a war-free country. Nour and her family had settled in an apartment; we settled in a house. A few neighbors started to respond to our greetings in a friendly way. We were naturalized. We received full healthcare. Gabriela earned some money and received some welfare support for our family. We could afford simple but good food. Still, fighting continued on other frontiers. Being accepted in Kastel seemed to require a lot of effort, resilience, and patience. Even though I did not feel very close to Onkel Walter, I was glad that he supported us. He typed another letter to the town council on March 6, expressing his consternation about the council's attempts to chase my family away.

> *I want to express my disappointment at the town council's decision to make use of the right of preemption after I had informed you about my sister's situation. Your decision lacked any legal basis. Still, it took you more than five months to adhere to the law and issue the negative certification. Further, it needs to be noted that a town council, led by the CDU, did not help my sister, who flew from war-torn Iraq and, instead of acting in the Christian command of love, tried to get in the way through dubious administrative behavior. Thanks to the Society of St. Pius, the purchase contract is still valid. After having experienced*

*this arbitrariness, I want to let you know that I still cannot be-lieve that all members of the town council back up this practice. Respectfully . . .*

# KASTEL

*March 1992–August 1993*

*Finally, we have you back!*

*March 1992*

I had just finished eating my breakfast cereal when Gabriela told me with a contented smile, "You'll start kindergarten today." Surprised by the promising news, I smiled back. I was happy and hopeful for the both of us. Her desperate search had been finally successful; I sensed that my acceptance into kindergarten could release some pressure from her and defuse the violent situation at home.

It would take years before she would tell me that, for five months, all three kindergartens of Kastel preferred German-speaking children to me. Her bakery colleagues repeatedly told her that their children had gotten a kindergarten place without delay. The unequal treatment tormented Gabriela's mind.

All the same, the Catholic kindergarten at the Goldbach creek accepted me at last, which brought a series of positive changes into my life. Around 9:00 a.m., Gabriela took me along to the one-story, flat-roofed building. Few buildings in Kastel had a flat roof; the construction reminded me of the houses in Mosul. Excited and nervous, I followed her into the entrance hall. A middle-aged woman approached us. She exchanged a few words with Gabriela, who shortly after ran on to work. For a second, I felt deserted, until the woman kneeled down. She took me by the hand and said with a gentle smile, "Willkommen, Junis! Ich bin Bärbel." Bärbel, my new kindergarten teacher, seemed to be a friendly person. I felt I was in safe hands.

She led me down a long corridor along some shoe racks. Some shoes were tidily put away inside the shoe rack; some were lying in front of it, I noticed. We stopped in front of a door that held a cardboard bear. "Du kommst in die Bärengruppe," she said. I looked at her with large eyes, aware that I did not fully understand her. My German was still too poor.

Since we had moved to Kastel, I had not heard or spoken a lot of German. Gabriela worked most of the time, and if she was at home, she did not speak much. Malik and Alim attended secondary school in Kastel, but preferred speaking Arabic when they were at home since they were still insecure in German. And Sophia, who was four years old, did not speak much at all.

I felt troubled. Would I make friends? Or would I end up like Malik and Alim on their first school day in Oslar?

I wanted to seize the chance to find a friend. Hopeful, I followed Bärbel into the room. She approached two boys at a table and said, "Ich habe einen neuen Freund für euch. Er heißt Junis. Er spricht kaum Deutsch, aber er ist sehr nett. Kann er bei euch sitzen?" The boys nodded and pulled back a chair for me. I sat down and shyly looked around. The two boys had blond hair, like most children in the room. Only three other boys looked similar to me. They were playing by themselves. Some other children were drawing at group tables. Some were sitting in the corner browsing books and talking with each other.

"Er ist Dominik und ich bin Marcus," Marcus said.

"Und wie heißt du?" Dominik asked me.

I kept silent, afraid to make a mistake.

Shortly, Bärbel called from behind: "Er heißt Junis. Spielt einfach mit ihm!"

"Willst du mit uns auf dem Teppich mit Autos spielen?" Dominik asked.

Since I knew that "spielen" meant playing, I nodded.

We got up and began to play on a carpet with matchbox-cars.

For almost two hours, we pushed the cars to each other and laughed happily again and again, thrilled by the speed of the cars. Once more, I noticed that connecting with others and having fun together did not depend on a common language. A little courage and mutual willingness were enough.

### Sunday, April 19, 1992

Two challenging and exhilarating weeks of kindergarten passed quickly. I needed some days to overcome my fear of making mistakes and see that I could have a pleasant time with most children without speaking perfect German. Still, I began to learn German quickly by playing and interacting with my classmates, listening to Bärbel's short stories and answering questions, and singing along with the German Easter songs we practiced every day. Easter drew near, and I was eager to learn more about it.

On Easter Sunday morning, my family and I left Kastel to visit Oma Erika and celebrate Easter together. We exited the freeway at Lutterberg and drove down meandering streets through the Solling uplands. Once again, I marveled at the green forest, which was dominated by spruces and beeches, as I could now tell after I had learned their names at school. I opened the window and inhaled the fresh forest air, entranced. When we entered the first village, we spotted bushes decorated with colored eggs in people's front gardens. Never before had I seen how Easter was celebrated. Gabriela saw our enthusiastic faces in the rearview mirror. She was pleased, stopped on a side street, and took a picture of us in front of a decorated bush.

We parked in Oma Erika's driveway around noon. She opened the front door before we could ring the bell; she was awaiting us. She gave me a big kiss on my cheek and a warm hug, like always. I felt happy and smiled, aware that everything was good in Amtal: Oma Erika would take great care of us, and she wouldn't allow Gabriela to beat us. Cheerful, I kissed and hugged Oma Erika back before we all went inside her house. We gathered in the kitchen. Oma Erika showed us the colored eggs she had bought for our egg hunt in the garden. Before we went outside, we sat down at the table, where she served venison goulash, red cabbage, and bread dumplings. She always cooked the freshest, most delicious food for us. We all smiled brightly. We were under a spell in her presence— it was her unconditional love.

After we had indulged ourselves, my siblings and I waited in the kitchen while Gabriela began to hide the eggs in the garden. Some minutes later, she joyfully called from the back yard, "You can come out now!" For reasons we didn't understand then, Gabriela behaved differently in Amtal compared to Kastel. She seemed to be more comfortable with herself, and she was kind and generous to us. We were glad for it, and we enjoyed the time with her in Amtal. Relieved and free like normal children, we ran outside—laughing, dashing in different directions, and trying to find the eggs. Easter in Amtal was a time of peaceful togetherness. Easter in Amtal was a time of joy. I wished every day could be like Easter in Amtal.

Some years later, during puberty, when recognition from others became more important, I would partially understand why Gabriela behaved differently in Amtal. She faced rather little social pressure and discrimination because of us in that remote village, which counted only about two hundred people. The peaceful silence of nature and the fresh air gently blew away the noise she carried along from Kastel. More importantly, Oma Erika was her safe haven. She accepted Gabriela unconditionally. She was her confidant, her mentor, and her friend. She helped her financially, and she lightened her workload by taking responsibility for us and the housework, which was mostly done by household help.

### *June 1992*

Unfortunately, not every day compared with Easter. Certain moments in my everyday life still terrified me. The first week after we had moved to Kastel, I ran to the basement for dear life and hid between the freezer and the gas oven when the Civil Defense siren sounded at noon. Seventeen months after the Second Gulf War, my heart still began to race whenever I heard a siren. I was still nervous even though I knew I was safe. The war, the terror, and the death from above were still ingrained in my mind.

Many things that reminded me of the war frightened me, such

as airplanes. But I didn't talk about it; I drew it. During the first months in kindergarten, my pictures showed warplanes, tanks, bombs, broken houses, and dead people lying on bloodstained streets. Bärbel observed me attentively. She carefully talked with me about every picture. She told me that what we had experienced was very bad and that she was glad we were in Germany and safe now. She reassured me that what we had experienced would not happen where we were now. Her care, her understanding, and her encouragement made me feel secure. It gave me strength and helped me slowly overcome my war traumas. She was one of my saviors.

Over time, my pictures became free of blood, even if they were not completely peaceful yet. In June 1992, shortly before the summer break, my drawings still contained random war elements, as if the war had somehow followed my family to Germany.

*Summer 1992*

Friends also helped me overcome my war traumas. Marcus, Dominik, and I had become good friends by the summer of 1992. In addition to playing together in class, we met in our free time very frequently. Dominik lived nearby. I visited him almost every day to play outside. Marcus usually joined us. That summer, we discovered the best hiding places in the thicket. "Ready or not, here I come!" one of us would yell, the others hiding in the bushes, silently observing the seeker and, if necessary, quietly changing positions. The more exciting and happy moments we shared, the more we connected, the more my war memories were pushed away. Besides, I was learning German at a high speed with their help.

In addition, my siblings and I had switched to speaking only German at home by the summer of 1992. We helped each other learn the language. When Gabriela was at home, she corrected and taught us as well, which improved our skills significantly. We still struggled to use the defined and undefined articles in all the different conjugations correctly, a major challenge for all German learners, but we got better in time. Skill comes with practice, Oma Erika used to say, and I learned that she was right.

A few weeks after I had been admitted to kindergarten, Sophia also got a place in kindergarten. She attended the neighboring group in my corridor—the dinosaurs. My family integrated more and more in Kastel, and yet we still faced random social attacks.

Malik and Alim normally picked us up from kindergarten after the end of their school day, 1:10 p.m., since Gabriela only had one hour-long midday break, in which she would rush back home, cook our food, eat, and go back to work. One day, on our way home, we passed a house that had a Great Dane lying in the driveway behind a metal fence. A boy my age was standing close by. He looked over us for a second before he shouted to his dog, "Attack! Foreigners!" The dog jumped up, hit the fence with his forepaws, and barked loudly. Standing next to Sophia, I held my breath and froze. Malik grabbed our hands and rapidly crossed the street with us. We walked away, scared and speechless.

Soon, my fright turned into embarrassment. Why did that boy despise us if he did not even know us? And why did some people still not see us as their neighbors, or at least as harmless strangers?

Two decades later, studying the "integration" of immigrants in Germany, I came to understand: A widespread fear of strangers was inflamed by continual negative, overgeneralizing, and false "news" about immigrants in the standard media, and fueled by nationalistic, in most cases, conservative politicians who didn't differentiate between asylum seekers, foreigners, and immigrants— let alone individual cases and mass phenomena—and who went out of their way to spread contradictory misinformation and racist prejudices. As if all "foreigners" (meaning all non-white and non-Christian people) in Germany took away career and housing opportunities, resources, and much more from native citizens. As if "they"—strangely enough at the same time—were almost always unemployed welfare recipients who lived lives of luxury, paid by the German taxpayers. As if "they" were fundamentally evil and a menace to society, being anti-democratic, uneducated, and uncivilized; rapists, gangsters, murderers, and so on. The consequences were fatal since the threshold of racist violence was low in an environment that fostered racist attitudes against non-white and non-Christian people.

### Sunday, September 20, 1992

In contrast to the fear of facing random attacks outside our house, our life at home maintained its routine. Even Sundays were strict working days. Gabriela let us sleep until 9:00 a.m. After breakfast, we tidied up and cleaned our house until noon. I was most commonly responsible for the bathrooms. After lunch, we continued cleaning the rest of the house before we met for tea and cake at 3:00 p.m., and then had some free time after.

One Sunday, Gabriela allowed us to go to an event in the Kasteler Freizeitpark[33]: "The Games in the Park." Clubs, church communities, schools, and kindergartens introduced themselves. The event was opened with a show of the Kasteler band. Surprised, I spotted Piero, a kindergarten friend of mine. He was wearing a red felt uniform and a pair of white gloves. We briefly smiled at each other before he started to play his horn with full confidence. The music got under my skin. I got goose bumps listening to the powerful composition. Fourteen people were playing horns; four people were on troop drums; and one young man played a snare drum that led the rhythm with a free and decisive beat. I, too, wanted to learn to play one of these instruments! After the

---

33  A recreational park with a swimming pool

fifteen-minute show, Piero came directly to me. We both smiled, and he gave me his horn to try playing. As I did, his father walked up to us.

"Not bad! You should join us, boy. You could play the horn, like Piero," he told me.

"I'd love to, but I have to ask my mother first. It's probably expensive, isn't it?" I asked.

"Nah, you're a kid. For you it's forty DM a year. If I can pay it, your mother can pay it too. And if you come, I'll take care of you like my son. Let me introduce you to my cousin, our maestro. He'll explain everything to you," he said and put his hand on my shoulder. At that moment I knew I absolutely wanted to become a member of that band. They seemed like a family that welcomed everybody with open arms.

When my siblings and I went home late afternoon, I wanted to share my wish with Gabriela, but I did not dare to approach her since I knew about our scarce financial resources. I was afraid she would get angry. At bedtime, however, I gathered my courage and approached her. My will was stronger than my fear. I told her about the Kasteler band and politely asked if she would allow and pay for me to join the band. She looked at me, deliberated for a moment, and then said, "Yes, you can. I'll pay for it." I was surprised. I thanked her and smiled shyly. Inside, though, I was unusually overjoyed!

*Monday, September 21, 1992*

At 7:00 p.m. I met Piero and Luigi, his younger brother, in front of the "Vereinshaus[34]" in Weinbergstraße, close to Gabriela's bakery. We went inside together. As we entered a smoke-filled rehearsal room, I looked around. Except for Piero, Luigi, and me, all the club members were adults. Many were drinking beer. I was alarmed. No one in my family drank alcohol. It was haram—forbidden—Adil used to say. For a second, I felt as if I should not be there. But then, all the club members approached me with a smile and introduced themselves. Some hugged me. Some were local Kastelers, some were relatives of Piero's, "originally" from Sicily. I felt warmly welcomed. Antonio, the maestro, bought me a Fanta at the counter before he announced, "I'm proud that young kids like Junis join us." Next, he handed me an instrument. "This horn is yours from now on. You can take it home and practice." The club members clapped their hands and smiled again. I beamed with joy. It felt like belonging to a second family, a family that appreciated me and that wanted me to thrive and become successful on a common journey.

Unfortunately, happy and peaceful multicultural coexistence wasn't a reality throughout all of Germany.

*Monday, November 23, 1992*

My siblings and I watched the evening news. "Two neo-Nazis attacked two houses in Mölln, Schleswig-Holstein, in which

---

34  Place or house where the members of a club meet

Turkish families lived, with Molotov cocktails. A ten-year-old, Yaliz Arslan, a fourteen-year-old, Ayse Yilmaz, and their fifty-one-year-old grandmother, Bahide Arslan, were killed in the flames. During the firefighting operation, the police received several responsibility calls, which ended with 'Heil Hitler.'"

We looked at each other, taken aback. Thoughts flooded my mind. The poor family! Their poor relatives! Why did these hate crimes reccur in Germany? Being six years old, I did not understand the political context, but I understood that the anger was toward "foreigners," and that we were potential targets. We looked like Turks too! We lived in a house too! I was horrified.

A third of all Germans supported the solution "Ausländer raus" before the murders in Mölln. After, the number dropped to nearly twenty percent, but that didn't take away my fear of being targeted in the future, maybe even in a deadly way. Slowly, a thought I had had before on similar occasions recaptured my mind. If we just tried harder to be like Germans, would we be fully accepted and safe?

## December 1992

I was willing to do anything to be fully accepted and safe. Gabriela would know what I had to do, I thought. She was born German, and I naturally trusted her words and her instructions.

At the beginning of December, Gabriela asked Sophia and me to act in a play in kindergarten, which we did. Sophia was wrapped in a white cloth, playing Maria. I was standing behind a crèche with a stick in my hand, playing a shepherd who came to see Maria's newborn, Jesus. Bärbel had read the story of Jesus to us a few weeks earlier. In Iraq I had been told about Allah and the Prophet Muhammad. I therefore felt somewhat confused the first time Bärbel read out the story of Jesus, but mostly I was astonished by the idea of "God's son." I accepted the ideological shift without much thinking. Also, I enjoyed our common play experience. After the play, parents congratulated us for the good show. I appreciated their recognition and felt as if I was on the right path to being fully accepted by others and safe in Germany.

### Sunday, December 13, 1992

We watched the evening news. "Three hundred thousand people marched in Hamburg with candles in their hands against xenophobia and for more tolerance. Marches are planned for Würzburg, Nuremberg, Stuttgart, Hanover, Leipzig, Frankfurt, Berlin, and more cities." The peoples' devotion to stop the violence moved me and gave me hope. Nonetheless, I still did not feel really safe in my skin in Germany. Like many times before, I wished my father would come and protect us.

### February 1993

Two wishes came true within two months. First, Oma Erika, Nour, and Gabriela unexpectedly reconciled. On Christmas Eve 1992, Oma Erika, Nour, Ammu Serhat, and Rahila suddenly stood at our front door, smiling and holding presents in their hands. They were part of our family again. I felt overjoyed about our reunification. Secondly, Adil retired in Iraq and came to live with us. He had, discreetly, arranged a successor for his posts. A sudden escape with us to Germany in 1991 would have put all of us in danger since it would have been seen as treason by Saddam Hussein, but Adil's past planning made this move to Germany more organic.

On his arrival day, we drew a Welcome Home poster and put it on our cupboard in the living room: "Endlich haben wir dich wieder." ("Finally, we have you back.") We also put flowers, candles, coffee, and pastries on the dining table. Onkel Walter, my aunt Ursula, and my cousins Moritz and Sabrina came as well to welcome him. We were all so looking forward to having him back.

When Adil arrived, we beamed almost non-stop, overwhelmed with joy that we were reunited and that he was healthy. Gabriela was smiling too, but Adil seemed to have difficulty recognizing her. Sometimes, he even stared at her. She had hollow cheeks, tired eyes, and completely gray hair by then. Before we started to eat, he took a deep breath. He raised his eyebrows and said in English, "God knows I would have done anything to spare us this painful experience, but now we're in security at last." Onkel Walter nodded. Adil looked at us and repeated his words in Arabic. Malik and Alim nodded, whereas Sophia and I just looked at him with big question marks on our faces. We already had difficulties understanding Arabic. Since we had entered kindergarten, we only heard and spoke German. I suddenly felt deeply troubled: I had learned German, but I hardly understood my father now.

### Spring 1993

My siblings and I now spent most of our time after school or kindergarten at home, helping Adil learn German and find his way. Normally, parent-child relationships work the other way around, but we had no choice. It was just another consequence of the war and part of our struggle to find a new home for our family, and we adapted without much talking about it. Sophia and I spoke German with Adil and Malik and Alim translated everything. Plenty of challenges awaited us. Adil's new job was to do the housework and take care of us, especially when Gabriela was at work. However, he struggled to meet his new responsibilities. He did not know how to cook, how to do the washing, how to dress us, how to get things done in the German health care system, how to help us with our homework, and much more. Many things were new and strange to him. He did not talk much, except to apologize for making mistakes. I often found him sitting in the living room, staring outside the window with a sad face and tears in his eyes. I felt sorry for him. I wanted to help him. Sometimes, I could convince him to go outside with me for a walk, even if our walks were only a temporary relief.

*Summer 1993*

One night, Adil called us to the living room. He announced in Arabic and then in poor German, "I need to speak with your mother tonight, and I want you to give your opinions too. I don't know what else to do. I am exhausted." We nodded and sat down. I felt nervous, not knowing what to say. When Gabriela came from her paper route, he confronted her right away. "Please, sit down. We need to speak. You need to spend more time at home," he said.

She sat down and looked at him, irritated, as they had had

the same argument many times before. "What do you want?" she asked.

Adil raised his voice. "A hundred DM more a month doesn't make a big difference. Our children need a mother. We need each other. We still have some money in Iraq, which I can bring if necessary."

"You can talk. I am the only one who earns money here, and I don't want them to walk around with clothes from the Red Cross[35] anymore. People laugh at us! Don't tell me what they need! And if you have money, bring it, now! What are you waiting for?" Gabriela said.

Adil turned to us. "Tell your mother that she should spend more time at home!"

Both of them looked at us, expectant.

Of course, we did not dare to say a word. We did not want to take sides. They were both our parents, and we loved both of them—and needed to be loved by both of them.

Since we kept silent, they told us to go to bed. Upstairs, we lay down and listened to them shouting at each other. Soon, they argued about things that had happened in Iraq. They called each other liars and other names. We felt miserable. Why were they being so mean to each other?

After their last words, an eerie silence occupied our house. I could not fall asleep. Could they figure out how to make our new life work? Would they reconcile?

---

35 German Red Cross Society offers a wide range of services within and outside Germany, such as care for the elderly, children, and youth.

Next morning, Alim asked around if anyone had seen his jeans. We searched the house. Eventually, Gabriela found them in the lowest drawer of his dresser. She blamed Adil. "You didn't put them in the correct place, and you ironed them poorly." He did not say a word. With an angry face, he went down to the kitchen to prepare our lunch boxes. I followed to help him. Shortly, Gabriela came after us. She pulled out a knife from the drawer and looked at it. "You can't even wash the dishes properly. Just leave all housework for me if you are unable to do it correctly!"

Adil beat his fists on his head several times, shouting, "Ya Allah!" I had never seen him like this before; I was scared. He was not the calm and strong father I used to know. Moreover, my parents did not get along at all, compared to our life in Iraq.

I had waited for my father's move to Germany with childlike anticipation, but instead it tested our family bonds. The relationship between my parents was increasingly plagued by disappointment, fighting, and resentment. It was almost impossible to find the emotional security my siblings and I needed in such an environment. Our family was in a critical situation.

It took my parents several months to compromise, allocate their new responsibilities, and adapt to their new roles. In the end, Adil started working nights as a cashier at the gas station of the Main-Taunus-Zentrum (MTZ), Germany's first and Hesse's biggest shopping mall. He was glad he could help to support us financially even if the work itself was a harsh social relegation for him. Gabriela, on the other hand, began a five-year kindergarten teacher's training, which included part-time work in a kindergarten. She enjoyed working with children even if the training itself was tough, since she had to write her papers late at night. It was an arrangement my parents seemed to be able to live with, and it improved our overall income, which finally allowed us to be independent from welfare checks.

Our security at home improved as well. My fear of being beaten by Gabriela diminished since Adil looked after us during the day; he usually protected us from Gabriela's rage, which had decreased since he had come to Kastel. Gabriela now habitually talked about her work and her children in kindergarten. Her emotional neglect and verbal assaults still occurred time and again in Kastel, but Adil tried to compensate for it.

Regarding the political developments in Germany, the public attacks on non-white people began to decrease in 1993 as a result of increasing pressure from the public, as well as from public authorities, which made me feel more secure in Germany, though I still felt the pressure to assimilate.

As the situation at home and around me developed in positive ways, I was able to move my focus from safety to other things: I would be starting primary school soon!

# KASTEL

*September 1993–August 1997*

*Rules of the game*

*September 1993*

The kitchen clock showed 7:30 a.m. when Adil and I were ready to go. He walked me to Pestalozzi Schule, my new school. I felt quite confident; so different from my first walk to kindergarten. I felt that my German was good enough that I would not be made fun of, and I knew Marcus and Dominik would be in my class too. I was looking forward to spending the next four years with my best friends.

When we sat down at a group table in our new classroom, we looked around with keen eyes. Our new class had twenty students, and everyone looked excited. I automatically noticed three boys who looked similar to me. As our class teacher, Ms. Schneider, asked us to introduce ourselves, I got to know their names: Ricardo, Hakim, and Nasir. The last two names were Arabic, I noted. Even though I did not know the three boys, it strangely put me at ease to see that I was not the only one who stuck out with a darker physical appearance and a non-German name.

*November 1993*

When I came home from school, Adil already had his jacket on. "I'm going to the town hall to work in the election committee of the first Kasteler Council of Foreigners," he said. Since I did not understand what he meant, I asked him to explain it to me. "The Hessian

Municipal Code prescribes for every municipality that counts more than one thousand foreigners to install a council that represents the interests of foreign citizens and advises the town in these matters," he said. I smiled, surprised by the existence of such a council and my father's new involvement in local politics. As he put on his shoes, I asked him for his reasons. "Despite the initial resistance, Kastel gave us a home. I want to give something back and help foreigners have an easier start here," he said. I was impressed by his willingness to take action and make a difference. He probably saw it in my eyes. "You can visit me with your brothers around eight," he said before he left.

We met him in the town hall that evening. The mayor stepped to the speaker's desk to proclaim the voter turnout, which was twenty-nine percent. He congratulated the nine elected representatives, who all had a different migration background. Their families and about sixty Kastelers clapped their hands before everyone bustled around the new representatives. Never before had I seen so many people with so many different skin colors, speaking different languages and wearing different kinds and colors of clothes—all gathering peacefully at one place in Kastel. Standing with Malik, Alim, and Adil in the midst of all of those people, I noticed that while we all looked different, we were the same: Kastelers. For the first time, I fully felt like Kastel was my new home; a place where I could be myself; a place where I could connect with people; a place where I belonged.

*December 1993*

When the Christmas season started, Ms. Schneider invited us to a baking event. I was looking forward to our community experience and to learning how to bake Christmas cookies. We met in the art room. My classmates and I were visibly excited about creating our sweets together. Some parents had come as well to help us prepare the dough. We rolled it out and cut out stars, moons, and hearts, smiling at our common creations and at each other. It was fun, and helped the social cohesion in the classroom. We all felt important as we shared this activity. Small activities like these were simple but powerful; they dispersed group boundaries and strengthened our group identity.

*Friday, July 15, 1994*

At the end of the term, my classmates and I waited impatiently at our tables while Ms. Schneider handed out our first report cards. Excited, I went over mine. She assessed my skills and my educational needs in a text, and I was impressed by her knowledge of me.

*Dear Junis,*

*You study diligently. You do your work accurately, most of the time independently, and by now, faster. Sometimes, however, you do not complete some tasks or you forget a part of your homework. You should always double-check the assignments. You behave in a companionable, cooperative, and responsible way toward your classmates. You can easily play and work together with other children. You follow the agreed upon rules. It annoys you when other children do not adhere to them. You should try to react a bit more calmly to those children. Most of the time, you follow the lessons attentively and with interest. In our narration circle, you are a good listener. You should participate more actively in discussions during the lessons. You have learned reading quickly. You read texts that we have practiced with a good flow and stress, and unknown texts slowly to grasp their meaning. Your printed letters and your cursive are clearly structured and neatly written. If we practice a word, you can write it error-free when dictated. In free writing, you write the words with phonetic accuracy. You complete exercises with numbers up to ten error-free. Sometimes, you use auxiliary material for addition and subtraction exercises with numbers up to twenty. With some practice, you will carry out these exercises faster in your head. You have a good sense of color and form in art. In physical education, you quickly grasp motion sequences and the rules of the games.*

After school, I showed my parents my report card. They read it, smiled, and congratulated me with kisses on my cheeks. I was grateful for their acknowledgment, and for the first time since we had come to Germany, I was somewhat proud of my abilities. With continuous hard work, resilience, and patience, I successfully met most requirements at school.

### August 1994

Like most children at Pestalozzi Schule, I had a diverse circle of friends. Friendship at school often started with common interests or other similarities. By September, I had become friends with Jonathan, a classmate of mine who collected stamps like I did. We began to meet after school at his big house in front of a strawberry field. His mother was a psychologist and had her practice in the loft. Jonathan's room was on the second floor. We often sat on his carpet, sorting and trading stamps. In addition to the latest German stamps, I had some from Iraq. Adil and Gabriela had given them to me, and I gave some of them to Jonathan, in many cases in exchange for some old German ones. Our hobby was fun and free.

Sometimes I visited Hakim, my other table neighbor. As a rule, he did not invite classmates to his home. His parents hardly spoke German and were shy toward German speaking people, but they made an exception for Nasir and me, probably because we were of Arab descent. Hakim lived on the fifth floor in a yellow tower block next to the railways, not far from Paul-Ehrlich-Straße. The first time I visited him, I was instantly allured by a spicy odor that escaped from his apartment door. When Hakim led me to the living room where his family awaited us, I found that the scent came from there. Plates of Kibbeh[36] and pots of vegetables were set on the floor. We sat down on the ground in a circle and began to eat a dish my family had often eaten in Iraq. I was eating Kibbeh for the first time since the war, and I vividly remembered the particularly spicy taste from my early childhood in Iraq. I smiled and felt like I was coming home.

Dinner at Marcus's home was different. His house lay near the

---

36  Arabic and Levantine dish—rice balls filled with spicy ground meat and fresh peppermint

Goldbach creek. From his living room, we could look through huge windowpanes at the small river. I only stayed for dinner when his father came home from work late. Marcus, his younger brother, his baby sister, and I would sit at a long table, far away from each other, while his mother served us small portions on white dishes. Dinner typically ended quickly and with no leftovers. At 6:30 p.m. sharp, I had to leave before his father came. "It's time for our family to be together and alone," his mother told me one time. Sometimes, his father came home early. He would then first drive me home before his family had dinner. The rule seemed weird to me at the beginning. If they had been of Arab descent, they would have probably insisted that I stay for dinner and spend time with the entire family, I thought. Anyway, I quickly adapted to the change. I appreciated Marcus, and I wanted to keep a good relationship with him. The dinner rule was insignificant in contrast to the joy we shared. That summer, we spent many hours on his garage roof, where we had built our own fort with wooden boards. We loved to sit side by side in our covert space, reading out jokes and laughing from our hearts. Shared joy helped us bond more and more each time we met.

### February 1995

Since my parents were able to save some money, we could afford to buy a new couch. We went to the Kasteler home improvement center and bought a green leather corner couch. Finally, we didn't have to sit on worn-out couches from the garbage anymore. We celebrated our modernized living room with chocolate cake and tea. Our ongoing efforts to turn our house into a home started to bear fruit.

### Summer 1995

As we modernized our house step by step, we made a new garden, which turned into a living jungle in the summer. Our grape vines became an impenetrable blanket of dark green leaves that grew together with our raspberry and blackberry bushes along the mesh wire fence. Together, they created a quiet, shadowy place, where blackbirds would hide from the midday sun and twitter every now and then. The dense canopy of our cherry tree threw another shadow over our lush lawn, where wild rabbits often grazed. Close by, parsley, chives, and rosemary spread a fresh odor underneath our young and thriving mirabelle tree. From all the beauties in our garden, our tall plum tree remained my favorite. During the summer months, I climbed it after school almost daily, rested on a high branch, and enjoyed some calm time with nature.

When Gabriela came from her teacher training in the late afternoons, we (sometimes the whole family that lived in Kastel) regularly picked our berries. She would squeeze herself along the bushes and the wire mesh fence, the hard to reach part, and pick berries with both hands. She never put them in the bowl before her hands were fully laden, and if one berry jumped out of the bowl, she would put it back right away. The bowls she returned to our kitchen contained so many berries that one more could have brought the entire mountain falling down. I admired her strong work ethic and her skills—her thoroughness, her speed, her efficiency—and tried to measure up. Her conduct and the results of her work carried me along.

### Beginning of August 1995

For the first time since we moved to Germany, my family could afford to go on a faraway vacation. Adil invested some of his old savings with the help of Onkel Walter in 1993. By 1995, they had already registered good returns. He was visibly happy that he could, once again, substantially contribute to our financial well-being and even pay for a trip abroad. My siblings and I were excited, although tensions between him and Gabriela regarding their new family responsibilities had flared up again.

Adil bought Onkel Walter's fifteen-year-old VW Passat for our six-hundred-mile journey to Eraclea Mare, a small coastal town in Northeast Italy. Hikmat, our former family doctor, had invited us for the summer break. After the war in 1991, Hikmat's family had fled from Mosul to San Dona, a town close to Eraclea Mare. We were looking forward to finally seeing them again.

In the late evening, after our eleven-hour trip, we arrived in Eraclea Mare. Hikmat and his family welcomed us at an ice cream parlor with many kisses on our cheeks. We were all smiling non-stop. I was glad to see them again, especially Hikmat. He was still a cheerful person.

Hikmat exchanged some words with my parents before he looked at me again, smiling. "Junis, make the adhan!" he said in Arabic and laughed. It was a joke he used to make since I habitually called for the prayer when he visited us in Mosul. However, I was unable to sufficiently understand and speak Arabic by 1995. I felt nervous and ashamed of myself. I owed him my life, but I just looked at him now—speechless, ignorant of what he said, and not knowing what to say.

"Junis and Sophia do not really speak Arabic anymore. We only spoke German with them in the last years after we had come to Germany. We wanted them to be successful in school," Adil said.

"Our children speak Italian and Arabic. We wanted them to maintain their language. I think they do okay in school," Hikmat said.

My parents shrugged their shoulders, somewhat embarrassed, before we sat down.

Sophia and I sat down on a white porch swing, our family and Hikmat's family around a table. I listened to their conversation in Arabic, which I hardly understood even though many words sounded familiar. Sometimes, they laughed about old stories and looked at us. Adil and Gabriela translated parts of what was said. I felt deficient and guilty. I should not have forgotten Arabic. After four years in Germany, I was separated from our former friends, from my past, and from who I used to be. It hurt.

Despite that incident, we had a good time. We spent many days at the beach, and we visited a couple of cities, such as Venice and Pisa. It was a great break from all the work and challenges at home.

## Fall 1995

One day when I came home from school, I found my parents fighting like I had never seen them fight before.

"I thought I'd be safe when I came to Iraq. I thought my husband would stand behind me, but you and your family betrayed me," Gabriela shouted.

"Betrayed? What did we do to you?" Adil shouted back.

"You never intervened when I was suppressed by your family."

"How were you suppressed?"

She remained silent.

Both glared at each other with contempt.

"My only escape was gardening and raising children." She paused. "If my religion had not taught me otherwise, I would have divorced you years ago!"

"Alright." Adil nodded. "If it was and is so excruciating to live with me, why torture yourself? Go get the divorce!" he said, embittered.

I felt weighed down. Everything I thought I knew about our past life was under heavy attack. How was she suppressed when we lived almost like kings in Iraq? What awful things had happened before I was born? How would I live as a nine-year-old, depending on parents who might never have loved each other? Would they separate? I felt doomed to insecurity.

My parents had quarreled on and off since we had come to Kastel, but fall 1995 was exceptionally damaging for all of us. A few weeks after their pivotal quarrel, Gabriela overdosed on pain killers. She alleged that she had been feeling sick and was admitted to a psychosomatic clinic for six weeks. We all briefly met in our living room after her initial treatment in the hospital. With packed bags in her hands, she said, "I need some time on my own. The family causes me too much stress." No one knew what to say. I did not understand why we were such a burden on her. "See you," she told us with an empty face before she left. We watched her leave. I felt helpless, guilty, and ashamed. Would she ever really want to see us again after what she had gone through because of us? As a child, I naturally took all the blame.

When she drove away, Malik and Alim told me how she had entered our house one day that summer, upset and full of shame. "I just heard from a neighbor that everyone thinks that we still live on welfare; that our house, your education, and everything is paid for by German taxpayers!" she had said. All those rumors in the neighborhood about us were lies, but the social pressure in addition to the personal and marital problems Gabriela continuously faced were too much for her to handle.

### February 1996

Two days after Gabriela returned from the clinic, Adil called my siblings and me to the living room. "You shall know what is happening between your parents," he said, before he began to read out a letter he held in his hand. In his letter, he told Gabriela that they would from now on only stay together because we, the children, still needed their assistance. He also said that all trust was destroyed because of the lies about our life in Iraq, and that they were thus no longer husband and wife. We looked at each other, shattered. Like Gabriela, he involved us in their marital conflict. We felt deeply troubled. Why could they not talk about the past and forgive each other? Why could we not be a normal family—happily united, living in the present and in peace with each other? Why were there accusations and resentment and pain where there should be love? Who could we rely on if not on our parents?

After our parents had ignored each other for some weeks, they seemed to give our family a second chance. They agreed to start family therapy as had been recommended by the doctors of the psychosomatic clinic Gabriela had visited. Since Gabriela didn't consider the therapist competent enough, she decided to stop our family therapy after a few sessions. Adil asked her to find someone else who she thought would be competent enough, but she unfortunately never did. There were many resources available to help our family: family therapy, parent-child care, parent counseling, household help, after-school centers, financial support (for club memberships, for instance), and much more—and free (free!); everything guaranteed by the Social Code. There were also private ways to get help: organizations, clubs, books, and much more, but it was not in my siblings' or my hands. Our parents would not seek external help. Maybe they were afraid of another stigma. Maybe they sensed it would take a lot of energy to deal with their personal and marital problems on top of everything else, and they were just tired of struggling. Whatever reasons they had, they could not void their natural responsibility and obligation toward us, toward their children. We naturally depended on their help, guidance, and problem-solving.

## *July 1996*

In contrast to the uncontrollable negativities at home, I felt in control at school. School was my opportunity to replace the ongoing misery in my family with positivity, with personal development, a sense of achievement, and recognition from others. I did not want to just pass my exams. I wanted to become an excellent, outstanding student. Quantitative grades were introduced in the third school year, and I was looking forward to receiving my report card, which included mostly A's and some B's. I ranked among the top five students in class.

## *January 1997*

After another successful school term, I would use my midyear report card to apply for secondary school. However, I was not sure which type of school I should apply for.

Aware that I needed advice, I showed my report card to Adil and told him that my class teacher recommended me for gymnasium[37].

He looked at me with surprised eyes. "You're the first one among your siblings."

"And the only immigrant of my class too," I said.

"Be proud!" Adil said. "I'm sorry I couldn't help you much. But you did it anyway."

Despite his recognition, I still doubted if I could be successful

---

37 Type of school in Germany with emphasis on academic learning—usually refers to secondary schools focused on preparing students to enter a university, similar to US high schools or British grammar schools

at gymnasium. Malik and Alim went to realschule[38], and their grades were average. "Baba, should I go to gymnasium or realschule?" I asked.

He contemplated for a moment before he said, "Look, son. We lost almost everything in the war, but thank God, we're in Germany, in security. We are privileged to live here. And you are a smart boy. I want you to make this decision on your own."

I was surprised he left this important decision to me although I was only ten years old. "In realschule I'd probably not have to study that hard, and I'd have more free time. In gymnasium, I'd have to deal with questions that are more difficult; I'd have to study more, and I'd have less free time."

"Yes, but it would be more rewarding too. Gymnasium would qualify you to study at university later. I don't worry about you. You can manage gymnasium and more. But whatever you decide, I stand behind you," Adil said. His unconditional support with respect to my personal development motivated me, helped ease some of the pressure I felt, and made me curious about what the future could bring. My father helped me build the confidence to take a risk and find out how far I could go. It was a good way to raise a mentally strong child, as I would learn later during my university studies.

*February 1997*

I reflected on my options for a few days before I decided to go to gymnasium. I believed higher education was my opportunity for

---

38  Type of secondary school, ranked below gymnasium; after completing the realschule, good students can attend a gymnasium or vocational school, or do an apprenticeship.

success in life. Adil was the proof, my role model. I believed if I studied hard enough, I, too, could attain the skills to build something good in the future.

In addition to my promising prospects at school, my parents surprised us with almost unbelievable news. After they had given each other a silent treatment for months, they started talking with each other again. One day, they called us to the kitchen to announce that they would extend our house. They showed us the construction plans, which included a front building with a guest bathroom and two dormers with two bedrooms, one for them and one for Sophia. "Everyone will finally have a private room," they told us, smiling. Our parents seemed to have reconciled, and we hoped that starting such a big project together meant they planned to stay together as a family.

### Saturday, February 22, 1997

The construction of the shed dormers started in the morning. We observed everything from the Park and Ride[39] behind our back yard. Around noon, the crane juggled roof beams to the opened roof. When Onkel Walter drove along Paul-Ehrlich-Straße, he spotted the construction as well. He parked behind us and rushed to my parents with an angry face. I was alarmed.

"What's happening with my house?" he asked.

"Didn't you tell him?" Adil asked Gabriela.

"No, I didn't find time to talk with him," she said.

"And I've got no time for your silliness. You can't extend the

---

39  Parking lots with public transport connections

house without informing me. You don't have the right. This is *my* house!" he shouted at them.

I was scared.

Adil approached him carefully. "I understand your anger. I assumed your sister talked with you about the extension of the house. Please calm down. What shall we do now?"

"It's too late to talk now." Onkel Walter turned his back on us, got in his car, and drove away.

We looked at each other with big eyes. Each time we made some headway, an obstacle appeared we had to surmount; this time it was self-imposed. My parents had made a profound mistake, and now we had to deal with the consequences.

### May 1997

One evening, Onkel Walter rang our bell. Tensed up, he handed Adil a fat, gray folder. "These documents show how much I spent on Paul-Ehrlich-Straße four, subtracting the sum of the rent—eight hundred DM per month—you have paid," he said, and left. Adil took the folder to our kitchen. We gathered around my parents. When they read aloud the documents, we learned what Onkel Walter had done before we moved in. He had organized a clearing out, installed two new windows, and bought insulating material for the loft. He had the chimney cleaned, ordered an electrician to build the wires into the wall, and laid tiles in the kitchen. He invested a lot of time and money and recorded every expense.

In 1991, we were thankful for his help. In 1997, we were stunned by his actions. He even put his "travel costs" and "undefined additional costs" on a debit note, a behavior that would have been regarded as unusually rude among our Iraqi relatives. It was normal among Iraqi families that family members helped each other for free, or at least not for profit. It was a question of honor. I felt disappointed in him. The last pages showed four options for how we could purchase the house. The fourth proposal, the cheapest one, detailed a price that inordinately exceeded the sum Onkel Walter paid in 1991. It also indicated that 100,000 DM was supposed to be paid in cash. We did not have many choices. Onkel Walter was ready to rent out the house to a German family who were willing to pay more rent if we refused to buy his house under his conditions. Finding a new, affordable housing arrangement as a family of six with a migration background in a conservative town like Kastel would be more than difficult. My parents were indignant, and I understood.

### June 1997

The conflict with Onkel Walter led to new conflicts between my parents. Sometimes, they were unresponsive and lost in thought; other times they yelled at each other. "Can your brother not give us more time to pay off the house, or offer us a better purchase price?" Adil asked again and again. But his desperate requests were not entertained.

"I cannot talk with him, again!" my mother would say.

To distract myself from my fear of possibly suffering from lack of money again, I began to write a fictional picture story that would receive the title *A Free Trip to Arabia*.

By 1997, however, my Arabic roots were so torn and diffused that I seemed strange to myself. I'd forgotten how to speak Arabic, and I didn't frequently think of Iraq or our relatives and friends, whom I hardly remembered. To many Germans who did not know me, I remained a "foreigner" because of my look and my name. Yet my sense of Iraqi identity had dwindled to a vague, romantic idea of home, diluted by images of deserts with cacti, flying carpets, and magic lamps.

### Wednesday, July 23, 1997

I received my final report card. Although most of my grades were excellent, I suddenly doubted my achievement; my grades were the reason I was about to lose some of my friends, who had been allocated to other school forms by our teachers.

Performance differences had already become apparent in the third school year when grades were introduced. Except for art, music, and physical education (PE), all other subjects more or less depended on German language skills. Students who mastered the German language well got good grades in those subjects in most cases. Those who did not master the German language, especially the socially disadvantaged and immigrants, often got C's or D's in those subjects—not grades that would earn a teacher's gymnasium recommendation.

But many teachers applied unfair double standards in the end. For students with well-educated, ethnically German parents, a C was good enough for a gymnasium recommendation. Less educated or immigrant parents were not considered a good enough support for their children with respect to the study requirements at gymnasium. For students like me, B's were the minimal requirement to receive a gymnasium recommendation.

I felt sorry for Nasir, Ricardo, and Hakim; their grades did not qualify them for gymnasium. At the age of only ten, an enormous obstacle to higher education was placed in their way. Hakim was recommended for hauptschule[40], a placement that significantly limited his opportunities for prosperity in his professional life since most well-paying jobs required a university degree. Very few hauptschüler reached university in Germany, and only after onerous educational detours. Hakim's grades reflected his struggle to learn in a system that didn't recognize his heritage or native language, a system that failed to sufficiently support the development of his German language skills. Nasir and Ricardo were recommended for realschule. They still had a chance to transfer to gymnasium with good grades, but even so, they ran twice the risk of being downgraded to hauptschule in the years to come.

I was seven years old when I started attending primary school, and I quickly figured out the rules of the game: 1. Learn German, 2. Adopt the expected behaviors. Years later, when attending university in Frankfurt, my studies on Pierre Bourdieu[41] confirmed my childhood observations: those who take over the "habitus" of the dominating class early at school receive the "right" school

---

40  Type of secondary school in Germany—ranked below realschule, offers lower secondary education; students spend five to six years at hauptschule

41  Pierre Bourdieu (Aug. 1, 1930–Jan. 23, 2002): French sociologist, anthropologist, philosopher, and public intellectual, concerned with the dynamics of power in society

certificate at the end. I knew what my path could look like after school, and how different my experience would be from what Hakim would likely face. That final day in Lindenschule, I felt like a traitor. I looked at him, concerned.

"Don't worry, Junis. We'll stay friends," he said.

"Of course," I said, even though I was afraid we would lose contact.

Strangely, I admired him despite everything. He was recommended for hauptschule, yes, but he was able to understand his relatives in their language and speak with them fluently, whereas I could not understand or speak with my Iraqi relatives. Instead, I was about to become likely the only immigrant in my new class; I would have to assimilate even more to succeed. The more I thought about it, the more I wondered: would I lose the last bits of my "Iraqiness" at gymnasium?

*August 1997*

Adil returned from a short trip to Mosul where he had, because of Onkel Walter's demand for a big cash payout, scraped some of our devalued savings together (the exchange rate for the Iraqi Dinar to the US Dollar had dropped over 6,000 percent by 1997 due to the UN sanction regime and hyperinflation), and sold some of our similarly devalued properties in a rush. Furthermore, we received an owner-occupied housing allowance in Germany, and Gabriela took on a big, long, high interest mortgage. With our savings, our sold properties, the housing allowance, and the mortgage, we were finally able to overcome the financial hurdle Onkel Walter had given us. We purchased the house in Paul-Ehrlich-Straße, but for an even higher price than we initially thought. Adil and Onkel Walter would despise each other after the ownership matter of Paul-Ehrlich-Straße for the rest of their lives. Our families thus broke apart.

Despite it all, Gabriela successfully completed her teacher training. Her new full-time position at a Catholic kindergarten in a village ten minutes away from Kastel improved our financial situation.

We celebrated our achievements with tea and pastries on our veranda. As we sat together, I began to prepare mentally for the new challenges that awaited me at gymnasium. A strange feeling told me that I might have to make difficult decisions in the new school that would deeply affect my identity.

# KASTEL

*September 1997–August 2003*

*The way to justice requires courage*

*Monday, September 8, 1997*

I transferred to Weinbergschule (WBS), a flat-roofed concrete
building. WBS included a hauptschule, a realschule, and a gymnasium. Malik and Alim attended the realschule. I was glad I could
see them on the school grounds during breaks. Marcus and I attended the same class at the gymnasium. We had become insepa-
rable friends, and were looking forward to spending the next six
years together.

On our first school day, we sat side by side in our new classroom when our new teacher, Mr. Siegert, asked us to introduce
ourselves. Marcus began. I followed, noticing that I stood out. Out
of thirty-one students, I was the only boy with black hair, brown
eyes, and relatively brown skin. When Mr. Siegert asked me where
I was "originally from," everyone, except Marcus, scrutinized me
from head to toe. I felt odd and quickly explained my parents'
nationalities. Mr. Siegert asked the same question only to three
girls who had a relatively brown skin. Their parents were born in
Mexico, Italy, and Turkey, respectively. When Mr. Siegert brought
attention to our different ethnic backgrounds, my fear of possible
rejection flared up again, which prevented me from seeing that he
actually intended to raise a positive awareness of our classroom's
diversity. Instead, I saw the possibility that my skills could easily
be linked to my different heritage, and if I didn't perform well, I

could easily be downgraded to realschule. I felt the need to prove to myself and others that I rightly belonged in gymnasium.

*December 1997*

My initial fears of failing at gymnasium were for naught. Most of my first grades were good, and I befriended more and more classmates. In addition to working together in the classrooms, we also played soccer together almost every break and met up in our free time, and usually we had great fun.

Marcus's eleventh birthday was a strange exception to our otherwise happy relationship. He invited five classmates to celebrate his birthday in a thermal bath. Shortly after we had entered the changing room, everyone began to take off their clothes—completely. I was taken by surprise, wondering what was happening. Marcus's father, also naked, approached me and said, "Junis, take off your clothes. We don't want to wait for you." I looked at him, baffled. I had never seen anyone in my family naked. It was considered obscene. To make things worse, I noticed that I was the only one who was circumcised, and remembered how my classmates had made fun of circumcision when we had talked about Judaism in religious instruction. I didn't know what to do.

"Don't be shy!" a boy named Finn said, making my classmates laugh. I felt out of my element, but there seemed to be no way out. Reluctantly, I turned my back to them, opened the locker door, stepped forward so no one could see my penis, and pulled down my pants. They saw my naked bottom, which felt embarrassing enough. My father would never have expected this of me—he would have even reprimanded me for it!

"What are you hiding?" another boy, Stephen, asked. Instead of answering, I turned red in the face while my classmates laughed again. Hastily, I put on my swimming trunks, closed the locker, and followed them. I felt ashamed of my strange body, ashamed of my strange shyness, and guilty about going against a behavior I had learned from my family. Apart from that moment in the changing room, we had a fun time in the thermal bath, playing all kinds of games.

### Fall 1998

After attending WBS for more than a year, my continuous efforts on my new path paid off. My grades were still good, and I had made many friends in class. The longer we knew each other, the more I understood that there was no reason to be ashamed of myself. I still avoided being naked in front of others, but I learned that to-show-or-not-to-show-your-penis was not an important question of character. My classmates appreciated who I was, and vice versa.

Our new friendships grew stronger in the course of the first school year. During our first summer break, we sent postcards to each other from our vacation places. We were looking forward to seeing each other again in the new school year. In the first week after summer break, a girl named Helena wrote in my friendship book, "Stay as funny as you are and keep dancing like Michael Jackson! I like you completely, my dear." Everyone wrote in it, and I wrote in their friendship books as well. "I wish we could stay

friends forever" was often our last line, our common wish. I enjoyed attending WBS.

### *Friday, January 15, 1999*

When Adil moved to Kastel in 1993, our next-door neighbors, an old German couple, abruptly stopped talking to us even
though we had slowly built a neighborly relationship. We could
only speculate about their change of mind; maybe they did not
accept having a full-blooded Iraqi as a neighbor. Either way, ignor-
ing our family was only the beginning of their hostilities. One day,
when I came home from school, Adil showed me a letter from our
neighbors. With a sad face, he asked me to read it.

> *Our clients wish, certainly more than you do, that the ren-
> ovation work on your house ends one day. The noise has stressed
> our clients' neighborly tolerance more than is acceptable.*
>
> *The town council has informed us that you are al-
> legedly interested in a good neighborly relationship. This is easily
> achieved if you adhere to the minimal requirement of social be-
> havior, taken as self-evident by every man in this country:*
>
> *1. Adhere to the rest periods.*
>
> *2. Inform your neighbors in advance of any noise-intense
> work so they can avoid this time by running errands.*
>
> *Our clients' health is already damaged because of your be-
> havior. This does not necessarily add to a good neighborly rela-
> tionship. Our clients informed me that you have been the
> chairman of the Kasteler "Council of Foreigners" since 1997
> and that you advise foreigners to adjust to local customs as far*

*as possible. Apparently, this recommendation ends at your front door as you act unreasonably ruthless.*

*In the interest of all parties, we ask you to show the little thoughtfulness that our clients expect. Since you ask our clients to tolerate the work, it would be only just if you paid consideration to their wish as well. If you lack this minimal social behavior, we will, unfortunately, advise our clients to sue you. We hope that this, as it is common with halfway civilized people, is not necessary.*

Halfway civilized? What humiliating language! I placed the letter on the kitchen table and looked at Adil with a serious face. "What are we going to do now?"

"We'll wait until your mother comes. We'll make a plan together."

When Gabriela came home from kindergarten, he gave her the letter. She read it, and told him, visibly upset, "We go to a lawyer right now!"

In the late evening, they returned with a copy of a letter written by a lawyer. I read it, slowly and attentively.

*It is correct that my clients hired construction companies to renovate the house in Paul-Ehrlich-Straße four. However, the structural alterations were conducted in regular working times. Also, a violation against the township law of rest hours did not occur since such a law does not exist in the first place. We are ready to receive a copy of this township law from you if it exists.*

*Further, a violation of the noise protection regulations of*

*Hesse did not occur. It is correct that nights (8 p.m. to 7 a.m.),*
*midday rest hours (1 p.m. to 3 p.m.), and holidays are protected*
*from noise. This generally affects private households. However, §*
*3 of the noise protection regulations says that services of registered*
*firms are excluded. If the rest periods had been violated, it was not*
*done by my clients but by the workers of registered firms, which*
*are excluded from the noise protection regulations.*

*With regard to your other arguments, it has to be noted that*
*they do not serve an objective dispute. This especially applies to*
*the note that my client is active in the "Council of Foreigners."*
*This note has no reasonable justification and shall apparently only*
*serve as cheap propaganda. At this juncture, I may note that any*
*further arguments in that direction will be prosecuted as libel.*

*For the reason of completeness, it has to be noted that your*
*clients gave you incorrect information. Over the years, my clients*
*have tried to build a neighborly relationship. Still, all their greet-*
*ings have been ignored in the last six years. No conversation could*
*be held with your clients, who told the town council that they do*
*not want to talk with my clients. When your clients telephone,*
*they call my clients "anti-social, uncivilized foreigners who should*
*go back where they came from," and hang up. When our clients*
*meet on the street, your clients switch to the other side of the street*
*with ostentation. Whether this is civilized behavior, shall not be*
*discussed here.*

*My clients will, like in the past, adhere to the rest hours. They*
*are also interested in improving their social contact with your cli-*
*ents. Your clients, however, should wish this as well. Last but not*

*least, it shall be noted that, despite an eight-year-long neighborly relationship, your clients do not know how to spell my clients' last name correctly.*

I looked at my parents, relieved that they asserted through official channels our correct behavior toward the given rules, and our willingness to have good relations with our neighbors. I even felt somewhat hopeful! Even if our neighbors were not interested in a neighborly relationship, our lawyer could at least prove our innocence if we had to go to court. And even if an acquittal could not heal the broken relationship with our neighbors, it could at least ease the sadness, the guilt, the shame, and the anger we carried due to their constant hostility.

### February 1999

Carnival season was now in full swing, and I looked forward to having a fun and carefree time to distract me from our neighbors' harassment.

By 1999, my siblings had joined the Kasteler band as well. Our performances in the Goldbachhalle[42] were the musical highlight of our year. We opened the first of what would be four carnival sessions at 8:00 p.m. After the traditional three beats of our drums, we started our march through the seating rows. The gym was packed with hundreds of people, and some started to scream as if they were at a concert. Even the elders got up and excitedly clapped their hands. Adrenaline shot through my veins. Soon, my heartbeat outran the beat of our forceful drums. We positioned ourselves on

---

42   Name of a Kasteler gym

the stage and raised our wind instruments. I stood in the front row, under the hot spotlight, when we began to play. Performing with the Kasteler band and captivating the audience was just electrifying! A unifying interaction!

After our performance, we got drinks and sandwiches for free backstage. With more than thirty active members, our band was the largest club of the Kasteler Karneval Klub. We were thus granted permission to spend the time between our two performances in the smaller adjoining gym.

There were almost no regulations during Carnival, and I liked that freedom. My parents let me stay out as long as I wanted. After our second performance at 10:30 p.m., most of the band members gathered on the stage in the adjoining gym. We arranged tables to spend the rest of the night together, snacking, drinking, laughing, and playing table games. Many members brought something along for our evenings. I brought my CD-player. Sometimes, especially when we put on *Top of the Pops*[43], some of us started to sing. No one told us to be quiet. We could just be ourselves and enjoy our time together. I felt warmly attached to every single person in the band. At midnight, all the young children were driven home, while I was allowed to stay for a few hours. Piero and I got drunk for the first time that year: one beer, one Jägermeister, one tequila, and cola for a change. Malik and Alim drank as well, and so did all the elders who checked that we teenagers didn't drink too much. I loved them all: happy, uncomplicated, and kind people.

In the dark of the early morning, Malik, Alim, and I started

43  Collection of popular current chart songs across all genres

to amble home. When we reached the railway station, a skinhead popped up behind a corner and started to harass us. I was probably too drunk to notice, but Malik did. "Hurry up, Junis!" he told me, and grabbed my hand. We walked faster. Fortunately, we were almost home. After our eight-year-long efforts to integrate, starting as notorious strangers and slowly becoming part of the Kasteler community, we were never completely safe from random attacks by radicalized strangers of the ethnic majority.

### January 2000

Nine years after the war, my family was finally completely reunited. Manal came to Kastel, Germany, with her children because her son had almost died from diarrhea. The ongoing UN sanctions were still silently killing people in Iraq in unknown, but high, numbers. Manal and her children moved into our house for the time being, and we were glad to be with them and see that their health was improving.

We all got along well. My siblings and I played with Asis, my four-year-old nephew, and Amal, my two-year-old niece, every day after school. On dry days, we put them in their buggies and raced on bicycle lanes to the next playground, and they'd laugh themselves to tears.

Despite the joy we shared, my family had new problems to solve. Our income was not sufficient to feed nine people and cover all our other expenses. Gabriela urged Adil to quickly find a solution; but even though he took more double shifts, and even though we were able to cover all our expenses, we still could not live in peace. Our next-door neighbors sent us more letters, complaining that our house was "overpopulated" and that "civilized people would never share a small house like ours with nine people." As if there were no larger problems in the world. I was sick of our neighbors' narrow-mindedness and racism, and yearned for an end to their harassment.

Our neighbors' attitude aligned with a re-enflamed populist and racist political movement against certain immigrants. After the Social Democratic Party of Germany (SPD) and the Alliance 90/The Greens (often simply called the Greens) won the federal elections in 1998, the CDU and the Christian Social Union (CSU) started a signature campaign against the planned reform of the German citizenship laws, which allowed for Jus Soli[44] and dual citizenship. In particular, the campaign aimed to prevent a dual German-Turkish citizenship, claiming that Turks would not be loyal to the German constitution or to democracy in general. The campaign polarized the entire country. In the end, the CDU and CSU got five million signatures, won the state election in Hesse and the majority in the Bundesrat[45], and deadened the reform.

### *Tuesday, September 19, 2000*

When I got home from school, I found a *Frankfurter Rundschau*[46] on our kitchen table. "Right-Wing Violence Claimed Ninety-Three

---

44 German: "Right of the soil"—the right of anyone born in the territory of a state to nationality or citizenship

45 Legislative body that represents the sixteen *Länder* (federated states) of Germany at the national level

46 German daily newspaper, based in Frankfurt am Main

Deaths in Germany from 1990 to 2000," was one title. For the first time, I was aware that the standard media acknowledged the numbers about *that* problem as well. I felt hopeful. Later, during my political science studies, I would understand why: widespread, balanced, and evidence-based information, combined with increased public awareness and a willingness to engage in open and possibly uncomfortable debates, are the first steps towards ending xenophobia, racism, or any social issue.

### Wednesday, November 1, 2000

After seven years of constant harassment from our neighbors, we had to appear before a local court in Frankfurt to testify in the case "Schmidt vs. Sultan." They had sued us for noise disturbances. We countersued them for:

1. *Putting up a six-foot-high wooden wall at the property border without informing us and without our agreement.*

2. *Bullying us in different ways, such as:*
   *a) Beating against the living room wall, chopping wood, hammering against the pipe in the basement, throwing around wooden objects in the veranda, playing loud marching songs and Heimatlieder on Saturday mornings before 7 a.m.*
   *b) Glaring at all family members and visitors through the kitchen window (or other windows) round the clock*
   *c) Frequently sending us insulting letters with lists about alleged violations against the noise regulations*

*d) Trying to intimidate us through insulting telephone calls and by talking to third parties . . .*

I felt exceptionally nervous and insecure. Never had I seen a courtroom from the inside, until I was sitting in one as a fourteen-year-old defendant!

When the judge entered the hall, everyone became silent. He read out the case. Next, he asked my parents to come to the front to testify on parts one and two a) of the lawsuit.

After their testimony, he called me to testify on part two b). When I sat down in front of him, I briefly turned around to my parents, who looked at me expectantly. I was worried I might say something that would get us into trouble, but I also knew that being silent was not an option. It would have not helped solve the problem; it would have only extended and aggravated it. I summoned my courage and took a deep breath. I said, "When we bring out the garbage, when we collect the mail, when someone rings the bell, the curtains in our neighbors' kitchen are moved aside and our neighbors glare at the person in our front garden. When we come home from school, they glare at us from behind their kitchen window. When we play in our back yard, they lower their roller blinds and observe us through a small gap. When we enter our veranda at night, they follow immediately and switch on the light on their veranda. They observe every step we make."

The judge took some notes before he looked at me with a stern face. "Can you comment on the noise disturbances?" he asked.

I looked at him for a moment, baffled. Did he think that we were criminals?

Our neighbors began to laugh.

"Be quiet! Otherwise, you will get a warning," he called out to them.

He seemed to be willing to solve the case quickly and according to the rules. Half-intimidated, half-confident, I continued, "I don't have the chance to make noteworthy noise. When I listen to music at medium volume, our neighbors call immediately. They call me 'anti-social' and request that I stop making noise. Next, they send insulting letters. This year, they also called the police, who sometimes appeared, in vain. My parents always urge me to stay quiet. In the rest periods, they don't allow me to listen to music at normal volume. I have to listen to music with earphones. When I move furniture, they come and tell me to stop it immediately, even outside the rest periods. They also urged me to inform my neighbors about my birthday party. When I called them, they hung up the phone right away."

I turned around and looked at my neighbors—suddenly feeling free. Finally, I was speaking up against their tormenting. Finally, I was heard by an authority after all these years of being persecuted at home, of having to stay silent or justify every tone, of being denied the right to be myself without constant constraints, insults, threats, and fear.

The judge asked me to sit down.

I sat next to Adil, who grabbed my hand.

"Good job, Junis," he whispered.

"Thank you. I gave it my best," I replied and began to reflect: The way to justice requires courage. It can be long and painful, but it's inevitable for a dignified life.

## Sunday, December 24, 2000

A few weeks after the stressful court experience, the Christmas season arrived. Manal had found a small apartment for low-income families in Kastel, so we decided to stay home and celebrate instead of spending Christmas in Amtal as we had in previous years. Oma Erika, Nour, and her family came to Paul-Ehrlich-Straße four as well. I was happy to have our big family together.

Delighted, I videotaped our festive living room. White pillar candles were shining on our brown marble windowsill. Our windows were decorated with colored paper stars, angels, and deer. Red pillar candles shone on our coffee table between plates of ambrosial almond cookies and kleicha while *Stille Nacht*, a classic German Christmas song, lightly filled the room with a harmonious chorus.

The music came from the speakers of our new thirty-two-inch television that had cost 1,800 DM. After we had struggled economically during our first four years in Germany, I was still aware of how much things cost, even though we were financially stable in 2000. In addition to the monthly bills and mortgage fee, we could afford to renovate our house step by step. We had gone on a two week vacation every summer since 1995, which meant reaching our financial limits most years, but the year 2000 was an exception. Gabriela got a pay raise and wanted to surprise us with a new television, a very generous present, a few days before Christmas. Our house was finally completely updated after nine years of hard, steady work.

Rahila was standing next to our shiny Christmas tree. Red and golden globes twinkled from the branches. She waved with both hands at the camera, smiling. Suddenly, Sophia jumped into the picture and blew kisses to Rahila. All three of us laughed full-heartedly.

Christmas was always one of the best times of the year; a time of togetherness, kindness, and joy.

Still, this Christmas was somewhat different. Ammu Amir had come to Kastel, and joined our Christmas feast for the first time, and we tried our best to make him feel comfortable. When he sat down on our couch, he began to silently observe everything. He was unable to understand or speak German. Adil brought him fruits from our kitchen. "People in Iraq typically sit together at night and eat fruits," he spoke into the camera. His remark instantly reminded me of our forgotten family evenings in Iraq.

When I videotaped Asis, Asis jumped up from the couch with a big smile. "I love Christmas. I want to be a snowman. I want to swim in snow." From the corner of my eye, I saw Ammu Amir staring at him with lowered eyebrows. Adil tried to distract him from Asis's enthusiasm by starting a conversation in Arabic while I wondered what Ammu Amir was thinking. Stupid Christmas? Maybe even stupid family?

For a short moment I videotaped Ammu Amir, who still looked like Saddam Hussein with his mustache and short, wiry hair combed to the back. Ammu Amir immediately glared at me.

"Don't videotape him! They don't like it in Iraq," Adil told me.

I switched off the camera straight away. Ammu Amir's behavior appeared strange to me. "Why?" I asked carefully. I felt guilty, since I had obviously done something wrong, but I was also perplexed; we used to take pictures in Iraq all the time.

"Taking pictures of humans and non-human animals is discouraged in the Hadith[47] to avoid adoring anyone or anything else but Allah," Adil said.

I respected Ammu Amir's wish, and yet I thought it was rather exaggerated: would I adore him only because I videotaped him? For the first time on Christmas, I felt at a loss. I had become ignorant of our common heritage, Islam, after spending most of my life in Kastel.

After everyone had eaten, Sophia lit two sparklers in front of our tree. Everyone, except Ammu Amir and Adil, clapped their hands. "The small ones will now hand out the presents," Sophia said in a sweet voice. We hugged and thanked each other for the presents. Ammu Amir received some presents as well. He looked at them suspiciously and asked Adil what the presents were about.

To my surprise, Adil acted as if Christmas was strange to him as well. When he received his presents, he said, "Presents for me? What for?" His behavior made me wonder. Was he trying to comfort Ammu Amir, who felt odd celebrating a Christian feast as a Muslim? Did he not want to celebrate Christmas as a Muslim anymore? If that was the case, then why did he celebrate Christmas with us in Iraq and in Germany for years? Did he feel a need to reaffirm his Muslim identity in dominantly Christian Germany? Why now? Was he holding onto the familiarity of the religion? Or

---

47  Record of the words, actions, and the silent approval of the Prophet Muhammad

did he feel somewhat pressured by Ammu Amir to assimilate?

## *February 2001*

For whatever reason, Adil was becoming more religious. A few days after Christmas, he announced during teatime that he would go to Mecca and do the pilgrimage. He said it meant a lot to him and that he wanted to go before he became too old and weak. He was sixty-one years old. Gabriela complained that the trip would be too expensive, but he had already booked it. So he went to Mecca.

One afternoon in February, we received a postcard from him. The picture showed thousands of Muslims in white garments encircling the Kaaba[48]. On the backside, Adil wrote, "Blessings to you from God. Maybe I shall reach you before this card does. I challenge you to try to find me in the crowd of this picture. I love you."

## *Mid-March 2001*

My father's trip to Mecca brought up many questions I had often asked myself over the years in Germany. What was Islam? Who was I? Was I a Muslim too? Since I had read a short text about Islam in religious instruction at school, I vaguely knew that going to Mecca was one of the five pillars of Islam. I was looking forward to finally learning more about Islam from Adil, but I also felt a bit uneasy about his return. Would he come back as a different person—one with strict religious beliefs and practices?

The bell rang in the afternoon. Adil was wearing a full, white beard. In Iraq, only old or religious people wore such a beard. He

---

48  Building at the center of Islam's most sacred mosque in Mecca, Saudi Arabia

was both now, I noticed, surprised. We smiled and hugged each other for an unusually long moment. I was glad to see him again despite my unspoken concerns. Adil, on the other hand, seemed completely relaxed. At a leisurely pace, he walked into our living room. He opened his suitcase and handed out a photo to everyone. In the photo, he was standing on a white marble floor, wearing a white cloth. His gaze into the camera was determined. It reminded me of his inner strength. He had struggled for a long time—like we all did—until he finally overcame the problems the war had brought, and I felt proud of him. Next, he handed out a gold necklace to everyone. I looked at it carefully. It held a pendant that looked like a scroll. "Allah" was engraved on one side, "Muhammad" on the other. Those were two of the few words, along with my name, that I had learned from him in Arabic years ago. Feeling honored, I put the necklace on. We smiled at each other.

"There's something else," he said. "You've asked me many times, and I always tried to dissuade you. But if you still want to box, I'll find a club for you."

I looked at him with large eyes, almost in disbelief.

Shortly, Gabriela left the room.

I was perplexed. Was she upset because I wore the necklace or because I would start boxing?

After a couple minutes, she returned with a small, red box in her hand.

"This is the cross my father used to wear. It's for you," she told me.

I was speechless. Her father had died from cancer in 1989; and from among all her children, she picked me to wear his cross. I had no idea why. I felt simultaneously honored and ashamed as my siblings looked at me without any presents from Gabriela in their own hands.

"Just take it," she said.

I hugged her and put the cross on as well.

From that day on, I carried two pendants, which represented my father's *and* my mother's religions; it felt good to cherish both. It felt as if I was able to bring together two worlds that appeared to be very different from each other, if not mutually incompatible.

### Wednesday, March 21, 2001

After school, Adil handed me a letter with a contented smile on his face. "Read this! It's by the local district court of Frankfurt," he said. I began to read.

> *In the name of the people: In the lawsuit: Mr. and Mrs. Schmidt (claimants) and Mr. and Mrs. Sultan (defendants) the court of Frankfurt adjudged to dismiss the case. The lawsuit's cost will be carried to 7/10 by the claimant and 3/10 by the accused. Grounds: The claims are without merit. The accused are owners of the property in Paul-Ehrlich-Straße four and have the right to renovate their property as they like. No third party can request that they reduce the renovation noise to a minimum as long as it does not violate public regulations.*

I smiled and hugged him, thankful that justice was finally

served. Our years-long struggle had come to a happy ending, and it felt as if nothing could come in our way now.

*Tuesday, September 11, 2001, around 3:00 p.m.*

I was eating rice with tomato-okra sauce at our kitchen table when the unexpected catastrophe happened. Adil was washing the dishes behind me. The radio was on. Suddenly, the radio announcer interrupted the music: "Attention! Breaking news—a plane accident just happened in Manhattan. One tower of the World Trade Center was damaged."

We went to the living room at once. Adil turned on the television and switched to CNN[49]. A picture of a smoky tower was shown. "A plane just crashed into the tower," the reporter said. I was shocked. The poor people inside the plane! The poor people inside the building! Their poor families and friends!

"How can such an accident happen in New York?" I asked Adil. He shrugged his shoulders. Shortly after, another plane flew into the second tower. I was horrified. When yet another plane crashed into the Pentagon half an hour later, I knew all this was no accident. *This* was a new era of warfare; I was scared.

*Wednesday, September 12, 2001*

The next morning, I had PE in the first two periods. It was chilly outside, and everyone was strangely silent and still as we waited for Mr. Siegert in front of the gym. Then Finn approached me. Finn was one of my close friends, a kind and well-behaved

---

49   Cable News Network: a liberal American basic cable and satellite television news channel

guy. We frequently met after school, just the two of us or in a small group. Our classmates appreciated and respected him. Finn's father was the principal of a vocational school in Hofheim.

"Junis, who do you think attacked the USA?" he asked.

"I've got no idea," I said.

He looked at me with large eyes. "My father said it was Saddam Hussein."

Baffled, I asked, "How can he know if not even the USA does?"

"Because Saddam is a criminal. He and the Iraqis will get punished for it. And Osama bin Laden[50] and everyone who was involved too. You'll see!" he told me with a raised finger.

I looked at him, perplexed. How could he be so convinced without having any evidence, and so intent on vengeance? And how could he treat me as if I was to blame? Did I belong to "the Iraqis" now as well?

I looked around and faced a number of judgmental eyes. Did my classmates think the same?

Their looks reminded me of the German chancellor Gerhard Schröder, who guaranteed unconditional solidarity with the USA and with the free and civilized world to fight the terrorists who stood behind the attacks and bring them to justice. I sensed that George W. Bush[51], Schröder, Finn, my classmates, and probably many other Germans confused justice with revenge. I was alarmed. Did they not know that revenge would only spread more and more violence, and eventually lead to the destruction of humanity?

---

50  Founder of al-Qaida, the organization that claimed responsibility for the 9/11 attacks on the United States

51  Served as the forty-third president of the United States from 2001 to 2009

Before I could respond, however, Mr. Siegert came to open the gym. All my classmates turned their backs on me and followed him. I could not believe what was happening. Were we not friends? Suddenly, I felt a piercing pain in my chest. I wanted to go home, but then Helena came back outside. "Junis, come in. They'll all calm down again," she said. We looked into each other's eyes. I hesitated, but then I followed her. I was scared, but my hope that she was right was stronger than my fear.

Still, what followed felt completely surreal. My classmates did not speak to me during our basketball game, as if we were playing on two separate teams: me, on my own team, and everyone else on the other team. The sudden silence between us felt agonizing.

As we crossed the grounds after PE, my classmates quickly walked ahead of me without looking back once. I felt that our bond was broken. Distraught, I stopped at the cafeteria, where I suddenly found myself in the middle of a huge brawl—white against non-white Germans. This type of fighting had happened before, but not at this magnitude. I stood rooted to the ground, aghast, while Marcus and some of my classmates fired their fists. All of a sudden, someone punched me in my kidneys. My black hair and brown skin were enough to make me a target. I turned toward my attacker and, in the heat of the moment, knocked him down. When his friends saw me, they immediately started chasing me through the building. I ran toward my classroom as fast as my legs could carry me. Luckily, Mr. Siegert was already approaching the classroom when I made it to the second floor. Even though I was safe that moment, I knew that it would be a different story when there were no teachers around. I was clearly outnumbered. 9/11 turned WBS into an unequal and open battlefield!

### Thursday, September 13, 2001

Our principal held a speech in the gym in front of the eight hundred students of WBS, but his words seemed to be fruitless. He mourned the victims of 9/11 and also asked us "to stop the attacks on foreign students, who are not to blame." Some students reacted promptly, shouting, "Ausländer raus!" ("Foreigners out of here!"). The other students remained silent.

Gradually I came to understand that group mentality can easily subdue individual awareness. Such visceral responses seemed to be exacerbated by modern media, spreading fear through multiple channels day and night. I and many other Middle Eastern-looking people were targeted because of our appearance, one that the standard media relentlessly linked with threat and terrorism.

With the exception of the Gulf War, I never felt more unsafe in my skin than the days and weeks in Kastel following 9/11.

### End of September 2001

Sitting in the classroom and facing my new reality, I felt betrayed, deeply disappointed, and tormented by anger. Were all those years of friendship meaningless? How could our bonds break so easily?

My classmates and I no longer approached each as much as we used to. We never talked about 9/11 again, but I sensed that who I was and which side I was on remained a fundamental question for them.

One day, during our five-minute break, a boy named Marek came up to my table. He gave me a portrait of me, which he had drawn during the lesson, and waited for a response.

"You observed my necklace well," I said.

"You carry a Quran pendant and a cross. I've never seen that before. I wonder—do you feel more Muslim or Christian? I mean, are these religions even compatible at all?"

"Why shouldn't they be?"

"Because they're so different and because I've never seen anyone who carried both."

"As regards the latter, you're probably right."

"But with which religion do you identify with more?"

"I don't have an 'either-or' attitude. I pick what I value from both religions. Christianity and Islam have much in common and can be complementary in beautiful ways if you allow them to be," I said, noticing how many of my classmates observed me attentively.

Did Marek and the others believe I was a stranger after all? Or were they trying to determine that I wasn't one? Why all those questions and looks when they had known me for years?

*Monday, October 15, 2001: First Diary Entry*

*I'm sitting at the white folding table in my room, in front of a blank paper. I'll start to write a diary now. Maybe it'll help me understand this life.*

*Today was my first school day after our two-week fall*

*vacation. Marcus asked our class teacher if he could sit in the front row next to Finn. He was allowed to do so. When he removed his books from under our table, he told me he could focus better in the front row. I know that we sometimes fooled around during lessons in the last row and that it wasn't helpful to follow along with class all the time, but I think there is more behind his decision.*

*After school, we always walked down Weinbergstraße together. It used to take us twenty minutes though it's only six hundred yards. We used to stroll and talk a lot. When we reached the Goldbachhallen, we normally stood there another fifteen minutes, chatting and laughing before we'd go in different directions. Since 9/11, it feels like our walk has become an unpleasant obligation for both of us. We don't talk enthusiastically anymore. Instead, Marcus accelerates our walking speed. Sometimes, it seems like he is concerned about being seen with me. It hurts. A few days ago, he started—without any reason— to kick Ali, a younger Hauptschüler who was walking home in front of us, in his legs. When I told Marcus to stop it, he blamed me for being on the wrong side and continued to kick Ali. Only after Ali had taken him in a deadlock did Marcus stop. It was such a weird situation. Marcus never used to target people like that, without any reason.*

*Why is Marcus suddenly willing to resort to violence? Am I now on "the wrong side" because of my religious heritage? Or because I don't randomly attack innocent people? I don't believe in religious exclusivism and holy war. I was raised with two religions. What about religious freedom, human rights, and dignity? Is our constitution only a piece of paper? What about human reason? Have I ever given him a reason to let religion come between us? He is a Christian; I'm not. So what? I went to his confirmation when we were thirteen years old. I ate pork and celebrated with his family. I appreciated him as he was: funny, sarcastic, and outgoing. We spent every season togeth-er. We played beach volleyball and threw each other into the swimming pool. We hung around with friends and drank beer from the gas station at night. We organized house parties. We dreamed of a lifelong friendship as neighbors living next door. How could our friendship suddenly have so little value?*

### Saturday, August 24, 2002: Diary Entry

*Two weeks ago, summer vacation ended. We were in Italy, for the fifth time. The weather was perfect, almost always sunny, the time at the beach so relaxing, and the food just de-licious—like always. I wish we could have just stayed there. I have survived school so far. My classmates and I talk again, but I feel the cold distance between us. I feel lonely.*

### Thursday, September 5, 2002: Diary Entry

*A lot of things will change because I want them to change, and they'll have to accept it. I'm no longer the four-year-old boy who is incapable of speaking German. Today, I'm sixteen years old, and I can hardly speak Arabic. It's a shame. How could I forget who I am and completely assimilate to this society? I*

*French-kissed several girls "to have fun." I smoked and got wasted every weekend with so-called friends who let me down when things got rough. After 9/11, I started hanging out and doing shit with my friends from hauptschule, mostly immigrants. Last weekend, we stole food from the supermarket and sprayed graffiti on the streets. I was rude, ignorant, and recently even criminal. I was everything but self-confident. I just followed along and tried to be like everyone else to get other people's acceptance without even knowing who I really was.*

*All this will stop today because I now know who I am. I AM JUNIS SULTAN! Does this sound like a typical German name? I am relatively brown. Do I look like an ethnic German? I am circumcised. Is this required by Christianity? I was born to be a Muslim. THIS WAY I can believe in myself again after all the discrimination and disappointment I've experienced in Germany and all the misdeeds I've committed.*

*In this society, many people live misguidedly and don't think about the meaning of life. I do criticize myself too. I've made many mistakes, but I want to live a meaningful life now. What is a meaningful life? Many people blindly strive to attain material things and then die at some point. But I want to create something meaningful, something I have dreamed of, something that hopefully stays for the benefit of other people as well. Oh, politicians, businessmen, and bankers, I don't merely want to attain material securities or increase my assets! I want to be who I want to be: Junis Sultan, the one who lives his dreams, the boxer, the son, the brother, the friend; someone who can bring people together.*

*I am not happy with the dysfunctional and false life I have lived. I need to be strong and take back some control of my life. On my journey to find and live a meaningful life, I now see that I have lacked something crucial that would give me inner strength. Since my classmates and I drifted apart, I have studied the Quran, and I found shelter, a sense of belonging, and guidance like never before, neither at home nor at school nor in friendships. Islam teaches me that we all belong to Allah's creation; that we have the right to life and the obligation to live in brotherhood; that we should be thankful and patient; that we should trust Allah, and that our lives are part of a divine, wonderful plan. Everything in my life happens for a good reason, I believe now even if I do not see it now. I'm thankful to Allah for everything I've experienced. Alhamdulillah.*

### Thursday, September 5, 2002, Afternoon

It was late afternoon. My parents were sitting at the kitchen table, drinking tea, when I positioned myself between them to declare my religious beliefs.

"I have to tell you something. From this day on, I'm a Muslim," I said.

"You—you what?" Gabriela said with wide eyes.

"I want to understand and speak Arabic. I want to study the Quran in its original language. I want to pray and live a good life. I thought you could support me."

Gabriela looked at Adil, perplexed. "Say something!"

"He's free to choose his religion. If he needs support, I'll help him," Adil said.

"Are you sure?" Gabriela asked me.

"Yes. I am a Muslim now."

"Why don't you first study Islam? Maybe you'll change your mind then," she said.

"I've read the Quran in German and many other books about Islam in the last few weeks. I'm not asking for permission. I just wanted to inform you," I said, sensing that Gabriela disapproved of my decision but also hoping that she would accept it eventually. Freedom of religion was my human right. They taught me so at school, and I strongly believed in it. Without another word, I went upstairs to my room.

### Friday, September 6, 2002

I came home from school to find Adil sitting in front of the television, watching Al Jazeera[52] with a tense face. A map of Iraq was shown. I asked what was going on.

"The USA bombed an Iraqi air base near Baghdad. It's their preparation for another big war. The war against the 'axis of evil,' as Bush claims," he said with contempt.

Worried, I let him read the news-banner before I said, "I watched the German news this morning. They said the US Congress had been informed that Saddam Hussein is close to developing a nuclear bomb and weapons of mass destruction."

"All lies and cheap propaganda[53] to cover up the real US

---

52  Arabic: "The Island"—refers to the Arabian Peninsula; Doha-based broadcaster

53  Hoeffel, Joseph M. *The Iraq Lie: How the White House Sold the War.* Progressive Press, 2014

political and economic interests; their Machiavellian[54] wish to get into Iraq, control the country and its oil, and if possible, gain control over the Middle East," he said.

"I pray there'll not be another war," I said, distressed and pondering. "I just can't believe it. It's so irrational what the United States claims, and so many countries decry it."

Adil shrugged his shoulders. "If they want that war, they'll get it, even if it means lying to the entire world. They have the strongest army. They will not lose. They will go to Iraq and destroy everything, once again."

After a moment of silent despair, I slowly went upstairs and grabbed my diary.

### Friday, September 6, 2002: Diary Entry

*George W. Bush and his partners in politics and economy think they can do whatever they want to enforce their interests. But what about other people's right to life? How come people in Iraq have to die in an unjust war that is based on lies? Until today, the USA has brought no solid proof that Saddam Hussein was responsible for 9/11 or that he possesses WMDs. Is this imminent war really about restoring "international peace and security"? No! Is it about the greed for crude oil? To a large degree, yes. Where is the justice in this world? How much is a human being worth in this petrodollar world? If this war becomes a reality, I don't know where we are going. This war would be completely illegitimate! A crime against humanity!*

---

54 Machiavellianism: employment of cunning and duplicity in statecraft or in general conduct, from Italian Renaissance diplomat and writer Niccolò Machiavelli (1469–1527)

## Sunday, September 8, 2002: Diary Entry

*My mother drove to Amtal yesterday after she quarreled with my father. She blamed him for watching the Arab news day and night and becoming more and more depressed. While what she noticed is right, I understand his worries as well. The war is not only about politics. It affects our relatives and friends in Iraq. Still, she doesn't want Iraq to become a permanent topic in our house. She also said Saddam and everyone who followed or tolerated him deserves punishment.*

*Regardless of the discussions about Iraq, the relationship with my mother has become very tense. After I declared my faith, I stopped wearing the cross, even though I felt bad about taking it off since it had belonged to her father. But it just seems impossible to follow two religions in this torn world. She has not spoken with me since then. When I came home after school on Friday, she ran to the basement with tears in her eyes and hid there for hours. She doesn't want me to be a Muslim. Our separation hurts me deep inside. I feel sad and helpless. I love her. I want to have a good relationship with her, but I also want to be me. How can I connect with her if she does not accept my personal freedom? I want to choose who I am.*

*I guess the only things I can control are myself, my attitude, and my goals. I wonder, who else do I want to be, and how do I become that person? I want to be an educated person, so I'll continue to study diligently. I want to be a modest and healthy person, so I'll distance myself from consumerism. I don't need to buy costly brand-name clothes anymore. I'm thankful for everything I already have and for the basic things I can obtain. My nutrition will also get simpler: water, organic food, and no more junk food and drinks. I'll take care of my physical health. Finally, yet importantly, I want to be a successful person. With respect to my dream of becoming a boxer, I'll apply a maximally efficient workout routine to perfect my boxing skills.*

### Monday, September 9, 2002: Diary Entry

*I'm gradually becoming the person I want to be. I've worked out very hard in the last few months. I've become faster, stronger, and technically more advanced. Consistency, progressive intensity, rest periods, and the study of boxing fights have improved my boxing skills significantly. I can already spar with adults without difficulty.*

*Moreover, I've become one of the best students in my class as a result of applying most of my workout principles at school or at home when I study. I rarely have any leisure time. Instead, I have success now.*

### Mid-September 2002

One afternoon, my family and I were drinking tea in the kitchen. As usual, Gabriela took the floor. She spoke about her work and told us about a colleague who had a baby. Smiling, she raved about the baby's soft, light skin and blue eyes.

Out of the blue, she announced, "I want to adopt a German baby."

I was stunned. Was she serious? I looked at Adil and my siblings, who slurped their tea, unimpressed. Did they understand what she had just said?

"You already have six children. Why would you adopt another child?" I asked.

Looking at her cup, she said, "Because I want to have someone who is like me."

"Are you saying that we're not like you?"

Malik threw me a stern look, but I did not care. I wanted to understand her.

"You're half-and-half, and I want a fully German child," she said, looking at me now.

"Are we not all the same, just human beings?" I looked at her with raised eyebrows.

"You're different, and I want to have a German child," she repeated, more to herself than to me.

My heart began to race. Did she still believe, as she had told us time after time, that we were different because of our connection to our father's allegedly "inferior culture"? I got up and spoke in a clear voice, "I don't have to sit here and listen to your degradations."

Everyone turned to stone, except Gabriela, who got up and raised her hand.

"Don't you ever dare touch me again! Those times are over now. Touch me one more time, and you will never see me again!" I said.

She stared at me with large eyes, as surprised as everyone else at the table, but I kept my strength of mind and left.

That was the last time Gabriela tried to beat me. She probably sensed that I was serious—that I would keep my word and leave for good at her next physical attack.

### *Thursday, September 19, 2002: Diary Entry*

*I have been unhappy the last few days. I only acted strong in front of my mother when, in fact, I felt hurt when she claimed that we're so different from her. She's our mother! Who on earth could be closer to us than our parents? Of course we're different in some ways. Otherwise, we would be nothing but clones. And yet we are family! Are we not supposed to love each other, unconditionally? Or do race, religion, and culture really come before blood?*

*My physical performance progresses, at least. Today, PE was cancelled because of excessively hot weather. My classmates went home, whereas I went to the athletic ground to run for one hour. The realization of my dreams requires constant and increasing efforts, pushing my own limits, and going the extra mile. I think I'm on the right track.*

*Moreover, I often talk with my father about Islam when we're alone. He answers most of my questions, but he's afraid to teach me Arabic. He said Gabriela would not approve, like in 1993 when she said that learning Arabic would distract us from learning German. I wish things were not so unnecessarily complicated in my family.*

### Wednesday, October 16, 2002: Diary Entry

*It's time to make a confession: I'm depressed, and I don't even really know why. This ungraspable feeling of helplessness assaults me again and again, and every time, I feel more hopeless. Maybe I'm depressed because I expect too much from myself and from other people. Maybe I have unrealistic dreams, like harmony and peace. Yes, I'll take the driving test in two weeks. I'll also start working as a salesman in a men's boutique. Soon, I'll be able to buy a scooter. I'll be mobile then. Still, I know mobility is not what I'm looking for deep inside. So what is my problem? Sometimes, I feel like I don't even know myself. Sometimes, I feel like I hate myself. Sometimes, I feel like I will never fully connect with people. Sometimes, I think I will never be happy. Sometimes, I feel like this world is just torn and messed up. Do many people feel that way? Why do I ponder so much? Why do I feel so lonely and sad? Am I too self-centered? Am I too negative about myself and the world?*

### Saturday, November 2, 2002: Diary Entry

*I won my first fight by unanimous decision, alhamdulillah. I pray five times a day. Also, I have ordered more books to learn more about the Prophet and the life of a Muslim. Islam gives me hope. Islam teaches me that I have intentionally been given life, that I'm no mistake of my parents, that Allah knows my life.*

*Monday, November 4, 2002*

Islam gave some meaning to my life in the aftermath of 9/11, and some hope in the face of the prolonged struggles in my environment; however, it did not entirely ease my mind, my heart, or my soul. I was still looking for deep connections with other people. I wanted to know and understand others; I wanted to be known and understood. I was tired of feeling lonely.

My relationship with my classmates indeed recovered over the course of the year. At some point, we began to talk with each other with more ease, and we gradually became closer again. Even though we had never verbalized our thoughts and feelings about what happened after 9/11, we eventually started to spend some of our breaks together again. Usually, our breaks were trouble-free, until one day.

It was 11:25 a.m. when the school bell rang for the fifteen-minute break. Stephen, Marek, Marcus, and I left our classroom together. We walked around the schoolyard until we stopped on the lawn in front of the faculty room. Stephen was telling a joke when five students from hauptschule approached us. I knew them through their older brothers. We greeted each other from a distance.

Suddenly, Marcus said, "Look at these guys! One older than the other and all attending the sixth grade in hauptschule. They're so desperately dumb."

Marek responded instantly, "I bet they all have the same father. It's one guy who fucks his three or four wives and all his daughters and cousins. They tup women like rabbits, even their own children."

My heart began to race at their disgusting words.

Before I could intervene, Marcus shouted to them, "Look at me, Osama! Alim! Malik! Saddam! Amir! You understand what I say?"

"No, they can't. It's German," Marek said, smirking.

"What the hell is wrong with you guys?" I confronted Marcus and Marek.

"Eyyo, I gangster. I dangerous, blah blah blah. Just watch them. They're even dumber than they look. Watch that guy! He's maybe just thirteen years old and already has beard growth. I guess his ass is also covered with black hair," Marek said.

Everyone in our group began to laugh, except me.

I looked at the guy who had once been my best friend. "Marcus! Seriously?"

He turned his head toward Marek.

"So what?" Marek said. "Their older brothers fuck with us too."

I looked at Marcus again. "You know the names of my brothers-in-law and of my brothers. You played with them for years. How can you call these guys by their names as if their names were insults? Have you completely lost your common good sense?"

He shrugged.

I felt completely betrayed. He was even ready to verbally abuse my family!

As the five boys were coming closer, I began to walk in their direction. The biggest one, half a head taller than me, shouted, "We didn't start it!"

"I know. Not this time," I said, stopping between both groups, who seemed ready for another brawl. I looked one boy after another in the eyes. "What the hell are you doing? When will you finally stop?" I shouted, hoping they would leave each other in peace.

Yet their faces showed only fear and the willingness to destroy the alleged threat in front of them: "the other." My words were fruitless. Upset, I walked back to my classroom alone. I couldn't understand why they did not just get out of each other's way. What would they have lost? Territory? Power? The title of "King of the Jungle"? A "Holy War"? At school, in the twenty-first century, they still looked for an enemy, with no efforts made toward peace. Maybe their behavior was a primal trial of strength. Maybe they adopted the opinions from the adults around them. Whatever caused their behavior, their hostility damaged our friendship.

*Monday, November 4, 2002: Diary Entry:*

*Do my classmates really believe they can humiliate non-white and Muslim immigrants AND stay friends with me, although I am a non-white Muslim immigrant as well? Did they really believe their behavior wouldn't affect me? Friends respect each other! Regardless of skin color, hair color, name, religion, or whatever. They don't disgrace each other, or each other's families. What happened is unacceptable. Period.*

*Once again, my classmates and I barely talk with each other. I only attend lessons and afterward leave school alone. Our separation breaks my heart, but I don't know what else to do. I will not deny my identity and sell my dignity and my rights to be friends with them. Whom can I trust these days? Ya Allah!*

## Late Fall 2002

A few weeks after the break with my male classmates, my Italian classmate, Laura—a polite girl who liked to hang out with a small group of other quiet and shy girls—and I began to see each other with new eyes. We had things in common; we were both in one way or the other "outsiders" in our class. Soon, I began to walk her home after school. We were each other's first love, but after two months of dating, her father found out. He told her that he wouldn't allow a "Taliban[55]" like me to date his Catholic daughter and that he'd send her to another school if we continued our relationship. His prejudices against me were ridiculous, but we learned that his worldview was fixed: Christians are better than Muslims, and they mustn't go together. Laura ended the relationship, and I was completely broken-hearted.

## End of January 2003: Diary Entry

*Anyone who observed me in the last few weeks could say that I'm a weird, quiet, and sad boy who often walks around with a black eye. All of it would be true. I want to connect with people and just be myself, but somehow I fail again and again. I am afraid I have neither real friends nor a real family. Sometimes, Manal invites us to her apartment on Sundays. When we are there, she and her husband are always hospitable and offer us*

---

55  A Sunni Islamic fundamentalist political movement and military organization in Afghanistan, which gave safe haven to Osama bin Laden in the years leading up to the attacks on the USA on September 11, 2001

*plenty of food; and still, Ammu Amir criticizes me (and others) in front of everyone almost every time. When I wear a T-shirt, he claims it's too revealing and allegedly haram. When I listen to music on my MP3-player, he claims that music seduces the senses and is thus allegedly haram. Even meeting, not to mention being friends with non-Muslims, is not okay for him. He abuses Islam with his radical interpretations to pseudo-justify his total-con- trol-over-everyone-agenda, while I'm tired of defending myself.*

*According to Ammu Serhat, I'm basically blameworthy as well. Yes, he and Nour are also hospitable and offer us plenty of food when we are there; but still he speaks to me in Arabic again and again, and then laughs at me because I can't understand him. When we're in private, he tells me that I'm a disgrace to the family and to myself because I forgot how to speak Arabic. Does he believe that putting me down makes me a better Arabic speak- er? Why does he not teach me Arabic? He says I forgot where I come from. He doesn't know anything. Only Allah knows. Only Allah—and no one else—can judge me. Still, I wish I could just have a friend who knows and understands me.*

### Beginning of February 2003: Diary Entry

*Piero and I have become close again. He attends hauptschule at WBS. One day, I met him at the cafeteria during our break. We began to talk about our good old times at the Kasteler band: carnival season, camping, and much more. I had left the band when I started boxing, since I decided to focus on my dream and put in all the work to become a successful boxer. Anyway, we now spend most of our breaks together. We also call each other almost every other day to meet up. We cruise around on my scooter and go to sports bars or to the cinema. We enjoy our time together. We always have something to laugh about. It feels good to be with Piero. He is funny and generous. I am thankful for knowing him.*

### Friday, February 14, 2003: Diary Entry

*The day of lovers? Sure. My parents are making our lives even more difficult than they are at the moment. They just don't stop fighting. Day and night, they blame each other for what happened with Sophia last weekend when she got so drunk at her friend's party that she had to be hospitalized due to alcohol intoxication. They quarrel over whether "the German culture" is to blame for what happened with her, whether "the Muslim upbringing" would have prevented it, whether "the Muslim way of life" is inferior anyway—blah blah blah. At least I have Piero. I need to get out of here!*

### A Saturday in March 2003, around 11:00 p.m.

Piero, his cousin Salvatore, and I had cooked Spaghetti and watched a movie at Salvatore's apartment before we both decided to walk Piero home. We were walking on the sidewalk of Bahnhofstraße, about two hundred yards away from Paul-Ehrlich-Straße, when a patrol car rapidly pulled up and stopped us.

"Put your hands on the wall! Spread your legs!" the officer shouted.

"What's the point of that? We didn't commit any crime," I said.

"Shut up!" he said. "We're looking for Mediterranean-looking guys who just robbed and beat up a person at the railway station."

"Shit," I said quietly, looking down at myself. I was wearing a hoody under a black leather jacket. Wrong look, wrong place, wrong time.

The officer patted us down. His colleague, standing close by, eyed us and kept her hand on her pistol. He first looked for my cell phone, then for Piero's. "Boom," he suddenly said. "The cell phone we're looking for." His colleague called reinforcement.

Salvatore did not understand German, but he understood what was going on. We were racially profiled and targeted by the police. "Porca puttana," he cursed.

The police officer pushed him against the wall, shouting, "Shut up!" We were in serious trouble.

Shortly after, another patrol car came from the railway station. As we were standing with our hands on the wall, flashing blue light lit up the street. I briefly looked over my shoulder as two more officers got out of the other patrol car—with Marcus.

"We got them," the officer said to Marcus, showing him Piero's red Nokia 7210. "Did these guys rob you and beat you up?"

Marcus eyed me suspiciously before he said no.

"Check the contacts! It's my cell phone," Piero said to Marcus.

"I told you to shut the fuck up!" the officer shouted at us. "Last warning, boys. One more word and we will take you to our police station and have a real fun night."

They checked the contact list and made a call to the police

station while a dozen roller blinds were raised. Half of my neighborhood was watching the show. I felt disgraced.

Eventually, Marcus got back in the patrol car.

"Lucky you!" the officer said to us before he got into the car as well. That was the third time in a month police had pulled me over for an identity check. I felt harassed, criminalized, and humiliated. None of my classmates had ever been pulled over so frequently; they were lucky. They were ethnic Germans; they would almost never be targeted by the police.

### *Thursday, March 20, 2003: Diary Entry*

*Last weekend, I had a tough fight and won by unanimous decision. Salem, my opponent, was rated among the top three lightweight boxers in Hesse. On Sunday, I'll participate in an advanced training camp of the Amateur Boxing Association . . . Today, the Iraq War started. I'm shocked. I can hardly write. Nothing is to be heard in our house except the sound of bombs exploding on the Arabic news reports. I'll go downstairs to my father now. My mother left the house.*

### *April 2003*

I came home from school, and once again, Gabriela tried to escape to the basement, as she had often done for the past months since I converted to Islam. Tired of her behavior, I confronted her.

"Why are you still avoiding me?" I asked.

"I'm not. It's your imagination," she said with one foot on the basement stairs.

"It's not. What's your problem?"

She looked over me and raised her head. "You decided against me and for your father."

"No," I said. "I made a religious decision for myself. This was my right, and you're still my mother. I rather think you have abandoned me because of my religious decision."

"Yeah, sure. I've got no place in this family anyway. I should just run away and drive against a tree. You all would finally get rid of me," she said.

I felt guilty every time she threatened to commit suicide, allegedly because of us, but I did not know how to take away her recurring death wishes.

"Nobody wants that. You are our mother!" I said, trying to understand once again. "What does religion have to do with the fact that we have a bond as mother and son?" I asked.

She turned her back on me and walked downstairs.

Once again, I felt deeply troubled, and wondered how I could fix my broken relationship with my mother without denying who I was. As I saw it, I had two options: to give up my personal freedom, assimilate, and live according to her expectations in the hope that one day she would deem me good enough; or to choose personal freedom and consequently live with the fact that my own mother deemed me a traitor, a bad person. Once again, I chose personal freedom; I believed that good relationships did not demand extensive control on one side and substantial assimilation on the other side, but rather that a deep form of bonding is built on mutual respect for shared humanity, for being individuals with equal rights who deserve to be loved unconditionally. That was what I still hoped for, against all odds.

Although I had reasons for my decision, I underestimated the impact of the recurring message then: "You are a bad person." It was a message I had received many times before, by my mother, our neighbors, the town council, politicians on the news, the police, and, after 9/11, also by classmates and other students. It was a message that increasingly and seriously damaged my self-worth. But in the end, I wasn't the only one in my family who got punished for his religion. Sophia's confirmation was also used as an excuse to deny her the thing that every human needs: unconditional love.

### June 2003: Diary Entry

*Sophia's confirmation was in May. My mother did not tell us when she signed her up for confirmation classes last winter. My father was in Iraq at the time. When he came back, he called in a family conference because of my mother's procedure. They yelled at each other for more than an hour. It was horrible. "At least one child shall be as I am—a Christian. This is my right as a mother. You have all your children on your side. She'll be on my side. I'm responsible for her!" she shouted.*

*"Well then, if you don't need me, you're not my wife anymore!" my father shouted back. The argument continued on and on.*

*On Sophia's confirmation day, my father participated in the church ceremony, but didn't join us in the restaurant as a sign of protest. I felt sorry for Sophia. Her father should have completely accompanied her in this important, identity-forming event.*

*Manal and Nour refused to show up at all. "According to Islam, Sophia should have inherited Baba's religion," they told me on the phone. I didn't agree. No verse of the Quran states that a child inherits the Islamic faith if one parent is Muslim. Instead, the Quran says there is no coercion in Islam. Thus, no one should be forced to be a Muslim. Being a Muslim is an attitude, a behavior; it's about service; it's about showing love to Allah, to Allah's creation, to other people, and to oneself. The passive-aggressive way my father, Manal, and Nour advocate Islam resembles the politicized Islams that were developed by so-called scholars after the Prophet's death to propagate the alleged rights and increase the power of an exclusive group: Muslims. The idea is human-made. It's grounded in the human greed for power. It is, like any other politicized religion, an unholy oppression of the freedom of religion and of "other" people.*

*It's sad how religion is used in my family to divide and exclude. Why are we ripping our family apart? How does anyone benefit from separation? From having less support? From being weaker and more vulnerable? Sophia suffers the most. She still cries sometimes. I've tried to comfort and distract her. Sometimes, I take her to my boxing club so we can work out together. I love her. Her happiness and her peace are important to me. When I see how the Christian faith helps her achieve that, I'm happy for her. I've got my faith; others have theirs. So what? It's not our business to judge others. We can only try to fully see and understand them, and that already goes beyond our human capacity in most* cases. *The Quran says that we shouldn't judge others, because we never know their intentions, let alone their subconscious mind. Only Allah does. So if we truly love Sophia, we should respect her choice and protect our bond—unconditionally.*

*I'm convinced, even if I don't see it now, that we can follow different religions and happily and peacefully co-exist in our family, in our communities, and in the heavens if we give more love. And if we truly want to serve Allah, God, or whatever we call it, we give love with pleasure to create a worthy life for everyone, a balanced life where we deeply connect with others, and give them, as well as ourselves, personal freedom. It's a choice we make, every day. In September, I'll transfer to high school. I look forward to making new friends and having new learning opportunities. Life is wonderful after all. Through all the struggles with our neighbors, my classmates, and my family, through all the losses and the despair, I feel like I have grown. I have found faith in Allah during my time at WBS. Also, I have learned to stand up for my rights, for human rights, and to fight for justice. I'm thankful for those challenging lessons. Alhamdulillah.*

# KASTEL

*September 2003–June 2006*

**When fall took its course**

*Monday, September 1, 2003: Diary Entry*

I transferred to the Friedrich Ebert Gymnasium (FEG), a high school in Frankfurt. I'm glad I decided to make a new start in an environment where diversity seems to be taken for granted. The openness I experienced in our class today was inspiring. When Mr. Müller, our new English teacher, asked us to introduce ourselves, I heard German, Arabic, Asian, Turkish, and American names. He didn't ask any of us where we were "originally" from. Instead, we were given time to get to know each other in private talks. We talked about our hobbies, what we liked and disliked, and much more. Our personal talks helped us see who the others were and vice versa; it brought us closer together. Some students were very talkative, while some listened attentively, like me. No one was objectified or gazed at. I like the FEG.

*Tuesday, November 25, 2003*

When I came home from school, Adil congratulated me for Eid al-Fitr[56]. He said he was proud that I practiced my religion faithfully, and wanted to hand me €100 when no one of the family was able to see and hear us. Though I was happy about his acknowledgement, I felt uncomfortable about receiving money or

---

56 Festival of breaking of the fast, celebrated by Muslims worldwide; marks the end of Ramadan

any extra treatment since I fasted to serve Allah, reflect, and heighten my awareness of God. Besides, none of my siblings fasted, and none of them got money on Eid. Still, Adil insisted that I take the money. "It's a gift from your father, who loves you," he said. I took the money, told him that I loved him as well, and that I appreciated his acknowledgement.

### *Tuesday, November 25, 2003: Diary Entry*

*I wonder how Islam became such a thorny issue in our family.*

*In Iraq, my father introduced us to Islam. According to my mother, he wasn't particularly religious until Malik died in 1977 of heart failure. After Malik's death, he began to read the Quran and go to the mosque on a regular basis. Sometimes he took us along or invited friends to listen to Quran recitations in our living room and pray together. My mother objected to the ritual prayers at home then and has continued to complain about them until today. She would say she didn't want our living room in Mosul to become a religious space, which seems odd considering that we celebrated Christian holidays in that room too, not to mention that she also sometimes had the Bishop of Mosul as her visitor in our living room. The last time I told her that she was applying unfair double standards, she just said, "Nonsense." I know my comment didn't change her attitude, but I believe that consistent confrontation with the facts can change an attitude in the long run.*

*After we had fled to Germany, she tried to keep us away from*

*Islam, and soon it seemed as if she rejected Islam overall. When my father joined us in 1993, she told him not to teach us about Islam, since it would allegedly distract us from learning German. Next, she claimed over and over—sometimes randomly, sometimes when my father still referred to the Quran—that Islam promoted the immoral idea of an-eye-for-an-eye, as well as many other problematic views. My father tried to convince her of the good in Islam during their recurrent fights, but without success. I share some of her concerns, for instance about retaliation, but the Holy Books need to be interpreted with "a good heart," I believe. The Quran, like the Bible, can be used to justify violence IF one chooses to do so and IF one reduces the entire religion to one sentence without considering the complete teachings. I know that retaliation is a topic in the Quran, but I believe that forgiveness and mercy weigh heavier. They are frequently favored over retaliation. However, only the strong and the faithful can forgive!*

*For the sake of peace, I don't start discussions about the teachings of Islam with my mother these days. Only when she puts Islam down do I briefly give her an alternative interpretation of the Quran and some real-life examples. I've seen how viciously my parents have quarreled about religion, using divisive good religion vs. bad religion arguments, and I don't want to engage in these disrespectful arguments, in which the other religion is only demeaned whereas one's own religion is praised to the sky. I practice Islam rather quietly and try to create peace within myself, in my relationships with others, and for Allah.*

*My siblings, with the exception of Nour, who is under*

*constant pressure by her conservative in-laws, seem to be more disconnected from Islam. Maybe they just don't believe in it. But I also think that they might fear my mother's possible rejection, as well as the social problems they could face as Muslims in Germany. Malik and Alim have not practiced Islam at all since we came to Germany. They only congratulate my brothers-in-law on Eid al-Fitr and join our family dinners. Manal used to wear a headscarf in Iraq, but stopped wearing it since she came to Germany. She could not stand people gazing at her. After 9/11 and the subsequent "War on Terror," an escalating number of people did not only gaze at veiled women, but also refused to talk with them, or give them work, or rent out a flat to them, and much more. I saw it, and I heard it not only from Muslims but also from Germans who talked and sometimes even bragged about it. I understand my siblings. We already look different. Why should we attract further negative social attention by practicing a notorious religion?*

*The social pressure we've continuously faced in Germany has had a self-denying and self-destructive impact on us. We never celebrate Eid as we did in Iraq anymore, with a huge barbecue, many guests, and an open-ended party. There are only a few Muslims in Kastel anyway. Still, even a small Eid dinner at our house leads to a useless quarrel about religion between my parents now. It feels so wrong. Why could we peacefully celebrate different religious holidays in Iraq but not in Germany? Because deviations from the so-called Leitkultur are largely not wanted and considered a threat in Germany? Because of how*

*Islam has constantly been pictured in Germany, as strange, out-dated, oppressive, violent, and evil? Why did we let ourselves be manipulated if it's self-evident that the problem is not Islam, with its inconsistent messages about the use of violence, but a few misguided, malicious wannabe "Muslims" who promote and do evil?*

*I still believe that different religions can enrich our lives—in our families, in our communities, and even worldwide—if we choose to let them do so, since every religion can teach us new ways. It begins with simple things like Iftar, the break of the fast at night. Since my father returned from Mecca, he has organized an open Iftar celebration in the town hall during Ramadan every year. A small group of probably seventy Christians and Muslims peacefully sit together, chat, eat, and laugh. The at-tending Christians don't just get to enjoy new foods and reci-pes, but also experience the gratitude the Kasteler Muslims show toward Allah, God, a principle both religions share, although the methods are different. Every year, some Christians invite all Muslims to join their Church ceremonies, which some Muslims, like me, do. Is our mutual curiosity and respect only pretense? I don't think so.*

### Thursday, January 1, 2004: Diary Entry

*Everything has gone well the last few months. I've made new friends at the FEG. My grades are good, and I've won most of my boxing fights. Only my family struggles continue. Three days ago, Oma Erika broke her hip when she fell in her kitchen. She underwent a lengthy surgery in Oslar hospital. After she had woken up from the anesthesia, we were allowed to visit her on the ward. Her arms were fixed on the bed rail. She was fidgeting with her hands. "Help! Where am I? I want to get out of here," she screamed. I was scared—we all were. We held her hands and stroked her hair, but we couldn't calm her down. Shortly, a doctor came in to give her a sedative shot. Tears rolled down my mother's face. Sophia was completely pale and almost threw up. My father took her out of the room. After a minute, Oma Erika stared at the ceiling, unresponsive.*

*The next day, the doctors diagnosed her with senile dementia. My mother has cried a lot over the last few days. I feel so sorry for her and for Oma Erika. Tomorrow, we'll bring Oma Erika to our house. She'll stay with us until we know what we can do for her. She certainly can't live alone anymore. Amtal belongs to the past, her growing mental weakness to the present. She often feels lost. She doesn't know who she is, who we are, or where we are. More and more things seem strange to her. I feel sad. Our bond with Oma Erika is dwindling away. Will we soon be total strangers to each other?*

### February 2004

My family, or rather, those of us who remained, kept together in the midst of our new family crisis. Alim had moved to Mainz with his girlfriend several months ago, and rarely visited us. He was studying music and focused on his dream of becoming an artist. Sophia officially still lived with us, but she mostly hung around outside with her friends, most of whom were drug dealers and addicts. Sometimes, we did not know where she was for days on end. She was inaccessible. I tried to talk with her and get her more connected with our family, but she seemed to hate us after all the pain she had experienced over the years. Since Manal and Nour looked after their families, it was up to my parents, Malik, and me to look after Oma Erika.

Our living room became Oma Erika's new bedroom. We put up a bed for her and built a small separating wall. In the mornings, Adil looked after her while we went to school or to work. He would wash her and change her clothes. Afterward, she would walk with her walker to a small table at the window, where he would serve her coffee and a sandwich before she took her medicine. "I'm thankful I can help her," he told me one day. "I wish I could have helped my mother the same way." In 1996, Adil's mother had fallen at home in Mosul and broken her hip. The doctors could not perform the necessary surgery on her; due to UN sanctions, the amount of available anesthesia was insufficient and only given to the young and strong. The doctors gave her expired painkillers and released her from the hospital to die at home. When we received the call in 1996, I saw Adil cry for the first time. I felt very sorry for him then. When that bitter memory returned in 2004, we were all the more thankful that we could help Oma Erika.

As a rule, I gave Adil a break in the afternoons when I came home from school. He would go upstairs to take a nap, and I would help Oma Erika go to bed. Sometimes, she slept for over an hour and I was able to do my homework at her table. But more often than not, she would have difficulties sleeping. "Help!" she would shout, again and again. I would sit next to her and stroke her hand. "You are in Kastel. You are Oma Erika. I am Junis, your grandson. Everything is fine," I would say. My gentle touch and my voice, which she almost always seemed to recognize as familiar, normally helped her calm down; if it didn't, I gave her a nice piece of chocolate, which always made her smile like a child.

"You're kind," she told me almost every day, grabbing my hand. It felt good to give something back to Oma Erika. She was like a mother to me, and despite her illness, we still had a deep, unbreakable connection. There was a basic trust between us.

Gabriela usually came home from work at 5 p.m., exhausted. Even though we faced each other more often, we did not talk about how we could improve our relationship. Oma Erika's illness was more urgent. Her constant confusion and shouting overwhelmed Gabriela, and I did not want to burden her with my needs as well. On most afternoons during the week, she let me look after Oma Erika while she went down to the basement.

### Saturday, February 7, 2004

Malik came home from his job at a computer company every evening at around 6:30 p.m. He and/or my parents looked after Oma Erika in the evening, and I was able to train at the boxing gym in Hochheim.

Rahman, my next opponent, was rated number one of the light welterweight division in Hesse. I worked out hard, since I absolutely wanted to win and qualify for the Southwest German Championship.

On the day of our fight, however, I was deeply worried about the burdens my family had to face. In addition to Oma Erika's illness, Sophia had escaped to Mannheim the previous night to meet a boy she had met online. My parents fought and blamed each other again—in particular each other's culture and religion—for what Sophia was doing, before they got in the car and left to search for her. A few hours later, Tariq, my coach, picked me up for the fight. I entered the gym with serious concerns about Sophia's safety. As I sat down on the bench in the changing room, I prayed silently and beseeched Allah to give my family the strength to overcome our battles, outside and within, and become better people. Praying gave me hope and changed my anxious, tormented state of mind. It encouraged me.

I got up and changed my clothes, feeling unusually intense, as if I was becoming another person, one who didn't know fear or pain. I couldn't afford to get distracted by personal concerns; I couldn't afford to be weak. I wrapped my hands and completely focused on the fight. The air in the changing room was full of different smells: the cold sweat of fighters waiting for their rounds, the salty heat of those who had just fought, the metallic blood that either gushed from open wounds or dried on leather gloves, and above all, the sharp Japanese peppermint concentrate that Tariq had dropped into my nose before he warmed me up. I hit the pads. Blood shot though my veins like burning petrol. The thick petroleum jelly on my eyebrows, cheeks, and nose felt like a protective shield. I knew I'd have to give a hundred percent to persevere, a hundred and twenty percent to win. Off and on, a fresh breeze snuck into the room through a small window and touched my hot skin. I breathed deeply in and out, concentrating.

Suddenly, someone shouted from the hallway, "Next fight, Junis Sultan, BC Hochheim."

Tariq whispered into my ear, "Go! No fear. No pain. Fight now!" I climbed up the stairs and entered the small gym, filled with a hundred people. All eyes turned to me; I focused on the ring. I felt my heartbeat; I was ready to fight for my life. Inside the ring, I went to my corner. After I had prayed the Surat al-Fatiha[57], the bell rang—*Ding*. Its echo inflamed my drive. I gave my entire physical and mental strength to those four three-minute rounds against an undefeated fighter, who had beaten me a year ago on the score cards.

After the final stroke of the bell, I walked back to my corner. Tariq beamed. "You made the fight!" he said. I felt the abrasions on my back, as if someone had whipped me with a cowhide. I had gotten them when I leaned back in the ropes, but for most of the fight, I dominated him from the middle of the ring with fast jabs. Tariq took off my headgear and my gloves, and my heartbeat eventually slowed down. I had no scratches on my face. Slowly, I felt myself becoming a normal human being again. People I knew in the first row and strangers in the back of the room all cheered, "Junis! Junis!" I smiled.

---

57  First chapter (*surah*) of the Quran; its seven verses (*ayat*) are a prayer for the guidance, lordship, and mercy of God.

Boxing, as I had already sensed when I started at age fifteen, became a lifelong passion. It taught me self-discipline, the key to success. Being successful in such a mentally and physically challenging sport gave me a sense of self-respect, recognition, and respect from others—even if only temporarily. I was never a heavy puncher, though; I was a technician. I always played by the rules, and won almost all my fights on the score cards. Furthermore, the intense workout gave me a break from everyday problems.

There were many reasons why I would hold on to boxing; most importantly, it prepared me for life, which was often damn hard. But I was not yet fully aware then that success in sports, in school, or any other activity was only a temporary relief from the pain I felt due to the problematic and failing relationships in my life.

### Tuesday, March 2, 2004: Diary Entry

*It's midnight. I'm sitting on our couch. My father is lying in Oma Erika's bed. His eyes are closed, but he can't sleep. He's still in pain. I can see it in his face. We picked him up today around noon after his eleven-day hospitalization, after taking Oma Erika to an old folks' home. I'm so sorry for her. She used to look after us with all her heart, and now we send her to such an unfamiliar place. We just can't look after two patients. It's too much for us.*

*It started Friday, February 20. My father had accompanied me to boxing training. I was sitting right here that night, watching the news when he returned to the living room from the toilet, pale. "I had a lot of blood in my stool," he said. My mother drove*

*him to the hospital right away. He underwent two emergen-
cy surgeries. The doctors removed an aggressive intestinal tumor.
The scar on his stomach is eight inches long. He has lost more
than thirty pounds and is still almost too weak to speak. I can
hardly grasp what has happened. Everything went so quickly.*

### Wednesday, March 3, 2004: Diary Entry

*I have to confess something awful. After the second surgery,
the doctors told us that my father would probably have only two
weeks to live, although they'd still try chemotherapy. I was instantly devastated. I couldn't cope with the idea of losing my
father—my most important confidant in the family, the one who
was almost always there for me, who always tried to understand
me, who respected me unconditionally. After the deadly message,
I skipped school and stayed at home. Sitting in my room, alone,
I felt so hopeless, so lost . . . that I took the knife from the drawer
and cut my arm. I don't know why I did it. I wasn't thinking.
I just put a bandage on my wounded arm, packed my gym bag,
and went to Hochheim as usual. After working out for ninety
minutes, I felt completely dizzy. I lurched to the changing room
to take off my blood-soaked bandage. Raid, my sparring partner,
entered the room after me. He gazed at my forearm with large
eyes. "What happened?" he asked. I told him. "You're crazy. You
mustn't do that!" he said. He's right! Ya Allah, what have I done?
WHY did I hurt myself? WHY did I make such a horrible mistake? Have I completely lost my mind and all sense of self-love?*

*Tuesday, March 30, 2004: Diary Entry*

*When I came home from school today, I found my mother sitting in the kitchen, crying. She told me that Sophia had just burned her forearms with cigarettes, and that she would be sending her to a locked psychiatric ward since all our family problems overburdened her. I went upstairs to Sophia and saw her arms. With tears in our eyes, I hugged her for a long moment. I'm so sick with regret. What happened is my fault. No one noticed that I had cut my arm, except Sophia one day—before she burned her arms. Ya Allah, I don't want to lose courage. Please, give me the strength to prevail. I'll fight for my family. I'll support and listen. I'll do the housework. I'll do everything I can. I want to be a pillar for my family, and not a disaster.*

*Monday, April 26, 2004: Diary Entry*

*Sophia is still locked up. Two days ago, she burned her forearms again. When we visited her, she threw my mother's flowers in a dustbin and ran away. The psychiatrist says that her problem is rooted in our family's cultural and religious conflicts, that she is torn between the two sides and thus lacks a feeling of belonging and psycho-emotional security. Is her psychiatrist right? I guess so. I think and feel the same way time and time again. Do I allow it to destroy me? It seems that way sometimes.*

*Yesterday, I felt this inner strife, this ripping pain and empty brokenness again. We brought Oma Erika to our house to celebrate her eighty-eighth birthday. Some of her friends visit-ed her. They drank champagne, ate pork sandwiches, and talked about German folk music. They had things in common, but I felt out of place, like I so often do. It automatically reminded me that I'm far from being a "normal Iraqi" either, especially according to my brothers-in-law. I'm so sick of thinking about not belonging anywhere. "It could be worse," I often tell myself. "Be thankful that you don't live in war," I often tell myself. "It's a shame that you're so hypersensitive and emotional," I often tell myself. This is how I go on, knowing I'm still lost. How can I connect with anyone if I don't love myself? How can I love myself again if I have, from early on and, over and over again, been taught to hate myself? How deeply is this self-hate embedded in my soul? The self-satisfaction I have experienced over the years has only been temporary, if not superficial. I was satisfied when I received good school grades or won a fight, but all this never gave me a stable sense of self-esteem—the feeling of being "enough and okay" — nor did it give me peace of mind. I wonder if I will ever reach that state.*

## May 2004

I should have sought psychological help to cope with the trau-mas in my life well before my act of physical self-harm, but I didn't, because I carried a burden that was already too heavy to bear: shame. I did not seek help because deep down, behind the veil of success at school and in boxing, my sense of self-worth and dignity was broken. I had allowed other people, and myself, to let it happen, and I didn't seek out psychotherapy because I feared more stigmatization and marginalization. Trapped in shame, I didn't see that getting help would have not only been the remedy to my trauma, but also to my feelings of inferiority.

At seventeen years old, I had difficulty developing a caring and understanding inner self. That kind of self-supporting inner voice had been almost drowned out by an increasingly relentless inner critic over the years, and it would take a lot of effort to rebuild a more positive, constructive inner self that could not be easily harmed or manipulated by the outside world, or turned against itself.

### May 2004: Diary Entry

*People need to connect. That's how we are wired. And people need to be free to be who they are and want to be. Otherwise, we get sick and destroy each other. If there is goodness in us, we will find ways to live together in peace.*

### May 2004: Diary Entry

*It doesn't make sense to be depressed, self-pitying, and afraid of failing in life, because it leads to failure here and now. I've missed more than fifty class hours, and I can hardly catch up now. I was barely admitted to the twelfth grade because of all my absences. Stop! I mustn't screw up my life. I am responsible for my life. I have to pull myself together! Giving up is easy. Remembering, following, and living my dreams is not, but it's necessary for a meaningful life. I'll focus on school again. Education is my ticket for a better future!*

## May 2004

After Oma Erika was diagnosed with senile dementia at the beginning of the year, my parents decided to bring her to Kastel and build a bungalow for her in our back yard. Her illness made them work together again, after giving each other the silent treatment for months in the aftermath of Sophia's confirmation. They gave our architect full freedom of planning in February, which led to a surprising outcome in May. One day Adil, who still received an intensive ambulatory chemotherapy and, surprisingly, seemed on the way of recovery, handed me the construction plan of a fourteen hundred-square-foot family house. I smiled and felt hopeful. Building had bound my parents together in 1997, and it could do the same in 2004, I believed. Their relationship already seemed to have improved because of Adil's illness. When he stayed in the hospital for eleven days, Gabriela cried almost every day. One day during our teatime, she said she couldn't live without him. It was the first time I heard her say such words about Adil. The way she said it sounded like she still loved him, despite all the great difficulties they faced in their marriage.

### Saturday, June 26, 2004: Diary Entry

*Lots of good news! My father's chemotherapy is finished. The doctors say he is healed. Alhamdulillah! He also applied to build that house in our back yard, which will give us more living space and make it easier to accommodate Oma Erika. Alhamdulillah!*

*We already brought Oma Erika back home to us. She is doing okay. Alhamdulillah! And last but not least, Sophia was released two days ago. She feels better now. Alhamdulillah!*

*Tomorrow, we'll all go to Italy for our summer vacation. The fresh ocean breeze, the salty water, and the warm sun will nurture our bodies and souls!*

### Friday, October 1, 2004

After the summer passed, we soon received our building permit from the authorities. On October 1, I watched the beginning of the demolition work before I went to school. Frankfurter Weg, the street behind our back yard, was cordoned off. An excavator evacuated the organic waste and the ruins of our garage with a rumbling noise that awakened our neighborhood. I was excited and even somewhat proud. We more than just settled in Kastel; we were already building our second, new house, which was a big achievement in our neighborhood. Even though I knew it was only a material success, optimism captured me. Our new house could be more than stones; it could be a place free from wall-to-wall harassment from xenophobic neighbors; a place where we could appreciate one another and ourselves; a place we could gladly call home.

Attending the FEG over the past year or so had been a challenge, as I coped with a number of private catastrophes, but it seemed like life was suddenly turning around for me. In addition to all the recent, positive developments in my family, I was about to meet a person who would lift me up in wonderful ways.

## *Monday, October 4, 2004*

The school bell rang for break. I went down to the cafeteria. My friends were already sitting in front of the counter. I shook hands with Payam, my sparring partner from Frankfurt, then with Samir, Sebastian, Andrej, Justina, Dorothy, and Helena. We were all either in the same English or PE advanced courses. On a normal day, I would have sat and talked with them, but that day I was so tired from my last workout that I excused myself. I walked to a free table in the back of the dining hall to have a power nap.

As I sat down, I saw a girl watching me with big, brown eyes, hiding behind her girlfriends. She stood up from her table. We looked at each other, unrestrained. She had straight, brown hair, a thin nose, and a well-developed figure. I was attracted to her, but physically so tired that I lay my head on the table and slowly closed my eyes.

After a minute, I sensed someone close to me. I opened my eyes. *She* was standing in front of me, smiling. She asked for my name, and I told her.

"Beautiful name. I like it," she said. She paused. "Are you Arab?" she asked, and immediately added, "I'm sorry, I'm just always so curious. You don't have to tell!"

"Well, half; and half German, if you want to see me that way," I said, somewhat irritated by her question but also sensing her genuine interest.

"Wow! German?" She laughed. "I would never have thought."

"I believe you," I said. "And what's your name, if I may ask?"

"Ceylin," she said, and smiled again.

I liked her kind manner.

"That's a beautiful name too. It's Turkish, right?" I asked, before I noticed that I had fallen into the same "identity" trap, although I believed that the question of ethnicity or nationality was rather superficial and intrusive, and should not be asked when meeting someone new—unless the other person wanted to talk about it to start a conversation. Either way, I wanted to know who Ceylin really was.

"Right. It means 'the door to heaven,'" she said.

I believed every word she said.

"Well, I have to go. I'll see you around here again, right?" she said.

"Yeah," I said, playing cool even though I was already falling for her. I wanted to see her again, rather sooner than later. What a woman! So charming and humorous! Out of nowhere, she had just entered my life and easily made me smile.

### Thursday, October 7, 2004

School ended at 4:00 p.m. I rode home on my yellow Gilera SP 50 scooter. Before I could enter the house, I heard my parents shouting. Alarmed, I quietly opened the front door.

"I was never accepted by any of your family in Iraq," Gabriela shouted.

"What about Ammu Nuri? He loved you and always cared for you. And my father was proud of you too," Adil shouted back.

"And your mother said that I was good-for-nothing and only a cheap European whore."

"I told you many times, don't talk like that about my mother!"

"I can say what I want. I've always been the one who was abused, and everyone who has abused me will pay for it here and on Judgment Day."

"Woe betide you if you are still talking about my mother!" Adil shouted with a raised finger, while I briefly glanced into the kitchen.

"I'm talking about you and everyone else in this family. I'll move out. I can't bear living here any longer. No one respects me."

Gabriela pushed me aside and ran to the front door.

Adil followed her, shouting, "Yeah, go! Nobody can stand your constant need to fight anyway. You just argue because Ramadan is coming and you want to ruin the atmosphere."

She slammed the door. My heart was racing. Like so many times before, I asked myself why they could not just get along.

Shortly after, Adil came to the kitchen and told me in a normal voice, "We've got rice and tomato sauce with zucchini, eggplant, and ground meat."

I put some food on my plate and sat down, upset and aware: Oma Erika's illness, his illness, and building a new house had not bound them closer together. "Why were you quarreling again?" I asked.

"Because I was listening to a Quran CD while I was cooking. I thought she would be at work until five, but she came home earlier. When she opened the door and heard the recitations, she started to shout at me. She doesn't want Quran recitations in our house."

I shook my head and swallowed. "She can't forbid you to be a Muslim. I mean, what are you going to do about it? Do you want to accept her behavior? She married you as a Muslim."

"I don't accept it, but I'm also tired of arguing. I listen to Quran recitations when she isn't at home, and when she is here, I don't. I just try not to provoke her."

"That's almost certainly the wrong strategy. We support her religious practice. We celebrate Christian holidays with her like Christians, including listening to Christmas music for weeks. We don't say anything when she eats pork or puts rum in her tea. We don't overplay our differences. What about our rights? Are we not free to practice our religion as well?"

"It's not that easy with her. You know that better than any of your siblings do."

"And it's still wrong," I insisted, looking at his distraught face. "Look, I'll go back to school now and meet a friend." I paused. "Baba, don't worry too much. It won't change a thing. You should tell her that she needs to accept your freedom as well, and then act upon it."

He sighed and looked at me as if he was considering my thoughts.

Upstairs, I quickly got ready for my first date with Ceylin. I changed, brushed my teeth, and dabbed Hugo Boss Bottled on my neck. We had exchanged numbers the other day, and since then we'd been texting each other constantly. Ceylin made me forget about the problems at home. She made me feel appreciated and special. Smiling, I put on my helmet and left Kastel at full throttle to meet her in Frankfurt.

She was waiting in front of the entrance to the train station. The moment our eyes met, we began to smile. I parked, took off my helmet, and slowly met her halfway while people hectically moved around us.

"You know what I have noticed?" she said with shiny eyes. "You used to look so serious, but since we have gotten to know each other, you can suddenly smile. Why?"

"It's because I'm happy to be with you," I said.

We looked into each other's eyes. My heart pounded. I was thrilled.

"Where can we go? I don't want you to get into trouble with your relatives for hanging out with me," I said, anticipating that she was a Muslim and that our date could be a risk.

According to the Sunnah, meeting with members of the opposite sex before marriage was not allowed without the presence of a third person. The rule is intended to keep a Muslim's chastity, which is demanded in the Quran. I considered this religious rule, not because I believed that our date would lead to premarital sexual intercourse and hellfire, but because I wanted to protect Ceylin from bad-mouthing and more serious consequences from her relatives, whom I did not know yet. I never would have allowed sexual intercourse on our first dates anyway. I wanted to get to know Ceylin in depth.

She smiled. "I appreciate your thoughtfulness. We shouldn't go to the central shopping area. My aunt works there. What about having a walk in the park, down to the River Main?"

"Great!" I said, and smiled back. It was a wonderful haven to get to know each other. Grassland, meandering footways, and tall deciduous trees next to a white church led down to the river.

As we meandered down the park, we talked about our hobbies, majors, goals, and wishes for the future. She spoke with ease, and I looked at her time and again, enjoying every word she said. Even though I did not speak as much she did, her eyes showed the same devotion when I spoke, and they captured me. We were connecting more and more.

After we had passed the old white church, we walked along the riverside to a small playground. "Let's stay. I used to play here when I was little," she said. She began to swing, like a child who enjoyed going higher and higher. Her light-heartedness inspired me. There was something in her smile that I had lost a long time ago. I sat down on the swing next to her. "Come on!" she said excitedly. Soon, we began to race. We couldn't stop laughing until we stopped to swing and turned to each other. "So what about your childhood?" she asked. When I told her about my first four happy years, and how they ended with war, she came closer. Her soft eye contact showed me how much she was able to empathize.

### *Friday, October 8, 2004*

When Ceylin entered the cafeteria, our eyes met for a short, intense moment. And yet we did not approach each other; we did not want others to know about us, since it could have meant trouble. Someone could tell her family about us, which we, by unspoken agreement, wanted to prevent.

Sitting with my friends, I began to ponder: could we ever act like the other couples at the FEG? Atheist or Christian couples were usually not subject to strict rules and constrictions. Jörg and Kathy from my English course, for instance, held hands and kissed each other in public as much as they liked. The FEG counted many couples like them. Non-Muslim-girl-and-Muslim-boy couples were rare, since Muslims constituted a minority. Still, these couples usually enjoyed more freedom as well, since Muslim boys, contrary to Muslim girls, were often given more freedom by their parents, as long as their girlfriends were non-Muslims. It didn't make any sense to me, and seemed completely unfair. As if non-Muslim girls had less honor than Muslim girls, who were expected to remain virgins until their wedding night. And as if it were not a sin for Muslim boys to sleep with non-Muslim girls for fun. I was still a virgin in 2004, but sex before marriage was okay for me if it came with love and the honest intention to stay together.

The longer I thought about everything, the more I realized how lucky Ceylin and I were. Our relationship was intense. It was neither easy nor phony. It was something precious we had to protect at all times, a bond just between us—the perfection of intimate togetherness.

### Sunday, October 10, 2004

Ceylin had to lie to her parents to be with me. She would most commonly tell them she was going to visit her best friend Derya, and then drive to Kastel instead.

I waited for her at the Park and Ride at sundown. She got out of her mother's car and grinned when she saw me. "I like your perfume!" she said. My neck smelled like citrus and sweet cinnamon with a touch of santal and vetiver.

"Thank you," I said, "I only use it on special occasions." We both laughed, knowing that she could not stay very long.

We began to walk down the bikeway next to the thicket that grew along the railways. Oblong serrated leaves in red, yellow, and brown crunched under our feet. Leaves also floated down from the blue sky as the golden sun was setting. Fall took its course.

"What a beautiful day!" I said, and deeply breathed in the cool air.

We stopped walking and looked into each other's eyes.

"I know that I want you, and no one else," Ceylin said.

Her openness gave me goosebumps. For a second, I thought about what to say, but then I lost and found myself again in her eyes. I was becoming like Ceylin—a free heart. "And I want you, and no one else," I said. Our lips came closer; we closed our eyes and let ourselves be carried away by our feelings. A stream of intense warmth filled my chest as I kissed her tender lips. She kissed me gently and passionately, and I found a kindred spirit in her strong emotionality. Love was alive.

## Wednesday, October 13, 2004

The builders poured the foundation of our new house in Frankfurter Weg when I came from school. I took a picture of the work with my cell phone, appreciating every step it took to build our new home.

*Friday, October 15, 2004*

As we had done on previous days, Ceylin and I met in the underground garage at school ten minutes before the first lesson started. I drove down the ramp and parked across from the staircase, where she was waiting for me. We smiled at each other. I walked to her and gave her a kiss.

"Why do I only get a quick kiss today?" she asked.

"Ramadan started. We should not kiss. I'm fasting," I said.

"Yes, it started, and I'm fasting too," she looked at me, puzzled.

"We should behave decently, especially during Ramadan."

"If you take Islam seriously, we're not allowed to kiss until we're married."

"I know, but according to Islam, there is also no compulsion in religion, and I interpret Islam in a liberal way. Our intention is good. We love each other, and we want to stay together."

"Then kiss me like you used to."

"I don't want to kiss you when I've got a bad breath."

She grabbed my hands and said, "I don't care about that, Junis."

I looked at her serious face, and found it hard not to smile. She was so beautiful and so strong-willed. "Why don't we kiss decently during the day like we just did? What can be wrong about showing love to each other as long as we don't go wild? And at night, when we don't fast, when we taste better, I'll kiss you as I used to. Would that be okay for you, my love?"

She smiled. "I was afraid you wouldn't want to kiss me for a whole month."

"You know I could never have done that," I said.

We both laughed, relieved, before she went up the staircase, and I walked up the ramp.

### Wednesday, October 20, 2004

The basement was built. I enjoyed watching the crane putting together the heavy, pre-assembled, armored concrete plates. In contrast to the walls of Paul-Ehrlich-Straße four, our new house was solid.

### End of October 2004

When Ceylin and I were in public, we never held hands or talked with each other in order to avoid speculation. By the end of October, though, some of our close friends noticed that we were a couple. Our eyes revealed our secret. Still, I knew I could count on my friends. They didn't make a topic of it, let alone tell Ceylin's parents. They just smiled sometimes and were happy for us.

One day, Ceylin and I briefly met under the staircase after our art course. I was wearing a T-shirt. We were talking about our next date when she suddenly froze. I tried to quickly hide my arm, but it was too late. "Junis, what's that on your arm?" she asked, concerned.

I felt tense. I had no idea what to tell her. I myself did not even know why I had cut my arm. Moreover, I did not want to make up a story like I normally did when people asked me about the scars.

My friend, Helena, had once asked me as well. I told her that I fell into a thorn bush. Of course, she did not believe me. She said I could talk to her anytime, but I always felt too embarrassed to talk about the scars.

To Ceylin, however, I wanted to tell the truth as far as I could. "An accident," I said.

"Did you cut yourself?"

I nodded, regretful.

She grabbed my arm and looked at it. "Why?"

"I don't really know. I had a lot of problems, and I was weak."

She let my arm go and stepped back. "How can I know you won't cut yourself the next time you're in trouble?"

"If I could undo one thing, it'd be these scars," I said. "I made a stupid mistake. It's haram to hurt oneself. The body is a gift from Allah. I will never do it again."

"I will have to believe you," she said.

I could see she was still shaken, though.

"Let's meet in Kastel tonight." I paused. "Give me a chance to explain myself. I know it's difficult to understand such crazy behavior, but let me try to explain everything."

She met me at nine. We sat in her car. I told her about the traumas I faced at an early age and the fears I developed thereafter. I told her about the war, the separation, and the losses within my family; of the discrimination in Kastel, the violence at home, my parents' constant fights, the recurring feeling of being torn and not belonging anywhere, Oma Erika's and Adil's sudden illnesses, and how I was, at one point, completely overwhelmed by hopelessness, which somehow made me cut my arm, as if the physical pain could take away the emotional pain. I had never told anyone about it, and I hoped she'd understand.

She held my cheeks with her hands. With tears in her eyes, she said, "You'll never stand alone again, because I'm on your side." I felt loved and secure, as if nothing could harm me anymore.

### Sunday, November 14, 2004

Ceylin and I met almost every other night in Kastel until Eid al-Fitr, when she asked if she could come around eight o'clock. I told her that I would first have to ask my father, since we had my family over.

I approached him in the kitchen.

"It's Eid al-Fitr, the end of Ramadan. What friend do you want to invite? Our family is together tonight," he said.

"She's a friend from high school," I said.

"A girl? A Muslim?" he asked, suspicious.

Suddenly, Ammu Serhat joined up with us. He had been listening to our talk from the living room. "Where does she come from?" he asked me.

"Her parents are from Turkey," I said, irritated by his question.

"I don't know if that's a good idea," he said, and looked at Adil.

"What about her parents? Is she not with her family on Eid?" Adil asked me.

"They already ate, and they said she was allowed to go out and celebrate with her friends," I said.

He thought about it for a second before he said, "If it's like that, she can come."

I smiled, happy about his decision and looking forward to seeing her.

Elders have to be respected and honored in Islam. Ammu Serhat therefore didn't contradict Adil. Even though I made use of this religious rule to bypass my brothers-in-law that night—anticipating that Adil would be more open to Ceylin's and my rather benign wish—I didn't believe in this rule unconditionally, after I had repeatedly witnessed how younger Muslims complied with their elders' ideas, even if the elders were wrong. I often wondered how this rule could build progressive relationships and societies: would it not make more sense to let the most reasonable argument win, as was usually done in the West?

Ceylin met me at the Park and Ride at eight. We congratulated each other for the end of Ramadan with a kiss. After I had briefly introduced her to my family as a friend from high school, we spent the evening in my room, talking, listening to Alicia Keys[58], our favorite singer, cuddling, and laughing again and again. I was deeply happy that our bond had grown so strong, and I felt positive about our common future.

### Wednesday, December 8, 2004

The shell construction of our two-and-a-half-story house was finished. Each floor contained fifty square meters; the rooms were

---

58  Born Alicia Augello Cook (January 25, 1981): an American musician, singer, and songwriter

neatly arranged. Our house was big enough for a family with three children. I was looking forward to moving into our new house the next year. Everything seemed to be going well.

### Sunday, December 12, 2004: Diary Entry

*Ceylin hasn't come to school for more than a week. I've called her a couple of times, but she didn't pick up. Three days ago, she texted me, "I have problems at home." I asked her what had happened, but she didn't reply. Last night, she texted me, "I can't talk." I was so upset that I got in my mother's car and drove toward Frankfurt through lightning, thunder, and heavy rain. When I entered an intersection, I hydroplaned and almost hit a silver Mercedes that was stopped at the traffic light. Fortunately, I only hit the traffic light. I reversed and drove back home with a broken axle, a distorted bumper, broken front lights, and a collateral bump on the driver's door. "The main thing is nobody got hurt," my mother said, startled when I showed her. CEYLIN, TALK WITH ME! I'M GOING CRAZY WITHOUT YOU.*

### Saturday, January 8, 2005

Even though Ceylin had warned me to never visit her at Woolworth, where she worked with her aunt, I asked Piero to give me a ride. I could not wait any longer. I wanted to know what was going on.

I entered the store at 7:45 p.m. and approached Ceylin at the cash register.

"I told you not to come here!" she whispered to me angrily.

"I won't leave until you tell me what is going on," I whispered back.

"Okay, go! Wait outside!" she said.

I waited outside next to some T-shirt stands, tense. After ten minutes, a saleswoman wheeled in the stands. At eight o'clock, she closed the shop, and Ceylin began to count the cash.

At 8:15 p.m., Ceylin came outside. We walked to a dark corner a few steps away from the shop door.

"I've got no time. Only five minutes," she said, stressed.

"Ceylin, what's going on? I've been trying to reach you for almost a month. Don't you remember? We wanted to be there for one another. Let me help you."

She looked to the ground. "You help me when you leave me alone."

"You mean for good?" I asked, not believing what she had said. "Say it to my face."

She raised her head. Tears rolled down her cheeks. "My father found out about us."

I looked at her, taken aback. Although I had been afraid of this reality for almost a month, I had always told myself that we had been careful enough in public, that there would be other issues in her family, anything, but not that. "Why didn't you tell me?" I asked quietly.

"Because he took away my cell phone. I'm not allowed to contact you anymore," she said. "If we continue to meet, he will take me out of school and marry me off to someone else."

I had heard a similar message before, from Laura, but this time

I was completely unprepared. Ceylin and I we were both Muslim, which I had thought should make our families more accepting. A sudden, heavy pressure on my chest made it difficult to breathe. "But we're of age. We're young adults now. Aren't we free to love?"

"No. My father wants me to marry a Turk," she said.

Her words felt like invisible blades stabbing in my heart. I still could not understand what was happening. "But I'm a Muslim, like you and your family. Isn't that good enough?"

She shook her head. "No."

That moment, my world fell apart. Ceylin and I were lost. Tears filled my eyes. "If it's like that, we're not a couple anymore," I said in a trembling voice.

"I think that's the best for everyone."

"No, it's not. You're wrong. And your father is wrong too. It doesn't matter, though, because you have already decided against us."

Silent tears streamed down both our faces.

"I've got to go now. Goodbye," she said, and left.

With shaking legs, I watched her walk away under orange shining street lamps until she disappeared behind a corner house.

I lurched to Piero's car, which was parked on a side street in the dark—looking back.

"Come on, that bitch is gone. Get in the car now!" Piero shouted.

I passed a metal trashcan and punched it so hard I dented it. Some lights in the houses around us came on. Piero rapidly got out of his car.

"Are you okay? Get in the damn car. Let's go now," he said.

I sat down on the passenger seat and looked at him, devastated.

"She's not a bitch." I paused. "I love her. How on earth could I let this happen?"

"What do you mean?"

"She broke up with me. It wasn't in our hands anymore."

"Champ, life's a bitch, and we need to be strong." He switched on the engine and drove me home.

### Monday, February 21, 2005

My parents went to the notary to register Frankfurter Weg seven, our new house, as part of the Paul-Ehrlich-Straße four property. Both houses were written in Gabriela's name. I took notice of it without interest. My mind and my body were completely occupied by Ceylin.

### Sunday, February 27, 2005: Diary Entry

*I'm falling. I see neither beginning nor end. At a lethal pace, I'm falling in the dark—trying to catch something, but I feel nothing. Ceylin and I, our wonderful bond, is destroyed. Since we broke up, I haven't prayed. I lost my motivation to practice religion. What should I pray for if I've already ended up in hell? There is no shelter for me, no mercy, no hope. Ceylin is carved into my bleeding heart. Happiness and peace have never been so far away. Why can't I simply be with Ceylin, my love? How can this torture ever be good for me, ya Allah? Where are you? Is this really what you have planned for me?*

## *Sunday, February 27, 2005, later that night*

Piero parked in front of Paul-Ehrlich-Straße four. He honked the horn a dozen times before he shouted from the street, "Junis. Come out! It's me, Piero. I know you're at home; I just talked to your father. You need to get out. I'll wait until you come out."

As he continued shouting, Adil knocked on my room door.

"I don't want to see anyone anymore," I said in a low voice.

"Junis, habibi, what happened? I feel so sorry for you. Please, let me help you. Piero wants to help you too. He's waiting for you outside." He paused. "We love you."

He waited in front of my door.

However, nobody and nothing mattered to me anymore at that moment. "Please, just leave me alone," I said.

Lying on my bed, I gazed at the poster of Mecca on the ceiling. Thousands of Muslims circled the Kaaba. Suddenly, the picture seemed to become real. I imagined walking with unknown people. In my mind's eye, I saw a teardrop fall down my face in slow motion, growing bigger and bigger until it hit the ground and created an ocean. I began to fight against raging waves while reality hit me full force. The overwhelming pain of having lost Ceylin captured almost my entire life; it was grounded in a deep feeling of worthlessness and shame. I had sought belonging and meaning in Islam in the aftermath of 9/11, but now I had to admit that unconditional love didn't exist among all Muslims either. In fact, a number of the closest Muslims in my life considered me not good enough, or even dumped me. Toxic thoughts reoccupied my mind: I remained an unwanted creature in a heartless and mindless world of random, human-made separations. My faith was broken, and tears rolled down my cheeks.

### *Friday, March 11, 2005: Diary Entry*

*Why do her parents not give us a chance? Why do they have so much power over her? Or does she share their view? Why then did she date me in the first place? Or is she afraid of her family, of being rejected, persecuted, or even killed for being with some-one like me? Is her family really that cruel? Or are they being pressured by their relatives to get her married to a Turk? Did Ceylin hope she would find a spirit of rebellion within herself against the oppression within her family? Why then did she lose her courage? What about our dream of togetherness and happi-ness? What about love? Today, her friends told me that her father already engaged her to a Turk in December 2004. I had thought only death could tear us apart. It was much less, though. It was our cowardice to fight for our dream. What cowards we were; what cowards we are.*

### *Saturday, March 12, 2005*

After three months of heartbreak, depression, and comfort eating, I forced myself to lose fifteen pounds in a week to box in the light welterweight division for which Tariq had registered me. I thought boxing would help me forget about her.

It was my seventeenth bout. Hartmann, my next opponent,

was a national league boxer. He had fought more than seventy bouts. Since I had lost against him by split decision a year ago, I knew I would have to put him under a lot of pressure and get into infighting to defeat him.

I had pushed too hard in the first round. After that, I was too weak to oppose him any longer in the second round.

"Keep your hands up, keep them up!" Tariq shouted.

My arms were too heavy, though. Hartmann broke my nose. Next, he pushed me in the corner.

"Get the fuck out of there!" Tariq shouted hysterically.

However, my feet were too tired. A staggering uppercut followed—a classic knockout, the first one in my life. I got up at eight, too late and stumbling. The referee counted me out.

After the official result of the fight had been announced, I walked back to the changing room with a low head. Tariq and Adil followed. "Junis," Tariq said carefully, but I was already losing myself.

"Ahhhhh shit!" I shouted, punching against the locker, again and again. Tariq and Adil quietly left the room. I was losing control of my life. The loss I had experienced outside the ring continued inside the ring.

*Friday, July 8, 2005: Diary Entry*

*I have hardly seen Ceylin at school for months now. Today, Helena told me in the cafeteria that Ceylin was married off. Ceylin was married off! CEYLIN WAS MARRIED OFF! I hate myself. I HATE MYSELF! And I hate her pseudo-religious, nationalistic father even more. Look what love has done! How low have I become? Has love really led me to self-loathing and hatred of another, or rather, is it that I am the problem myself?*

### End of July 2005

Shortly before summer break, our new house was completed. The facade was painted ocher, a unique color in our neighborhood. Our kitchen contained built-in, high-end devices, such as a ceran stove, a dishwasher, a microwave, and more. The floors were laid with gray granite tiles and heated. Fourteen floor-to-ceiling casement windows allowed plenty of natural light to enter our new house, which was a luxury in contrast to our old one. Gabriela, Malik, and Oma Erika stayed in Paul-Ehrlich-Straße four for the time being, whereas Adil, Sophia, and I moved into Frankfurter Weg seven. And still, my initial optimism was gone. The fact that I could directly see the Park and Ride from the kitchen window already reminded me of her—Ceylin.

During summer break, I spent many hours on our new roof terrace, pondering what to do with my life. I wanted to do something meaningful.

### Thursday, November 3, 2005: Diary Entry

*What shall I do after high school? I'll certainly not do military service and support the killing of innocent people. I'll do civil service. Today, I talked with my father about my options. He told me that I could contact a friend of his in the USA who works on projects that aid developing countries. I'd like to help other people. Maybe I could carry out my civil service in the USA Since I learned about the US civil rights movement at WBS, I've been impressed by the political struggles of the US King's[59] dream still inspires me. I'm also for the pursuit of happiness, for liberty and brotherhood, for acknowledging the truth that we are all created equal. I have often missed these truths in Germany.*

*But maybe I'm all wrong. Maybe I failed in the German society. Maybe I even failed as a human being. Maybe I'm the reason I've remained a stranger here. Maybe I should have assimilated more. Maybe I should have communicated better. Maybe I should not have taken life so seriously. Maybe my attitude has been too critical, too negative. Even Piero got sick of my self-pitying Ceylin story. He said I should just take another girl and join him partying. I just can't. I still love her.*

### Tuesday, March 14, 2006: Diary Entry

*I had a talk with my father about my plan to go to the USA Now, he's suddenly changed his mind. He said I had to stay to look after the houses and after my siblings since he was too old and wouldn't have much longer to live. WHY, oh WHY does he select me to be the future caretaker? I don't want that role! He said Manal and Nour have their family duties. So what about my other siblings? How come Malik sits in front of his computer almost all the time, playing games? How come Sophia is usually drunk or high, if she is at home at all? How come Alim usually*

---

59   Martin Luther King Jr. (January 15, 1929–April 4, 1968): American Baptist minister and activist who became the most visible spokesperson and leader of the civil rights movement from 1955 until his assassination in 1968

*only calls when he cannot pay his debts? How come I must take the responsibility for all that? What about my life? What about my dream of happiness and peace? How can I live in Germany? In cold isolation and depression, like I have in previous years?*

### Wednesday, June 14, 2006

On our last school day, Mr. Müller handed out our high school diplomas in our classroom. I had a 2.5 GPA[60], a mediocre, rather disappointing, but well-deserved final result. After the break up with Ceylin, I had skipped school frequently. Depressed and unable to focus, I had done poorly on a couple of tests, which all counted toward the final grades. I put the diploma in my bag and left the classroom as soon as we were dismissed. Most students stayed on the school grounds to celebrate the end of schooling with music, dances, and plenty of liquor, but I jumped on my scooter and drove home. I was sick of the FEG, sick of Frankfurt, sick of myself. Everything reminded me of her—Ceylin.

Since Adil had not allowed me to go to the USA, I applied to do a nine-month civil service period in the Hofheim hospital. Fortunately, I got accepted. These nine months, I hoped, would give me time to learn my life lesson, move on with a new and stronger mindset, and do something meaningful with my life.

---

60  Grade Point Average

# KASTEL

*July 2006–October 2007*

*Life is a constant comeback*

*Wednesday, July 26, 2006: Diary Entry*

*I want to share my love, but I can't because I'm alone. I can't even call our new house a home. My family is drifting further and further apart. Sophia is locked up in psychiatric ward again because she seriously burned her arms with cigarettes yet again. Tears are rolling down my cheeks. I tried to convince her a couple of times that hurting herself doesn't make anything better, but I failed. I feel so guilty. I should have tried more to build her up. I thought she'd manage somehow. I was wrong, though. And Malik? Today, my father requested me, like so often, to look after him since he locks himself in his room every day after work to play computer games. All my attempts in the last years to get him out of the house have failed, though. He doesn't want to play basketball, or rollerblade, or go for a walk, or spend time in the MTZ, or go to the cinema like we used to in the 1990s. He's lost in the world of gaming. And my parents? Since my father moved into our new house, they have fought almost every day. My mother is tired of going between our houses, and yet she doesn't know whether she wants to live with my father either. Today, they fought so viciously that they wanted to get a divorce again. I'm so sick of it. I wonder: why do I still let their problems burden me all the time? I'm almost twenty years old. It's time to finally find my own way.*

## Sunday, January 28, 2007: Diary Entry

Last night I went to the cinema. It first felt somewhat embarrassing because I had never gone to the cinema alone. But since I had no one to accompany me, I just went. I needed to get out of the house. I watched Rocky Balboa, the sixth part of the film series. Since we came to Germany, I have watched the Rocky movies many times and always sought inspiration from them. Rocky taught me to always keep on fighting and to never give up. The new movie encouraged me once again. I got goosebumps in one particular scene. Rocky was talking to his grown-up son, and it felt as if he was talking to me. They were standing on a deserted street at night when Rocky told his son:

"You grew up good and wonderful . . . Then the time came for you to be your own man and take on the world, and you did. But somewhere along the line, you changed. You stopped being you. You let people stick a finger in your face and tell you you're no good. And when things got hard, you started looking for something to blame, like a big shadow. Let me tell you something you already know. The world ain't all sunshine and rainbows. It's a very mean and nasty place, and I don't care how tough you are, it will beat you to your knees and keep you there permanently if you let it. You, me, or nobody is gonna hit as hard as life. But it ain't about how hard you hit. It's about how hard you can get hit and keep moving forward. How much you can take and keep moving forward. That's how winning is done! Now if you know what *you're worth, then go out and get what you're worth. But you gotta be willing to take the hits, and not pointing fingers saying, you ain't where you wanna be because of him, or her, or anybody! Cowards do that, and that ain't you! You're better than that!"*

*To hell with my depression! I need to leave behind all anger and regret if I want to live a successful life. Life is a constant comeback. I need to make the best of it.*

## *Saturday, February 10, 2007: Diary Entry*

*If I really want to live a successful life, I need to know myself first, so that I don't get in my own way. I need to be aware of 1) who I am, 2) who I want to be, 3) how I can be that person, and, 4) what I want to achieve.*

*1) So, who am I? What are my strengths? I am, I believe, a person who is thoughtful and committed. These principles have helped me support my family since my childhood, and they've helped me reach goals at school and in boxing. So why should I run away from Germany when I can count on these strengths? I can also develop these strengths further and reach more goals right here. There is no better place to be when it comes to becoming the best version of myself—period. I just start with what I have here and now, take step after step, see how far I can get, and from there, go further.*

*But I also need to know my weaknesses and their roots if I want to stop self-sabotaging my life. My biggest weaknesses are probably my fears of being rejected and abandoned. Maybe these fears derive from childhood. Maybe my parents were overcritical* toward us in Mosul. Maybe the personal losses caused by the war left wounds that never healed. Maybe being discriminated against in Kastel time and time again destroyed my sense of self-worth, of belonging. Maybe the abuse I experienced at home was the deciding trigger. Maybe these fears are cultivated by my parents' constant fights, depressions, and inaccessibilities. Maybe they are grounded in the emotional insecurities at home, which have made me feel overly responsible for my family. Maybe they derive from the combination of everything and more. Whatever the reasons are, I cannot play the people-pleaser anymore to get acceptance from the outside, since it only manifests my fears, weak boundaries, and low self-esteem. In this poor condition, I cannot live a successful life! Moreover, I have to change my negative mindset. I've almost certainly adopted the idea that I'm not good enough and that I'm generally a victim. Both ideas are wrong and dangerous. They keep me trapped in feeling like a failure and in blaming others, both of which don't improve anything! They kill my sense of self-competence and self-esteem. If I don't change my way of thinking, I'll never achieve my dreams.

2) After all these years, I still just want to be a person who is happy and at peace.

3) The critical question is how I get there with my strengths and weaknesses. I now see that too much thoughtfulness and commitment can be self-destructive, especially when committing to negativity. I'll need to make healthier decisions. I'll need to see and embrace more positive thoughts, emotions, and people. I'll need to continually remind myself that I deserve to be happy,

*that I am worthy and lovable. If I can make it a habit to think more positively, my emotions will also get more positive. Also, it'll help to be around people who do not constantly try to control me or pull me down. I'll need to spend more time with encouraging companions when I direct my strengths toward realizing my dreams. Tackling my weaknesses will not be easy, though. It'll probably be a lifelong struggle. I'll need to compassionately remind myself again and again that I'm an adult now, that my wellbeing does not depend on anyone anymore, that I can care for myself, and that I am fully responsible for my life. And if the validation of being worthy and lovable comes from within, I can also change my ways of connecting with other people. I can be more optimistic and open, but also more self-supporting. Saying no to others is okay and necessary sometimes to protect myself. I need to be my own best friend and not listen to that relentless inner critic if I want to live a happy and peaceful life.*

*4) Even though I absolutely wanted to leave Frankfurt, I am once again attracted by this city. Yesterday, I visited Goethe University Frankfurt. It is a huge educational institution, and they offer a number of fascinating study paths. I am positive I could find a program that would help me develop myself, and give back something positive to other people.*

### Monday, April 12, 2007: Diary Entry

*I made a decision. I would like to study at Goethe University Frankfurt and become a teacher. I'd like to study, teach, and discuss the human experience. I'd like to foster mutual understanding and respect. I'd like to work with children and teenagers, and teach them as best I can. They are our hope for a better future. They are usually open, idealistic, and not yet deadened by social prejudice and divide. They are our companions in building what will hopefully be a more happy and peaceful society.*

### Saturday, October 6, 2007

I received a letter from the Goethe University Frankfurt, and only read the beginning of the first line: "We are glad to inform you that you are accepted . . ."

With a thankful smile, I put the letter back on the table.

# KASTEL

*October 2007–December 2008*

*Disturbed relationships*

*Monday, October 15, 2007*

Excited about striking out on my new path, I entered Campus Westend and crossed a large green area, heading toward the travertine, flat-roofed main building. It had six wings connected by bent corridors. The warm colors of the facade, a mix of yellows and browns, made the construct look warm despite its huge size. Even though I had seen the campus before, I was still impressed by the beautiful and spacious sight. I entered the central portico. Many voices resounded in the hall. Students were rushing back and forth. Some were sitting on the stairs to the rotunda. About thirty-seven thousand students were enrolled, and I was looking forward to making new friends and realizing my goal: to study and discuss the human experience.

*Tuesday, April 29, 2008: Diary Entry*

*I enjoy my studies. The more knowledge I acquire, the better I can grasp the world. Today, I gave a presentation on family structures in a sociology seminar. I talked about the transition from a dyad (couple relationship) to a triad (couple with a child). The research I did helped me understand how the relationships in my family are disturbed. I've recognized it before, but now I see how it affects us in our different roles. Malik listens to our mother's stories every day after work (before he disappears to play World of Warcraft) and on the weekends during teatime. He substitutes my father to some extent as a partner. Sophia's boyfriends are typically more than ten years older than she is. They also seem like a substitute for my father, who has never really recovered from the loss of our home in Iraq. The memories of the past and the news about the unending civil war in Iraq that followed the 2003 US invasion pull him down continuously. He has almost no more resources to face our family problems. So he usually asks me to tackle them, and convince everyone to change their mind for the sake of peace. But I can't and won't do it any longer to the full extent that he wishes, because I'm not the parent or the partner. I'm the grown-up son, who needs to look for a relationship outside the family. I want to create my own dyad and triad. I want to live my own life.*

### *Friday, May 2, 2008*

While my boxing workouts helped me stay balanced and fit, I decided to stop fighting in the ring and focus on my new path. My reinvention and intended personal development came with a price, though.

### *Friday, May 2, 2008: Diary Entry:*

*My membership in the boxing club has become problematic. Last week, I skipped training twice since I needed time to write a paper. This evening, I told Tariq that I would work out only when I have time, and not fight anymore so that I can focus on my studies. He called me a "loser" and shouted at me in front of everyone, "Then you better never show up again!" Everyone stopped working out. I told him to his face that he didn't care about my future or the future of anyone in our club, but only about us stepping into the ring and representing him. He stared at me, probably as surprised as everyone else in the gym that I defended myself. I stared back at him before I turned around and left. It was not an easy decision, especially after he taught me so much, but I want to go to the next level and achieve the best possible results in my higher education.*

*Most of the club members are Arabs, Turks, and Russians, in many ways strangers in Germany like me. But I'm also becoming an academic now, in contrast to most other club members. Their reactions to my new path challenge me. Some said, "What? You want to become a teacher? I hated my teachers." Some added that their teachers had prejudices against them, and that was why they made their teachers' lives hell, which made their teachers hate them even more. Some said, "I hope you don't become as arrogant as the students I know." I understand the bitterness they carry inside, but I hope I can make a positive change by following my new path, staying friends with them and with Tarik, and hopefully giving back one day, maybe as a coach.*

### Beginning of August 2008

I started to write a paper on child poverty in Iraq. Ever since the 2003 Iraq war, I often wondered how Iraqi children were living. I only had a vague idea from Adil's accounts. My research helped me understand why he wanted us to leave Iraq in 1991. In 1990,

Iraq was about to become an industrial state. The mortality rate of children under the age of five was at 5.6 percent[61]. When Saddam Hussein illegally invaded Kuwait, the UN Security Council imposed economic sanctions on Iraq. As a result, Iraq lost ninety-seven percent of its exports and ninety percent of its imports[62]. A three-hundred-page document banned the import of "dual use" items, meaning items that did not only have a civil use, but also a possible military use. The list included medicines to treat cancer, X-ray units, laboratory equipment, scientific books, machines for agriculture, spare parts for oil refineries, chemicals to clean water, and much more. The most vulnerable, especially children under the age of five, were hit the hardest, while there have been international disputes about how much the child mortality rate increased exclusively because of the sanctions.

As a young boy in the 1990s, I did not understand the impact or the implications of the UN sanctions regime. In 2008, I did. Iraqis were indefinitely denied their basic human needs and, as a result, their value and dignity as human beings. Due to the widespread lack of clean water, an increasing number of people suffered from diarrhea and gastroenteritis, as well as pandemic diseases like cholera and thypus, which had almost been defeated before the sanctions.

During my research, I also read an article by Hillel Cohen[63],

---

61  Hilfiker, David. "Biologische Kriegsführer." *IPPNW forum*, 79/2003.

62  Melby, Eric D.K. "Iraq." *Economic Sanctions and American Diplomacy*, edited by Haass, Richard N. Council on Foreign Relations Book, 1998.

63  Cohen, Hillel. "A Weapon That Keeps Killing." *Challenge to Genocide*, edited by Ramsey Clark. Intl Action Center, 1998.

which shocked me with an almost unbelievable crime against humanity. The bombs the USA dropped in 1991 on Iraq continued to kill Iraqis even long after they had exploded, as if the sudden death from above were not inhumane enough. They contained depleted uranium, which contaminated the air, the groundwater, and thus, the food chain. As a result, the rate of children suffering from blood cancer shot up over four hundred percent during the first ten years after the war. Miscarriages and births of dysplastic children exploded in similar numbers.

I was just in the middle of reading another article when Adil called me for lunch. I got up and looked at a book that was lying on my desk, *The Children Are Dying*[64]. It pictured a young girl holding her head low, with hopeless eyes and arms that looked like sticks. I could count her ribs. I felt terribly sorry for all the children in Iraq. They were innocent in contrast to most of us. How could so many people dogmatically blame Saddam Hussein—one person—for the suffering of an entire people? Why did we not rescue the Iraqi people? Why did we ignore our common humanity and the human rights of Iraqis? What happened to empathy? What about Kant's categorical imperative; what about *universal* moral principles? Did they not apply to strangers? What about religion; what about *universal* love and compassion? How hypocritical, how egoistic was that? It was a horrifying example of human failure.

"Junis, please come now! Stop working!" he shouted again.

We went to Paul-Ehrlich-Straße four. Malik and Gabriela were

---

64   Clark, Ramsey. *The Impact of Sanctions on Iraq: The Children Are Dying.* World View Forum Pub, 1996.

already at the kitchen table. We sat down. Everyone began to eat, except for Gabriela.

"I can't live like this anymore," she said, and got up.

"We're all together. We're healthy. We live in peace. What's the problem?" I said.

"I just can't live with this family anymore," she said, and went to the hallway.

I put down my fork and followed her. "What have we done to you?" I asked.

She left the house without a word. I went back to the kitchen.

"Why can she not even look at us?" I asked.

No one responded, but I finally understood. She was right. It couldn't go on like this anymore. She still didn't seem to value us. How were we supposed to live under these conditions? Malik played computer games every night and almost all weekend long. Sophia was still a mess. And Adil constantly quarreled with Gabriela, or else hid, inaccessible, like the rest of us. If I stayed at "home," I knew it was only a matter of time before I became depressed again. I had to free myself from the continuous negativity around me if I wanted to live a happy and peaceful life.

*Monday, August 11, 2008: Diary Entry*

> *When I move out and pay rent for the rest of my studies, I'll toss at least €10,000 out of the window, money that I will never see again. I have saved up €12,000 in my bank account. Last night, I did some research on the internet. I could buy a small studio for around €30,000 in the Main-Taunus district.*

*I'll ask my father if he can help me finance it. The plan is to buy a studio and move out by the end of 2008. I need peace and freedom to study and to develop myself.*

### November—December 2008

I found a studio in Liederbach, a small village between Kastel and Frankfurt. Adil accompanied me when I met the realtor the first time in November. On our way back home, Adil told me that he liked the place, and that he could lend me €10,000. I was deeply grateful for his tremendous support. When we told Gabriela that we wanted to try to buy that studio, she surprised me with unexpected news as well: "You have €8,000 with me from your grandmother. She saved up money for all of you. You can use it." I looked at her with big eyes, aware that Oma Erika was one of the greatest people in my life. She saved me once again, even if she could not realize it anymore.

"Well, then I'd very thankfully use it," I said, and smiled blissfully. While I didn't know what this new chapter in my life would bring, I was looking forward to it: I would finally have more freedom to follow my own path.

# PART IV

# LIEDERBACH

*January 2009–August 2010*

*Something big*

*Beginning of January 2009: Diary Entry*

*Today, I moved into my studio. My father and Asis helped me transport my belongings from Kastel to Liederbach. Liederbach is a rural village with about 8,500 inhabitants. I enjoy the quiet here—it's relaxing. My apartment is on the fifth floor of a ten-story Plattenbau, which was built in 1975. The property contains altogether four apartment towers strung together. The building complex doesn't look very inviting from the outside: the facade is clad with washed concrete slabs, and the windows are positioned like a grid. Each apartment looks like the other from the outside, a dry spectacle across from a Coca-Cola factory with a red cooling tower. But living in the Plattenbau is affordable. In contrast to Paul-Ehrlich-Straße, quite a number of residents are immigrants here. Next to the apartment towers, there is also a three-story parking lot, which is occupied most of the time. Since I can't afford to buy a car, I'll try to rent out my parking space to improve my financial situation.*

*Freedom is not free. It comes with a price, and I am willing to pay for it. I pay back €200 a month to my father. Utilities are another €200. With my current income, that leaves €20 a week for eating. I have to live very economically, like in 1991 when we came to Germany. My father told me that I don't need to put myself under pressure with regards to paying back. But I do. It wouldn't be right to owe him so much money and live as if I had all the time in the world to pay my debts. Moreover, owing is a dependent and weak position, which I do not like. The sooner I am debt-free, the sooner I can freely make my own financial decisions. And with all the problems going on in my family, I need to become independent rather soon. I'm aware that it was risky to finance a studio with no stable work contract. None of my fellow students took such a risk. When they get to know about my housing conditions, they usually look at me with large eyes and ask how I could handle the financial burden in addition to studying. "I have two jobs, and work hard to achieve my goals," I usually tell them. In fact, the first time I saw the studio last November, I already knew I would go for it, no matter what.*

*I'm satisfied with my choice. The property is well maintained. My studio is 370 square feet. It has new oak laminate flooring, white woodchip wallpaper, floor-to-ceiling windows, and a new, white tiled bathroom. From my balcony, I can see a creek, a beautiful park, and an Italian-style villa. I can even watch the sunset behind the forested Taunus mountain range on the horizon. It amazes me every time; it's a natural wonder. The train station is only a five-minute walk away. During the week, I ride to university by train. When I come home, I eat, study, and go running in the fields. I train in Hochheim every other day. Tarik has accepted my decision and is glad that I assist him. I'm glad I'm finally free to be who I am and develop myself.*

*February 2009*

In addition to working as a salesman in the MTZ on the weekends, and as a tutor and boxing coach at a comprehensive school in Hofheim during the week, I also started working as a substitute teacher at a gymnasium in Frankfurt to improve my financial situation.

One day, I was supposed to teach a fifth-grade class in English. When I introduced myself, three girls from the last row immediately started asking me questions: "Where are you from? Are you Turk? Are you Muslim? Do you fast? Do you pray?" I noticed that the three girls were wearing scarves. Their tactlessness irritated me, and yet I thought I understood their excitement. I was probably one of the very few teachers who had a visible migration background and with whom they could identify. I had not noticed any teacher who looked like an immigrant when I walked through the staff room before classes began.

On the one hand, I did not want to be objectified and share parts of my private life in front of the class. On the other hand, I wanted to give these girls something that could encourage them for their future careers.

Before I could comment, however, a boy shouted at the girls, "Shut the fuck up, Aisha!"

"None of us are called Aisha, you asshole!" the girls chorused at once.

Their violent language shocked me. I had thought that

diversity would rather be seen as normal among students in an international city like Frankfurt.

With a serious voice, I said to all the students, "To make it clear from the beginning, I don't accept discrimination and bullying. You treat each other with respect. You understand?" I sensed that if I had not reacted immediately, it would have been very difficult to establish a socially acceptable, positive working climate afterward. And if I could not establish such a climate, the students would not learn anything at all.

Indeed, the class turned quiet at once. I proceeded with the lesson. When I asked the students about their happiest day during their Christmas vacation, they participated actively. They chose a classmate and listened to what they wanted to share.

Everything worked out as planned until I initiated a partner work phase. I supported each pair with their writing assignment. When I reached the last row where the three girls sat, who absolutely wanted to work together for some reason I had not quite figured out yet, a letter began to make its round behind my back. It reached Yafet, a boy in the front. Suddenly, another boy, named Sebastian, laughed out loud. "You better check what's going on. They're bullying him again," one of the girls said.

As I walked to the front, the class turned dead silent. Yafet was holding his head low. I asked him to show me the letter, which he had crumpled up. He looked at me, worried and expectant, before he gave me a drawing that showed him with pitch-black skin and extra thick, red lips.

"Who drew this?" I asked, looking at the class with a serious face.

The class remained silent, as if they anticipated what was on the letter.

I waited—until a girl named Lena asked carefully, "Who drew what?"

"I've got a racist picture here that I'll not show you. But I want to know who drew it."

Still, the class remained quiet. They looked at me with large eyes, almost surprised how much I was determined not to let them get away with it.

"I'll keep the picture with me," I said, looking around. "The one who drew it can come to me after the lesson, or meet me in the staff room. I'll wait there for five minutes. If no one shows up, I'll give the picture to your class teacher." I paused and thought about what else to say. I did not want to make too much of the drawing and open Yafet up for additional torments, but I also sensed that the class needed more guidance to create another reality in their classroom. So I revealed my feelings. "I find it sad how you treat each other. Where is respect and solidarity? You should keep together as one class! This could be one of the best times of your life if you allow it, and work together and not against each other."

The students behaved respectfully toward each other after my words. However, I had doubts if they fully embraced the sense of community I was trying to make accessible for them. I was just a random substitute teacher who had no regular contact with them.

## June 2009: Diary Entry

I've got a financial problem. My expenses exceed my income, but I do not want to stop paying off the apartment. Being a substitute teacher does not bring enough income. In May, it brought only €100. The school did not need more substitutes. I need to look for a job that brings a higher and more regular income; hopefully, a job that contributes to transforming our society from divisiveness and violence to more connectedness, happiness, and peace. What can I do in addition to teaching?

## Tuesday, August 6, 2009: Diary Entry

*My mother asked me if I was interested in going to Italy. I said yes. I hope we can improve our relationship. I know that she loves the beach, and I love it as well. It's something that connects us. Since I moved out, the tension between us has decreased. We don't fight that much anymore. Sometimes, distance helps heal relationships. Yet healing takes more than that. Forgiveness, good will, and constant effort are necessary as well. I visit my parents once a week, and I try to avoid the critical talking points: religion, politics, and money. I want to strengthen our connection by focusing on the things we have in common and enjoy. I try to show that I appreciate both of them. I try to build up trust. My father will go to Italy as well. The last time we went together on vacation was in the summer of 2004—before I met Ceylin. Too long ago!*

### Sunday, October 11, 2009: Diary Entry

*We had a beautiful time in Italy, like back in the 1990s. We enjoyed the warm weather. We walked on the beach. We swam together in the ocean. We ate ice cream almost every night. We also spent an entire day walking in the small alleys of our beloved Venice. We had a happy and peaceful time together, alhamdulillah!*

*Before we went to Italy, I had applied for two scholarships—HORIZONTE and FULBRIGHT. I spotted the first Horizonte poster as I was walking along a corridor in the IG Farben building (Campus Westend). The poster pictured three fine-dressed students: a lightly tanned male student with black hair, an Asian female student with black hair, and another lightly tanned female student with black hair. Their looks attracted me subconsciously. I read the text: "Did you choose teacher training? Are you a teacher trainee? Did you or your parents migrate to Germany? Today thirty-three percent of pupils but only one per-cent of teachers in German schools has a migration background. The Horizonte scholarship financially and ideationally supports outstanding prospective teachers who have a migration back-ground." Horizonte seemed to be looking for someone like me, I thought. Without a doubt, I needed the money. So I applied.*

*This week, I received a positive answer to my applica-tion. From November on, I'll be a Horizonte scholar and get €650 per month over the course of two years. End of financial crisis, alhamdulillah! Two hundred and fifty students applied in Berlin, Hamburg, and Frankfurt for the scholarship. Eleven people were accepted in Berlin, nine in Hamburg, and only three in Frankfurt. All the hard work on my new path pays off, alhamdulillah!*

*On top of that, my mother surprised me again. She said she was proud of my achievements at university and that she bought me a car for €600, a 1991 black VW Golf GT Special. It's sporty and I love it. It belonged to the friendly owner of the gas station in the MTZ, where my father used to work before he got cancer. The car gives me more freedom of mobility. I thanked her with a big hug. I am so happy that I am on good terms with her again, alhamdulillah!*

### Mid-October 2009

In January 2005, heartbreak and cognitive dissonance (due to the gaps I had observed between the theory and the human practices of Islam) made me drift away from traditional religious practices. Many alleged Islamic rules, I realized, were not religious but rather cultural and political, and thus crippled by the human weakness for power without love. I did not pray on a regular basis anymore. I did not fast, either. I drifted toward free spiritual practices, pondering the meaning of human existence, sometimes talking to Allah in silence, and trying to understand truths beyond those of our physical existence. I still had faith in a higher power. The ninety-nine names of Allah still enchanted me, especially those that express the face of love: beneficent, providing, gentle and kind, grateful, watchful, responsive, steadfast, merciful, and eternally forgiving. The message of love, I understood, connects all religions. Love, I believed, is what almost all people inherently strive for; it is the key to a meaningful human life. It is a principle, a condition for interpersonal happiness and peace. I strived for love and tried to exude love, despite my imperfections; and through love, I tried to improve my relationships with others, with Allah, and with myself. Moreover, I kept reminding myself of two core Islamic virtues: Sabr (patience and endurance) would motivate me to keep trying on my imperfect journey, and Shukr (thankfulness) made me more content. I thanked Allah quite often for providing my basic needs: food, clean water, fresh air, a calm walk in the forest, a warm bed to sleep in, and much more. And when my relationships improved or my personal dreams became reality, I thanked Allah from my inmost soul.

*Wednesday, October 21, 2009: Diary Entry*

*Next Monday, I'll participate in the final assessment at the Fulbright center in Berlin. I have already successfully competed against all the applicants at Goethe University. If I am successful in Berlin, one of my long-time dreams will come true.*

*Saturday, November 14, 2009: Diary Entry*

*Today is a good day. Today is probably the greatest day of my life. After I came home from university, I opened my mailbox and found a blue letter from Berlin. I opened it and only read the first line before I jumped into the air with the brightest* *smile! What a life! I am so blessed. I am nominated by the Berlin Fulbright Commission for a nine-month scholarship, including up to $30,400, alhamdulillah! In August 2010, I will go to the USA! The land where people have sought liberty and happiness from all around the world for centuries! Dreams become true in 2010!*

### December 2009

In contrast to the recent positive developments, my family was hit by a heavy stroke of fate. Oma Erika died a few weeks after she had been diagnosed with esophageal cancer. Her death cut a deep wound into our family. Not only did we lose our beloved Oma Erika, who took care of us in every sense and bound us together, but her passing also increased the division within my family once more. While we tried to assure Gabriela that we would always be there for her, she felt she had lost her last confidant in our family.

### Beginning of August 2010

When the summer term ended, I went to Onkel Walter and Tante Ursula to say goodbye before leaving for the USA. Even though our families—except Gabriela, who visited Onkel Walter and Tante Ursula once a month—did not keep close contact anymore after the dispute over Paul-Ehrlich-Straße four in 1997, I thought it would be appropriate to visit them because we still invited each other to important celebrations, such as milestone birthdays. Going to the USA would be just as special, I thought.

We were sitting in his living room, opposite each other, when

Onkel Walter asked me, "How did you get this scholarship? Was it your migration background again?"

His question made me recollect how my English professor had opened her eyes wide when I told her I had qualified for a Fulbright scholarship. She said the number of applicants had decreased and that it would be easier to get a scholarship these days. I never understood this behavior. What did envy offer people besides burdening their relationships? How would anyone benefit from such negativity?

Controlled, I said to Onkel Walter, "No, it was not my migration background. My grades were excellent. Further, I ran through various assessments and convinced the committee. The same actually applied for the Horizonte scholarship as well."

He looked at me with a raised eyebrow. "So how exactly did you convince the Fulbright committee?"

"I don't know. Probably with my knowledge of the USA and with my intercultural competencies."

"Was the competition tough?"

"Well, every German university student was able to apply. In the end, only six students received a nine-month full scholarship for university-level studies."

"You're lucky. You've been given an exceptional opportunity. Congratulations."

"Thank you," I said with a friendly smile, knowing that I was not lucky. I had started from almost nothing in 1991, and now I had achieved something big.

# PART V

# FULLERTON

*August 2010–April 2011*

*Peaceful rise*

*Friday, August 6, 2010*

I landed at Los Angeles around noon, after an eleven-hour flight. Even though I lacked sleep, I got up from my seat with energy, full of hope: USA, the nation of immigrants! As they say, at least. With a bright smile, I thanked the flight attendants and followed the passengers into the airport. When it was my turn at the access control counter, I showed my passport. "Wait a minute, sir. Something showed up here. We need to check you," the officer said. He dialed a number, merely said, "Junis Sultan is here," and asked me to wait off to the side. The passengers behind me were allowed to enter, and I began to feel nervous. I had never had any problems with flying in Europe.

After a couple of minutes, two officers in black uniforms came and asked me to follow them. When I read their tags—Homeland Security—I understood what was going on. The officers represented the institution that was installed under George W. Bush after 9/11 to protect the USA from terrorists. I had not expected they would want to examine me too. Walking between the officers, I briefly looked over my shoulder. The remaining passengers at the desk stared at me while I was led off like a criminal. I felt harassed.

The officers led me to a small interrogation room, which had no windows. "Take a seat. Your documents, please," said the younger officer in a serious tone. He looked at them for a minute before he started asking me questions: "Who are you? Where are you from? Where were you born? Who are your parents? What are they doing? Where were they born? Have you ever been to the USA? Do you have contacts in the USA? What are you planning to do here? Where? Why are you in the USA? Do you have a religious background? Knowledge in chemistry? Are you planning a terrorist attack? Are you telling the truth?"

The interrogation took about fifteen minutes. I answered all questions as calmly as I could, even though I was quite worried I could say something wrong or behave in a way that might get me into trouble. I had nothing to hide, and yet whether I should be allowed to enter the country, or considered a threat to the public and sent back depended on his assessment of my behavior.

"You know why we ask you all these questions?" he said.

"I guess because I possess the Iraqi passport as well," I said, though I had not travelled with the Iraqi passport since my naturalization in Germany in 1991.

"Correct. Your country and your name are on the black list," he said and looked deeply into my eyes.

I knew we had reached the critical part of the interrogation. Questions shot through my head: Was he testing me for honesty and moral fiber? Did he believe that I was a terrorist? I had no idea how I was supposed to respond, so I firmly kept eye contact and hoped he would believe me.

After a tense moment, he said, "But you're okay. Enjoy your time at California State University, Fullerton. I've heard they like partying there. Welcome to America!"

"Thank you," I said, relieved that he would finally let me go.

We got up and shook hands. It felt odd. I did not take the interrogation personally. I knew the officer was required by law to target me. Nonetheless, it did not assuage the stress I felt.

After I had gone through customs, I went outside. Many people were bustling about on the curb. Some were picked up by family. Some caught a taxi. I located a person who wore a blue T-shirt. She put me on the list for a "Super-Shuttle." The international office of CSUF had recommended this shuttle service. Shortly, a blue Ford van stopped by. I sat down in the rear seat. After five other passengers had boarded, the driver hit the road. He turned up the volume of his radio a little bit. A famous saxophonist, whom I did not know, was announced. Smooth jazz music began to play. It relaxed my mind. Through the window, I looked out at the "New World." Cars and streets were wider here than in Europe. Along the freeway, I saw trimmed palm trees peacefully rising from the horizon into the light blue sky. What a beautiful sight! Every now and then, my eyelids dropped. I was jetlagged, but curiosity always made me open my eyes again. I felt like I was in a trance.

After ninety minutes of driving and dropping off passengers, we arrived in Fullerton. I tipped the driver twenty percent, as I had been advised. "Thanks, brother," he said.

"You're welcome, brother," I replied, surprised by our words. No German driver had ever called me brother; it felt good to be treated kindly. We smiled at each other before we continued our separate journeys.

I waited with my baggage in front of the Fullerton Marriot Hotel. Across the street, a display showed one hundred degrees Fahrenheit. I did not know exactly how many degrees Celsius that was, but it certainly felt like more than 30 degrees Celsius. The hot air warmed me up immediately. This was my kind of weather! In all those years in Germany, I never fully got used to its weather; it was far too cloudy, gray, and chilly. Hours-long cloud covers were normal from October to March, and the sun would shine less than four hours a day for half the year. Even in summer, the sun was covered by clouds from time to time. Now, I was looking at the golden star, gloriously shining. Blue sky and sunlight, what a great delight! My face shone.

Across the street, I beheld the campus of CSUF. Students were walking in the sun on a smooth, pre-fabricated pathway that meandered through a neatly cut lawn. Fullerton and Mosul almost lay on the same latitude, I knew from my travel planning. Both places had more than two hundred sunny days in a year; Fullerton even closer to three hundred. I looked at the trimmed palm trees on the campus that grandly rose into the sky. They sweetly reminded me of my childhood in Iraq.

Suddenly, someone called me from behind. I turned around and saw a middle-aged, clean-shaven man, smiling.

"Tom?" I asked, smiling back.

"Yay, I found you. Welcome to America, my friend!" he said.

We shook hands, smiling nonstop. I was excited to meet my temporary host father. Tom wore a nice dress shirt and suit pants. His hair was short and brown. He was my height, a bit overweight, and his big, brown eyes told me that he was glad to meet me. I felt warmly welcomed.

"Let's get in the car. I'll take you to your new home, to Yorba Linda," he said.

As we were driving through Yorba Linda, I spotted large residential lots. Many front gardens were not enclosed by fences or walls like in Germany. Instead, they were open, manicured, and planted with flowers or palm trees. Some properties even contained a swimming pool in the back yard. Horse trails lined the road in places, and we even saw a few equestrians out riding.

"What a beautiful place to live!" I said.

"Oh, you like it. That's good to hear," he said, and laughed.

Tom seemed to be a fun-loving person, and I easily took a shine to him.

As we kept driving, we began to talk about our families. I sensed that Tom was a family man. He told me, with a big smile, how excited everyone was to meet me. Of course, I was as much excited to meet them. Tom had sent me a picture of his young family before my departure.

After our ten-minute drive, I saw them in person. His family was awaiting us on the lawn in front of their huge house, which had a sloping roof. We got out of the car and met the family halfway. We were all smiling. Janel, his wife, gave me a warm hug. Their three children hugged me as well. Christine was six, John, three, and Cathy one year old. They were my new family. I counted myself lucky.

## Mid-August 2010

Tom's family also hosted another student from Germany, Emmanuel. He came from Herrenberg, in the south of Germany, and arrived one day after me. Tom's family actually had not volunteered in the seven-day homestay program that year, because they were busy attending to their baby. But since no family had consented to host Emmanuel and me, the program supervisor had contacted Tom two days before my arrival. They agreed to host us right away. Their readiness to help and welcome us amazed me. It made me feel safe and appreciated even before I arrived.

When Emmanuel and I met in the living room for the first time, we briefly examined each other and just said, "Hi." We both thought that we would only be staying together for seven days.

Our initial chilly greetings thawed within a few days, though, as we became closer and integrated into the family. We easily played with Christine and John, and we sometimes fed Cathy in her baby high chair when we all sat down to eat. Almost every day, Janel cooked for us, and we would help her. Janel was what many Americans called "Korean-American." One day, we helped her prepare kimchi, a traditional Korean food. We chopped cabbage and cut garlic, chives, and an onion while she prepared a special sauce. Another day, we helped Tom prepare a US barbecue. We seasoned juicy steaks and plenty of vegetables and put them on the grill in their back yard after we had done some yard work together. In addition to all the activities at home, Tom and Janel drove us around whenever possible. They took us to our campus so we could explore it. They drove us to malls and helped us choose cell phone providers. We also went with the entire family to Downtown Disney District, to Legoland, to Fashion Island, and to some beautiful beaches of Orange County, or "OC" as they called it. They paid for everything without ever talking about money. Instead, they explained to us how things worked in the USA; for instance getting a driver's license or health care. They helped us find our way in a new country and were eager to learn how things worked in Germany. After our talks in the evening, the kids always kissed us goodnight. Sometimes, Emmanuel or I read a bedtime story to them before we, the adults, all met in the living room. We would sit on a pillowy couch, snack, talk, and laugh time and again. The love we received deeply touched and inspired me. Emmanuel and I became a part of the family.

When Tom drove Emmanuel and me around during the day, he frequently received calls from vendors, which did not prevent him from showing us OC. Sometimes, he also stopped at his favorite cafes and bought us coffee and bagels. Being with Tom was a gift.

During our drives, I spotted oil wells over and over again, even in the middle of neighborhoods. It made me ponder over the 2003 Iraq war. If the USA drilled their own oil without visible restrictions, why did they invade Iraq in 2003? Was it really the insatiable and reckless greed of a highly industrialized economy that had to go beyond national borders to get oil and grow further? Or was it the political struggle for a new US-controlled world order? Or perhaps it was both—a win-win situation?

One day, I asked Tom how much oil the USA produced. He said, "Almost half of what we consume. The bigger half is imported from countries like Canada, Venezuela, and Iraq." At that point, I told him that my father was born in Iraq. Without delay, he said, "I'm sorry for what happened. The USA had no good reason to invade Iraq. It's a catastrophe for the people." I appreciated his empathy.

My studies in Germany helped me analyze political conflicts and consider solutions. In the USA, I rediscovered the yet unresolved problem of power in the international arena. Tom was a committed Republican and a Christian. He believed in the Christian command to "love your neighbor as yourself." And though he voted for George W. Bush as president in 2000, he condemned the destructive US foreign policies that followed 9/11. The legitimacy of power was questionable even in a democracy, and especially with respect to international affairs, I now noticed plainly, as never before. It made me ponder over world politics once again: Has the time not come to prevent Machiavellian wars? Has the time not come to create a more just "world order"? Has the time not come to extend the UN Security Council and make it more representative, more legitimate? Has the time not come to always put the right to life and the dignity of human beings first when we face questions of international peace?

## *Friday, August 20, 2010*

Emmanuel and I enjoyed our time together with our host family, but we looked for separate dwellings. We wanted to live with US Americans and enhance our cultural horizons and our English language skills. Since we could not find anything workable and affordable in seven days, however, Tom and Janel invited us to stay as long as we wanted. I was moved by their unconditional support.

In addition to our search for a suitable apartment, Emmanuel and I attended orientation week, which ended with a feast at the CSUF president's house. We, like hundreds of other international students, were gathered in a white tent that was put up in the president's huge back yard. In his speech, the president welcomed everyone before he proudly announced that three international Fulbright students were enrolled at CSUF that term. Next, he called my name and asked me to stand up. I could hardly believe what was happening. When I got up, everyone applauded for a long moment. I was treated with extra respect for my achievement. I felt very much honored. A photographer took a picture of us three Fulbrighters with the president, who stood in the center and laid his hand on my shoulder. With a bright smile, I embraced the American dream: USA, the land of opportunity. Tom was present as well. He was standing next to the international student supervisor and told her how lucky he felt to host me. After the photo shoot, Tom approached me. He put his hand on my shoulder and said, "I've hosted lots of students throughout the years, but never a Fulbrighter. I have respect for you. Not only because of what you've achieved, but because I can tell that you're a very thoughtful person." He touched me with his words. I felt appreciated.

"Thank you, Tom," I said. "And you are a very loving person—I can tell."

### End of August 2010

Since Emmanuel and I did not find separate dwellings, we decided to share an apartment in a residence across from CSUF. After we had moved into our one-bedroom apartment, he bought us beer and chips from the supermarket close by. One beer would not be too bad, I thought. However, it was the first alcoholic drink I'd had in years. We were sitting on the beige, fluffy carpet in the living room, watching a movie on his Mac Book, when I began to feel dizzy. Emmanuel noticed it. As I weaved to the kitchen, he followed me, grabbed my shoulders, and laughed out so loud, like he often did, that I began to laugh as well. What a hilarious guy! We were building a friendship, and I was glad to live with him.

### September 2010

After we had furnished our apartment, Tom invited Emmanuel and me over for a barbecue. He called me and asked what I wanted to eat. I told him that I ate just about everything, except pork. There were two reasons: Though I had distanced myself from religious practices, I still tried not to eat pork since my stomach didn't tolerate it anymore. Second, I knew that pork was not the healthiest meat. Tom answered easily, "Alright, I'll take care of that!" No pork was not a big deal for him, I noticed gladly, remembering how Gabriela sometimes hid somewhere in our house so no one could see her when she ate pork. She said she felt bad about it since Adil and I were Muslims, whereas I felt sorry that she ate alone. I told her almost every time that she could, of course, eat whatever she wanted in our presence. It was difficult for me to understand why it was not possible to be together and eat a different meal. Or maybe she still felt bad about eating pork since many of our Iraqi relatives had not tolerated it back then.

Tom, his family, and Emmanuel were fortunately more open and easygoing. Tom picked us up, and we had a delicious pork-free and pork-rich barbecue. We sat at their round table in the back yard. As we did every time, we first held our hands and praised and thanked God for the food before we began to eat. I enjoyed our ritual. It reminded me of the prayer Adil used to speak in Arabic before we would break the fast in Ramadan. And it showed me, once again, that people have more in common than they often imagine. In fact, there are a number of human virtues, like gratitude and love, that go beyond religious and cultural borders and that deeply connect people. After having lived in OC for two months, I felt very connected to Tom's family, to Emmanuel, and to the beautiful area. I enjoyed living in OC.

### Saturday, October 16, 2010

Sitting at my desk and eating cereal, I watched the German news on my laptop. The German chancellor and CDU leader,

Angela Merkel, was speaking to young CDU members. She said, "Of course the multi-cultural approach, the idea of people with different cultural backgrounds living happily side by side, has utterly failed in Germany." As she was talking, she nodded vehemently and moved her hand. Indignant, I swallowed the cereal. Never before had I seen such a committed performance by her and such an excited audience. She continued, "It's not acceptable that twice as many of them [meaning all foreigners, immigrants, and asylum seekers] don't graduate from school. It's not acceptable that twice as many of them don't have an associate degree. This is causing our social problems of the future, and this is why integration is so important, and this means, in the first place, that those who want to live in our society do not only have to abide to our laws, but they have to, above all, learn our language!"

I shut down my laptop and walked to the mirror on the wardrobe. My pulse shot up: Mrs. Merkel, of course people need to learn the national language to integrate into society! So why did Germany not run obligatory integration courses until 2005? And what about the highly selective German education system that allocates children largely on the basis of their German skills when they are only ten years old? Why don't you address how non-ethnic-German children are severely disadvantaged at this early age? Why don't you address how your state-sponsored and state-organized system fosters ethnic segregation after primary school and, consequently, for life? Why don't you address the real reasons for the large gaps between ethnic German students and non-ethnic German students as regards school performances, career opportunities, and income?

Do you really believe non-ethnic German children fail at school because they don't want to learn German? Have you not seen the results of the PISA[65] studies since 2001? How can you blame those who you fail to serve for the failure of your system to provide more equal opportunities? Why don't you finally reform the German education system? How about an integrated school system and long common learning like it's done in all other successful education systems? How about a multilingual education system that embraces the linguistic backgrounds migrants bring along? That, in addition to German, promotes the use of non-European languages in the student body? Would that not only be democratic and just? How many children could we effectively and inexpensively promote according to their natural abilities already through e-learning alone? If linguists have proven that learning the first language helps migrants learn the national language, why don't you listen to the scientist? How successful could Germany be? And what about the hard-working immigrants who prevailed in your intolerant system? Is it coincidence that you left them out in your divisive, oversimplified speech? Who benefits from your half-truths, your disparaging view on non-ethnic Germans, and its political implications? What about the constitutional promise of freedom, equality, and the human right not to be discriminated against, because of one's ethnicity and language? Do you know how much your immigrant-baiting damages social cohesion in Germany? Can you take the responsibility for the consequences in the future?

---

65 "Programme for International Student Assessment" is a worldwide study by the Organisation for Economic Cooperation and Development (OECD).

After a moment of indignation, I became aware of how lucky I was to live in the USA In contrast to Mrs. Merkel and the majority in Germany, Mr. Obama[66] and the majority in the USA acknowledged and valued the fact that they were a nation of immigrants—a truth that was valid for all modern nations in our globalized world, and which could not be reversed by nationalistic, racist, and oppressive identity politics. Quite the opposite: the more people embraced this reality, the more people and nations benefited from it.

I whole-heartedly embraced how diversity was lived at CSUF. I attended three evening classes with about twenty students in each class. We had different skin colors, dialects, ages, work experiences, religious beliefs, political views, and relationship statuses. Everyone accepted it as a matter of course, and no one made a big deal out of it. Diversity was accepted as the self-evident reality of our human existence. First and foremost, we were all the same—students. In my first three weeks at CSUF, I developed more contacts than I had in three years at Goethe University. My classmates and I called each other regularly. We met in groups at cafes to do our homework. We chatted, read, philosophized, and laughed together. When we had questions, we contacted our professors, who always quickly replied to our e-mails and invited us to their offices. They were glad to see our interest and, in most cases, equipped us with more resources. After our discussions in our evening classes, my friends and I sometimes spontaneously went for a drink somewhere. We also met for the cinema just two weeks after classes started. I frequently wore

---

66   Barack Hussein Obama II: served as the forty-fourth President of the United States from 2009 to 2017; first African American to be elected President

a T-shirt when we were together. None of them stared at my scars or asked what happened. We just enjoyed our time together. I felt like a normal human being again. Studying at CSUF was a much richer experience than I had ever expected. I had the opportunity to fully develop myself and connect with others without unnecessary complications.

### Sunday, October 31, 2010

I also had many international friends. Some came for their studies from Japan or the Philippines, others from Greece, Mexico, and France. In addition to Emmanuel, I befriended more exchange students from Tübingen University, Germany. We often had lots of fun together.

On Halloween, we all headed to Isla Vista to join a street party that attracted thousands of students every year. We drove with three cars. I picked up Christina, Natalie, and Cornelia in the morning with my green 1999 model VW Golf convertible. I had bought the car at the beginning of October, since public transportation in OC was, unfortunately, insufficient compared to Frankfurt. It took ninety minutes, for instance, to get from our apartment to the beach by bus, whereas it was a thirty-minute ride by car.

The warm sun was shining brightly as we drove down the 101 along the Pacific coast that morning. Fresh ocean air was blowing in our faces. It was perfect weather—not chilly, but not too hot. Countless waves washed along the sandy beach that stretched for miles right next to us while palm trees popped into view, one after another, creating a fantastic dream. Christina, sitting next to

me, and Natalie and Cornelia, sitting on the rear seats, were singing along with Katy Perry's[67] *Teenage Dream*. Time and again, we
stopped and took photos of each other, posing and laughing in
front of my car with the dark blue ocean in the background. It was
the car ride of my life!

In Isla Vista, we danced and sang all night long. I felt more
happy and free than I ever had before.

### *Beginning of November 2010*

Life was colorful. Life was cultivating. Life was vibrant at
CSUF. Even though my schedule was packed with assignments,
I was eager to enrich my campus experience as much as possible.
After classes had begun, I became a member of a campus association: the Middle Eastern Student Society. Most members had a
Middle Eastern background. We largely communicated in English,
and soon, we all became friends. In November, we organized an information day on campus. On posters and flip charts, we presented our countries of origin and other topics, such as "Arabs in the
USA" and "The Palestine Conflict." We also provided Arabic food
and music. Hundreds of students joined and enjoyed our event. In
the afternoon, we all danced together to belly dance music. I was
thrilled; it was possible to celebrate diversity!

### *Thursday, November 11, 2010*

Tom's family went to church every Sunday; from time to time,
they invited Emmanuel and me to join them. On Thanksgiving

---

67  Born Oct. 25, 1984: American singer and songwriter

Day, we went to the evening dinner their church had organized. We were served typical American food: turkey with cran-
berry sauce, yams, and pumpkin pie for dessert. Until that day,
Thanksgiving was a part of American culture that I had only seen
in the movies. Paul, Tom's middle-aged friend, who had asked
me in church two weeks earlier whether I was a Christian, was
present too. I had told him that I was a Muslim to make things
easier, since I assumed that my identity was relatively complex
and contradictory.

When I lined up at the buffet, he handed me a book and said,
*Inside the Revolution*. It says that Islam isn't the answer, and that
not Jihad, but Jesus is the way." I looked at him, perplexed. Did
he think he was morally superior because he was Christian? Did
he want me to distance myself from all pseudo-legitimized terrorist acts that were conducted "in the name of Islam?" What gave
him the right? Of course I did not support terrorism!

Tom intervened immediately. "Paul, this is just a book written by someone. People can believe what they want and that's
fine. We're all people, right?"

"Sure," Paul said, and disappeared, while I felt lost for a
moment. I couldn't understand why people used religion to clas-
sify people they did not even know as wrong and inferior.

Tom must have seen it in my eyes. He put his hand on my
shoulder. "Don't take his insensitivity personally. I like you," he
said. Tom was my hero. He protected me from Paul's arrogance
and from my self-pity. He calmed me down with sympathy, and
he made me smile with a compliment and his unwavering positive

attitude. Smiling at him, I was convinced that we needed more Toms in this world.

## End of March 2011

I hardly noticed how fast time went by while I was studying, thriving, running, celebrating, traveling, and discovering California with my friends. At the end of February, I flew to New Orleans to participate in a four-day Fulbright enrichment seminar titled "Greening of the Planet: Global Challenges, Local Solutions." I worked together with Fulbright students from all over the world. It was an incredibly empowering experience to see how we, without really knowing each other, could create and develop ideas together that could help all of humanity. After the seminar, there were only four weeks left before the final exams at CSUF, and the reality of my return journey became inescapable; the realization troubled me more than I expected.

### Sunday, March 27, 2011: Diary Entry

*It's 4:00 a.m. and I can't sleep. I was just standing at the end of the long corridor that leads to room G25—Emmanuel's and my apartment. I was looking at the city in front of me, pondering, for one hour. Orange clouds were flying away from light pollution, while heavy thoughts encircled my mind. Why can't I escape reality? Why am I who I am? Ungraspable, painful emotions pull me down from deep inside. Tonight, I went through many cigarettes. It has been years since I smoked and I still feel dizzy, but I just need to write. Maybe it'll help me understand what it is that bothers me so much. I hear the far-away horn of the Amtrak . . . Return journey! Soon, I'll have to go back to Germany. Then WHAT? I thought distance would help me forget. It didn't, though. All at once, it feels as if my old traumas have become alive again. My family, Marcus, Laura, Ceylin, and all the places and scars inside of me. Ya Allah, what crimes have I committed to be haunted by those demons? I am tired of being myself. I DON'T WANT TO GO BACK TO GERMANY!*

### Saturday, April 23, 2011

On my last day in the USA, my friends and I went to the *Exchange Club* in Los Angeles to celebrate together one last time. We danced on the huge dance floor. Green lights shot from a tall black dome into the dancing masses as the DJ was playing electronic beats. Around 1:00 a.m., Emmanuel and I went outside to a small, fenced-in area next to a back street. We smoked a cigarette and looked at each other.

Suddenly, Emmanuel broke the silence. "I'm gonna miss you man."

"I'm gonna miss you too. One year together. Best time of my life."

"Are you ready to go home?"

"I don't know." I paused. "I miss my family. But I rather feel like staying here."

"Okay, stop! Otherwise, I will start to cry. You shouldn't leave now. I will visit you in Germany when I come next month. Let's go and celebrate, my friend."

I smiled although I, all of a sudden, felt dizzy. I hardly managed to follow Emmanuel inside. When I reached the dance floor, my friends looked at me with concerned faces. "Dude, are you okay? You're pale. You're sweating. Sit down! We'll get you water," they said. I sat down on the floor in front of the bar for fifteen minutes, too weak to get up.

Chiara, Emmanuel's Italian-German girlfriend, who was visiting us from Germany, sat next to me. "It's the stress. You've been here for almost a whole year. Now you suddenly realize that you will leave everything behind and go back. I went through it last year when I studied in Niagara Falls. I didn't want to go back to Germany, either. But don't worry! You'll manage!" she said.

"You're probably right," I said. "I guess many things will be the same when I go back, except for me. I have changed. I felt so good here." I paused. "I met so many kind and open people. I had so much joy and freedom."

"Don't worry! You'll manage!" she said again, and smiled.

I smiled back, hoping she was right. Wistful, I got up to enjoy my last few hours in the USA.

After we had danced for the rest of the night, my friends dropped me off at LAX[68]. In the gray of dawn, when the sun slowly began to rise, we said goodybe to each other with a long embrace.

---

68  Los Angeles International Airport

# PART VI

# KASTEL

*April 2011–May 2011*

*Jus sanguinis*

*Monday, April 25, 2011*

After I had gone through customs at Frankfurt International Airport, I spotted Malik standing in the arrival hall in a crowd of people. We both smiled at each other and met halfway; we were glad to see each other again. We talked about the flight and his work for a moment before I asked him if he had come alone to the airport.

"Yes. Baba flew to Iraq. Mama is at home. She's tired," he said.

I said was surprised to hear about Adil's sudden departure. "How come? He e-mailed me two weeks ago that he would pick me up at the airport."

"I don't know," Malik said, avoiding eye contact.

I was alarmed. His evasive behavior almost certainly pointed to a new problem at home, I thought. Did my parents fight again?

While he led me to his car, more questions came to my mind: what happened during the time I was away? Could I continue from where I left in August 2010? Or would unforeseen challenges await me? A sense of foreboding gradually diminished the pleasant anticipation of seeing my family again. Even though we skyped regularly when I lived in Fullerton, I reckoned that they might have withheld some problems from me, probably because

I was too far away and unable to help on the ground.

After a fifteen-minute drive, we arrived in Kastel. It was an un-usually sunny day and almost thirty degrees Celsius, which made it easy to acclimate. I entered Frankfurter Weg seven. "Hello, I'm back," I called out, and waited—but no one responded. Malik went upstairs to the bathroom. I dropped my baggage on the floor and looked for Gabriela. When I stepped inside the kitchen, I spotted a book on the table: *The Great Cover Up. For Integration, against Islamism* by Alice Schwarzer—an iconic German feminist who had published many texts on that subject area. I felt weary. Was this just another source that fed Gabriela's negative thoughts and feelings about Islam? Disheartened, I opened the book.

As I skimmed through the text, I recalled the book review, which I had read in Fullerton. According to Ms. Schwarzer, the integration of immigrants failed because Germany applied the wrong kind of tolerance: an allegedly uncritical sympathy for all immigrants, motivated by the history of Nazi Germany. Ms. Schwarzer thus celebrated the 2009 court ruling, which revoked the possible exemption from co-educational swimming lessons for Muslim girls, as a victory for good and hard-fought Western de-mocracy against the "evil Islamism" that allegedly contaminated all Germany. As if there were only *one* political Islam; as if the ma-jority of German Muslims followed this antidemocratic political Islam; and as if the 2009 ruling made the German society more integrated, safe, and peaceful. It was the old, divisive, and dema-gogic narrative—Us against Them; Good against Evil.

Pictures flashed through my mind: I entered the staff room

of the Frankfurter gymnasium where I used to work. A teacher put an article on the wall and proudly proclaimed, "The Higher Administrative Court of Münster forces female Muslim students to participate in co-educational swimming classes. They can wear a burkini if they wish. The ruling is just and legitimate."

Three other teachers rejoiced with mischievous comments: "Now their stinky parents can complain as much as they want."

"Thank God the law is on our side."

"Finally our Aishas have to swim with boys."

I was perplexed and wondered: did these three teachers really feel better after expressing their hatred against a radical minority of Muslims? And did the silent majority of teachers in the staff room feel the same way? Why were they silent?

I put down the book and took a deep breath, aware that I needed to calm down.

Pensive, I looked outside the window at the Park and Ride where Ceylin and I used to meet. Was she all right? What was she doing? Where did she live? I took another deep breath, filled with old regret—Ceylin.

Suddenly, Gabriela entered the kitchen and said hello.

I replied and smiled, even though her look almost frightened me. Her face was swollen. Her eyes were tired. We kissed each other's cheeks.

"How are you?" I asked, watchfully.

"I'm okay," she said in a low voice.

She wasn't, I knew. She had dark rings under her eyes. "When does Baba come back?" I asked, cautiously.

"I don't know." She raised her shoulders.

I hesitated, but I could not hold back the question: "Did you quarrel again?"

"It has been difficult with him while you have been in America."

"Why? What happened?"

"He talked about properties and money all the time, and I don't want to talk about it."

What properties, and why not? I wondered, but I did not ask. I did not want to bother her with more unpleasant questions. In addition, I knew I would be confronted with it sooner or later.

### *End of April 2011*

After Oma Erika's sudden death in December 2009, Gabriela and Malik moved into Frankfurter Weg seven. There was no need to keep two houses for only three people—Gabriela, Adil, and Malik. Also, it would have been difficult for Gabriela and Adil to keep the two houses after her death, since Paul-Ehrlich-Straße four was partially run by a portion of Oma Erika's pension. My parents' pensions would have barely closed that financial gap. Gabriela had worked only seventeen years in Germany and hence did not accumulate many pension points, and Adil's Iraqi pension was even lower due the almost worthless Iraqi Dinar. I had thus pushed them to rent out Paul-Ehrlich-Straße four before I went to Fullerton, so that they would be financially well set again. I advertised it on the internet and helped empty the house. We had many potential renters and agreed to rent it to a young family from Montenegro.

Frankfurter Weg seven was big enough for us anyway. Sophia had lived in Bad Homburg, a thirty-minute drive away, with her alcoholic friend since winter 2008, while Alim had been doing pop art in Kuwait since summer 2006. And I was only staying temporarily in Kastel until I could move back to my studio, which I was renting out.

One afternoon, I saw the renters of Paul-Ehrlich-Straße four loading a transporter with their belongings. Startled, I approached their twenty-year-old daughter and asked if they were moving out. "Yes. Your mother terminated the rental contract, effective immediately," she said. I looked at her with big, unbelieving eyes. Suddenly, the entire family met me under the grapevine. They told me what had happened as Gabriela was watching us from the living room.

After they had finished, I excused myself and went back to Frankfurter Weg seven.

I confronted Gabriela in the living room. "Did you really terminate the rental contract?"

She looked at me as if that was none of my business.

"How could you do that without informing us? Our family, especially you and Baba, depend on this rental income!" I said, upset.

"Oh please! You have no idea. My pension is enough for me; I have a private supplementary pension. I made the right decision. Last month they didn't pay the rent on time; this month they didn't pay at all."

I looked at her, stunned. "They just told me that the woman

stayed in the intensive care unit for two weeks, that her husband was unemployed for a month, and that his new building contractor had not paid him yet. Did you know that?"

"Yes. But I am no welfare organization! I also have bills to pay!" she shouted.

I shook my head. "The family over there was and still is in an emergency. It's not that you couldn't survive six weeks without the rental income. And ending the contract was not a decision you should have made alone. It might not affect you that much, but Baba! His pension is not only much smaller than yours; it doesn't even come on a regular basis. Why didn't you at least wait for him? You know he comes back next week. You could've made a reasonable decision together."

That was the moment she started raging: "I knew it! You are a traitor. You've always been against me. You only take sides with our renters because they are foreigners from Montenegro and Muslims like you and your damn father!"

I looked at her furious eyes. "What you're saying about me is not true. I'm talking about compassion and reasonable decision making," I said.

She turned her back on me and ran out of the house.

Welcome back to my old life!

*Friday, May 6, 2011*

During the time I was in Fullerton, my Horizonte scholarship was on hold. In May, it resumed, and I was looking forward to receiving more education and training.

The Horizonte scholarship holders were invited for a training course in project management at the foundation's villa in Frankfurt on May 6. We sat at a long table in the meeting room while the director gave her welcome speech. "I'm glad to present to you our new flyers and posters, which will be distributed and presented nationwide," she said. Next, she turned a page on the flip chart. I spotted three students on a poster. They kept the two females of the first version, but changed the male in the center. I was looking at a picture of me! It had been taken at our training course in conflict management before I went to Fullerton. That day, I had been wearing a white dress shirt with bronze stripes.

The new scholarship holders looked at me with large eyes. "Wow, beautiful! Junis, this is you," they said. Taken by surprise, I did not know what to say. I had mixed feelings.

"Please, help distribute the flyers and poster. We've already sent them to twelve hundred addresses nationwide, including all universities and institutions that educate teachers, as well as many schools and the cooperation partners of the Horizonte scholarship," the director said.

Next, she put a box on the front table and left the room. All the students got up and grabbed some flyers and posters, except Faris, who approached me.

"Did they ask you whether they could put you on these posters and flyers?" he asked.

"No. It was written somewhere in the contract that they could use pictures of me, but I thought they would ask me first. I just came from the USA and I had no idea! Damn!" I said.

"Come on, I'd love to be on this poster. Be happy! You're a celebrity now."

"Yes. The prototype of an exceptional immigrant who somehow managed in Germany," I said. Being a "successful" immigrant wasn't necessarily something to be proud of, though. It should be rather normal in every society, I thought. Or was this poster necessary for that same reason, to change the image of immigrants in Germany and inspire immigrant students to apply for the scholarship and attain their educational goals? Could programs like Horizonte improve the integration of immigrants?

*Monday, May 16, 2011*

The study regulations at Goethe University for prospective teachers included an obligatory eight-week internship in a non-pedagogical institution. The purpose was to broaden the horizons of prospective teachers, which I thought was a good idea. Since I was interested in policy-making processes, I applied for an internship at the Ministry for Justice and Integration, or MJI. I was glad when I was accepted.

The week before the internship began, I bought black and light blue fitted dress shirts, black patent leather shoes, and a black leather belt at an upscale fashion boutique in the MTZ. I also went to the barber to get a regular men's haircut, since I wanted to look neat and tidy. After studying politics for almost four years, I was looking forward to my first experience in state politics.

On my first working day, I arrived at the Wiesbadener central station thirty minutes prior to my registration appointment to make sure I would be on time. I headed toward the ministry and crossed a park. The morning sun gently touched my face, which was still gold-brown from OC. To my left, tall oak trees bordered the park and threw a shadow on the sidewalk. To my right, fountains sprang water every five yards, encircling a large green area. My eyes lingered on the beautiful sight.

Suddenly, I heard my shoes on the sidewalk, tick-tock. They were stiff, like my dress shirt. Did I look right? I wondered. I did not want to overdress, but I also did not want to look too casual. I was wearing dark blue jeans, a light blue dress shirt, black patent leather shoes, a black leather belt, and an anthracite suit coat. *I should look right,* I thought.

The ministry stuck out with its natural stone facade and arched windows. Next to the security entrance door, I read on a golden plate "Hessian Criminal Court." The ministry for the integration of immigrants and the rehabilitation funds for offenders were located in the same building. It reminded me of my studies on Foucault[69] at CSUF, about how power served to control and punish the minority. The joint building subtly fit with the standard media coverage[70] and public discourse, which predominantly portrayed certain immigrants as a burden, if not a menace, to the democratic German society. My heart began to race. I wondered: did I, Junis Sultan, have a place here?

I rang the bell. Shortly, a wide electronic door opened. I stepped

---

69   Paul-Michel Foucault (Oct. 15, 1926–June 25, 1984): French philosopher, historian of ideas, social theorist, philologist, and literary critic

70   "Prejudices." Information on Political Education

into a small, shady entrance hall. An officer was sitting in a cabin in front of me, behind a security glass. "Your ID, please," he asked. I gave it to him. "Take a seat. You'll be called," he said. I sat down, nervous.

After a couple minutes, the personnel manager came downstairs. She introduced herself and asked me to follow her. We took the spiral stairs to the fourth floor, where I was supposed to meet a member of the leading team. "Dr. Hoffmann" was written on the door sign. She entered his room, introduced me, and left, while Dr. Hoffmann came around his table to shake my hand. As we faced each other, he eyed me from head to toe. I felt uneasy.

"Your name is interesting," he said, half-questioning and half-skeptical.

"Pardon?" I said, though I understood him accurately. It was a defense I had developed after experiencing countless embarrassing interactions in Germany because of my name and outward appearance. Was he sincerely interested in me, or was he suspiciously aiming at my ethnicity? I waited for his restatement to find out.

"Sultan is an interesting name. Where are you *originally* from?"

The classic question I frequently received in Germany. After all those years, I still did not seem to *really* belong to Germany. I asked more clearly to find out what he was looking for: "What do you mean?"

"Where were you and your parents born? You look Mediterranean or Middle Eastern."

"My father was born in Iraq. I was too, and my mother in Germany," I said, suddenly feeling my heart pounding. He forced me to explain my ethnic background as if the reason for my non-German name and my non-whiteness was the most important thing about me. Could he not wait until I felt like sharing a private part of me? And what did my ethnicity tell him about me anyway?

"Interesting. Your German is really good. How come?" he asked, seriously.

As if I had to be uneducated because of my ethnicity. I should have said something smart ("Thank you. *Your* German is also good!"), but I did not, because anger flared up inside of me. "I went to kindergarten, primary school, gymnasium, and university in Germany," I said before I noticed that I was explaining and defending myself, once again, even though it should have been unnecessary in a democratic country where people are protected from discrimination and racism.

"Still, your German is really good. Many immigrants, especially Turks, have stayed here for decades, but they still live only among themselves and can hardly speak as accent-free as you do," he said.

I raised my eyebrows. Did he just really say that about *all* Turks? When would we finally reach post-racial Germany? And did he, in his high position, really not know about the decades of unjust and failed integration policies in Germany[71]? I wondered while he brought forth a book from his antique table.

"Do you know this book?" he asked.

"No."

"It was a bestseller in the USA It's about 9/11 and the terrorists

---

71  Raimann, Anna. "30 Years Lost."

who were on the plane. And it's about other terrorists who confess their activities in al-Qaeda and who left the organization and became normal people again. One even converted to Christianity. You should read it. It's really good," he told me with his eyes wide open.

I looked at the title. *Inside the Revolution.* Wasn't this the book Tom's friend Paul had wanted me to read because I was a Muslim? Had Dr. Hoffmann anticipated that I was a Muslim? Did he want to educate and save me, like Paul, from the allegedly most evil religion on the planet? Or did he even recommend that book to everyone he met?

I did not reply. I had enough of his attitude, and he did not even notice. Smiling, he shook my hand and wished me a good time in my internship. I just wanted to leave his office.

### *Wednesday, May 18, 2011*

At around 10:00 p.m., I approached Adil, who had returned from Iraq a few days earlier. He was in the kitchen drinking a cup of warm water, as he usually did before going to bed, when I asked him for some advice. He was listening carefully as I told him what had happened at the ministry.

"I'm sorry to hear that," he said. "You're in an exhausting position. You constantly have to prove that you're better than many people here think you are."

"Do I really have to prove this to people?" I looked at him with raised eyebrows.

"I know how you feel, but you need to be patient and work

hard. Give it more time."

"And then what? Patience and hard work don't seem to change other people's attitudes. All my hard work and achievements over the last twenty years don't seem to matter in Germany. I am still treated like a stranger. In the United States, I was almost always treated with respect—regardless of my name, my skin color, or whatever superficial thing. What I experience here is simply wrong. I see it more clearly than ever before. It's inhumane. It's intolerable. It's absolutely unacceptable."

"Look, I've met many politicians here as the chairman of the Council of Foreigners, and more than a few had prejudices against me and treated me like dirt. But in the course of time, even some of the tough ones changed their attitude toward me once they saw that I wasn't primitive, uncultured, and lazy. It's not that we all became friends, but we can work together today."

"But I'm sick of their power games. I bow out. They can think whatever they want in their deadlocked brains. I will not prove anything to them anymore, because integration is not a one-way street. It's about mutual respect and meeting others halfway. Look, I did what I could to integrate, and still, I've remained a stranger. Why? Am I a complete failure? If so-called 'successful' immigrants like me have difficulties becoming accepted and getting respect in society at large, how shall immigrants with a low socio-economic status ever be integrated? Is this what we call the free, developed world?"

Adil looked at me with raised eyebrows. "You've always weighed your options carefully before you made a decision. This internship is a good chance for your career. Don't lose it because of some idiots. But if you do, you should know why, and whether it's worth it."

I nodded. "I know what principles I stand for."

Adil put his hand on my shoulder. "I appreciate that you come and ask your old man about what he thinks. You know, whatever you decide, I stand behind you," he said.

At that moment, I knew I would turn my back on the so-called Ministry for Justice and Integration. I slowly calmed down, and yet I knew that what I would do was not going to be easy.

### Thursday, May 19, 2011

At 8:00 a.m. I entered the personnel manager's office to give her my termination letter. She looked at me with large eyes. I told her that the letter contained an explanation. Since she insisted that she wanted to talk with me in person, I commented on what I had written down.

*1. The "welcoming" by Dr. Hoffmann was marked by negative stereotypes. I'm disappointed that a leading member of the Ministry for Justice and Integration has such a biased, disrespectful attitude toward a particular group of immigrants.*

*2. Scientific work was unwanted. I intended to do this internship to gain and create more knowledge of the Hessian integration efforts. Indeed, I was asked to measure the integration projects in quantitative and qualitative terms from 1999 onward. To do that properly, I would have had to request data sets from the Ministry for Social Affairs, which initiated integration projects from 1999 to 2009 under the CDU before the FDP took over the MJI and became responsible for integration. When I asked my superior for permission to make that request, however, I was told that such a detailed data analysis was unnecessary, and that I should show numbers that put the current ruling party (FDP) in a good light. These cover-up tactics are untold.*

*3. Independent work was unwanted due to the coercion of promoting a party's political agenda. More precisely, I was also asked to investigate the immigration policies of Canada and Australia to develop a similar, point-based concept for German immigration policies. This intended concept belongs to the political agenda of the FDP and is in the best scenario market-oriented, but not human-rights-oriented. Regardless of the fact that I do not belong to any political party and that I do not want to promote any party's political agenda, I can't identify with this concept, because I believe in humanitarian ideals.*

In the end, she told me that she understood my decision.

"I'll also quit my job when I go on maternity leave. I've got a Polish migration background, and I frequently experience it in my everyday work too," she said.

Her name and her dark hair must have affected her in similar ways.

"Jus sanguinis, the right of blood, still governs Germany," she said.

I got up, shook her hand, and left the ministry.

## *End of May 2011: Diary Entry*

*I'm sitting in the basement at our old dining table. It's midnight. The curtains are closed. I just crossed out the internship from my calendar on the wall. I have arrived in Germany, and it's still the same crap. I am still a stranger in Germany, and my family is still a mess. My parents are upstairs. I can hear their unending fight over houses, properties, money, and things that happened in Iraq nearly forty years ago . . . I wonder: what shall I do now? WHAT SHALL I DO NOW?*

# PART VII

# LIEDERBACH

*June 2011–November 2011*

*Goodbye*

*June 2011*

I was looking forward to moving back to Liederbach, my old refuge. When I opened the apartment door, a feeling of relief overcame me. I deeply breathed in, aware that I needed peace even more now than in January 2009. Being back in Germany burdened me much more than I had expected. Old traumas, emotional flashbacks, and a sense of reverse-culture shock almost overwhelmed me. I fled from those negative thoughts and emotions into a numb work mode. The final state exams were coming up, and I set myself a goal to achieve excellent grades; I still believed that a university degree was my ticket for a better future.

*Monday, August 1, 2011*

After teaching at the comprehensive school in Hofheim, I stopped by in Frankfurter Weg seven to congratulate my parents for their forty-eighth wedding anniversary. However, I only found Adil. He was sitting in the kitchen, glaring at the table. He raised his head and stared at me as if the world would end today. "I quarreled with your mother. She ran away," he said. I looked at him, wordless and helpless. In all these years, dozens of family meetings, family therapy, and constant efforts to understand and accommodate each other still hadn't brought peace. Somehow, fighting always came back to us—tearing us apart.

### Tuesday, August 23, 2011: Diary Entry

*My mother moved out on August 1. She has been living with Onkel Walter since then. She hasn't contacted me, and I'm afraid to contact her. What should I say? She probably abandoned us for good. She has never run away for such a long time.*

### Monday, August 29, 2011: Diary Entry

*This morning, my father said he would file for divorce. It's not the first time my parents have taken official steps to separate. Since my father came to Germany, my mother repeatedly contacted a women's aid organization and lawyers to get advice on the question of separation. Each time, though, she changed her mind. I often wondered why she always came back to us, even if I've never dared to ask her. It wasn't that I didn't want her to live with us, but everyone knew she felt unhappy with us. Maybe she always came back because she wanted to keep the promise of marriage. Maybe she was afraid she would be alone. Maybe she loved us and hoped that everything would become better somehow. Maybe she had other reasons.*

*Or maybe I am completely wrong. Maybe we all didn't love each other as much as we should have in order to live happily and peacefully together. Maybe cultural differences were only an excuse for our human failures. Whatever it was, all I know is that our struggles over the years, our efforts to stay together despite our painful conflicts, were in vain. Now, all hope is gone and written law will decide how we will be divided. I wonder: what is the lesson to learn?*

### Sunday, September 4, 2011, at midnight: Diary Entry

*I'm sitting at my table. The white laptop screen illuminates my tense face while the dark night surrounds me. I'm trying to catch my wild thoughts and emotions. I'm trying to understand. I lost my parents, my siblings, my childhood—a central part of me. None of my siblings call me anymore. They don't want to talk about the family. I feel so lonely, so sad.*

### Thursday, September 22, 2011: Diary Entry

*Next week, my father will go back to Iraq for an indefinite period of time. He wants to secure our property rights, at least in Mosul. His lawyer told him that it would be difficult to get a share of the property in Kastel even though my father has invested about $300,000 over the years (mostly money from Iraq) to help buy and renovate Paul-Ehrlich-Straße four and build Frankfurter Weg seven. However, my mother refuses to split the ownership in Kastel because Onkel Walter advises her so.*

*Today, I told my father that he shouldn't stress himself out for property issues since keeping up our relationships was more important in this tough time. But he is obsessed with the idea that he will die soon and that he has to leave some secured property for us. He said, "Maybe you're too young, but you'll understand when you're old, when you have children, and when you unjustly lose everything you've built up for them over the years."*

*I could not say a word. I understood his position as well.*

*I wonder what would have happened if we had never come to Germany—a place where differences have frequently been viewed as a threat for the so-called Leitkultur. Maybe my parents would still be together. They didn't rip each other and our family apart in Iraq. Maybe my mother wouldn't have felt ashamed for what we often are in Germany—an ethnic minority, the allegedly strange, unintegrated, inferior, vulnerable "other." If I had the money, I would take the next plane to California.*

### Monday, September 26, 2011: Diary Entry

*Ya Allah, I haven't prayed for your help for some time, but please, if you can, help me.*

### November 2011

It was already dark when I stopped by at Frankfurter Weg seven to check how Malik was doing. To my big surprise, I didn't meet him, but Gabriela. She was sitting at the dining table, working her way through stacks of paper. I had not seen her for three months. Did she move back because Adil stayed in Iraq? We briefly looked at each other. I said hello and went to the kitchen to take a breath and think about how to behave. But I had no idea. Nervous, I opened a magazine that was lying on the kitchen table.

Suddenly, Gabriela approached me from behind. "The magazine lists the prices for solar panels. I want to buy some for Amtal," she said.

"Okay," I said, wondering how she could talk as if nothing had happened.

"Or maybe I'll buy a studio. You could help me find a good investment," she said.

I put down the magazine and decided to speak up for the family. "No, I won't help you with investing *your* money. If I may remind you, you deny all of us a share of what we have built up together."

"*We?*" she said with large eyes. "*I* had to work day and night, not you or your father."

"That's not true. We all paid the price. We renovated, built, and maintained the houses together. Even as young children we helped as much as we could. And Baba often worked double shifts and brought thousands of dollars from Mosul over the years. And now you simply want to kick us out of the house as if we had no rights whatsoever."

"Your father told you this stupid stuff. It's a lie."

"I wish it was." I paused. "I still can't understand why you and Baba can't split your finances like adults. We wanted to talk with you about it as a family, but you ran away to Amtal. Why?"

"It's not your business, and I don't want to talk about it." She turned her back on me and walked toward the front door.

I grabbed her arm firmly, for the first time. Anger got the best of me. "You can't just run away and not take any responsibility!"

"Don't grab me! That hurts!"

I let her go.

"I ran away because he held a knife to himself on August 1

and threatened to commit suicide if I didn't agree to his offer. You weren't there!" she shouted.

"No, I wasn't, and either Baba or you are lying about August 1. He showed me his affidavit in which he stated that none of that happened. Either way, I can't understand you. He proposed that you keep one house and write the other one in the name of all children. Why couldn't you agree on that?"

She came toward me. "Because I can't trust you. You have always betrayed me. My own children have always been on their father's side."

Her words cut like an old knife. "We have not always betrayed you. We tried to be on the side of who was right, not because we wanted, but because you and Baba forced us. And if we didn't take sides, or the wrong side, you blamed or ignored us." I paused. "Don't you know how painful it is to hear these sweeping accusations after all the years we've lived together?"

"In my entire life, I was suppressed by my family and not allowed to be who I am. The houses in Kastel are my only security for the future. You'll not care for me once one house is in your names, because your father has drummed into you that you cannot count on me or anyone in Germany, because you are 'foreigners' here and not accepted."

"What? Suppressed? How? When? I went to church with you many times, even as a Muslim. We celebrated Christmas and Easter more than anything. You were free to be who you are, do what you wanted, and go where you wished. We were not. And in regard to Germany, discrimination was not Baba's invention, but part of our experience here. Why don't you finally show some understanding?"

"Yeah, the Germans are always the bad guys, right? I have no bad conscience. I bought you food and clothes. I worked only for you. Still, my own children were like strangers to me. They grew up with their father's religion and culture, while I never had a say in anything! And that's also why I never had motherly feelings!"

"'Never had motherly feelings'? 'They'? Who are we in your eyes?" I waited for an answer, but I didn't receive any. "I did not say all Germans are bad. I enjoyed a good education here, and I had good times with some good friends here. And if I may remind you, you raised us as well."

"And you still became a Muslim. You decided against me and for your father."

Tears filled my eyes. "This doesn't make sense. I told you many times I did not decide against you. I made a religious decision for myself, which is my right. And I respected your faith and always will. All I expected from you was that you respect me as a human being with equal rights."

"I will never accept Islam. Islam lacks basic human principles."

Although this was not the first time she had said these words, I once again felt deeply hurt. "So are we all incomplete, inferior creatures, who are on the wrong side?" I asked.

She picked up the book by Alice Schwarzer. Searching for a page, she said, "I can quote it: Islam says that a woman's witness report doesn't count as much as a man's witness report."

"Please! How does this relate to our family? Did we ever treat you like that?" I asked and waited, but I did not receive an answer.

I packed my bag and, without looking back, left the house.

As I was walking away, she came to the garden fence. "Junis, you don't say goodbye?"

I looked over my shoulder and saw her waiting in the distance.

"Goodbye," I said quietly, not for the sake of courtesy, but because I meant it.

# EPILOGUE

*A sense of warmth*

*Friday, November 11, 2011*

The news anchor announced, "According to the German federal bar, the thirty-six-year-old Beate Zschäpe, who is a member
of the neo-Nazi group 'National Socialist Underground,' and who
burned down her apartment in Zwickau on November 4, is connected to the murder of a policewoman in 2007 and the serial murders of nine immigrants—including five Kurdish, three Turkish,
and one Greek kebab store owners—between 2000 and 2006."

Junis Sultan had already assumed in 2006 that the murderers
were neo-Nazis. It was almost obvious. The only things the victims,
except the policewoman, had in common were their migration
background and their darker physical appearances. It was rather
easy for neo-Nazis to operate in a toxic atmosphere. Chronically
negative and overgeneralizing news reports about certain "foreigners"—typically problematizing or demonizing non-white and
non-Christian immigrants and asylum seekers—in addition to recurring foreigner-bashing by nationalistic and conservative politicians, didn't only spread fear and hatred among citizens, but also

served to normalize certain prejudices. Accordingly, even the investigating authorities wrongly accused the victims and their relatives of having mafia business connections and being responsible for the murders. The hasty accusations had never been about solving the cases, he sensed, but rather, they reflected the racist attitudes which had deeply infested the state. One of the murders had even been witnessed by an undercover agent who worked for the "Federal Office for the Protection of the Constitution," the institution that would later shred relevant documents, among other dubious actions, when Beate Zschäpe burned down her house, at which point some parts of the truth had to be revealed to the manipulated, fear-conditioned public.

All this racist propaganda and violence had scarred his heart much deeper than his arm. He felt the pain of injustice and human failure on many days, but on this day, he felt utterly lonely and helpless—abandoned by his natural confidants, his family, the most trusted people in his life.

Junis turned off the television to go out for a walk, thinking that maybe nature could calm him down. But nature had already withdrawn back into itself. Fall had taken its course. Trees faced him as leafless skeletons. Struggle-weary, he bought cigarettes from a vending machine. Even though he wanted to quit smoking, he didn't care about his health anymore. His mental state was a devastated, contaminated battlefield. He lit a cigarette, inhaled the smoke, and thought about his mother's final words to him the last time they spoke. Full of toxic shame, he started to walk through Liederbach. A kindergarten teacher saw him approaching. Tears were rolling down his cheeks. She stared at him for a moment before she went back inside the building. Demoralized by the indifference and callousness of strangers, he kept walking until, almost exhausted, he reached a field. As he stared at the brown soil, total despair overcame him. How could he live without his family? Without a friend nearby?

Hopeless, Junis slowly walked back to his apartment. He opened his laptop. Angelo Milli's[72] *Requiem* resumed. Piano tones and dramatic strings heralded the end. He stepped onto his balcony and looked into the sky. It was clear for the first time in weeks. Cold wind blew gently into his face while doves flew in the blue heavens. How beautiful, he thought for second, but he was too weak to hold his body up any longer. He went down on the cold concrete. His heart was pounding painfully. His spirit seemed to be flying away. His life was meaningless because he was all alone; he might as well be dead, he thought. But would he dare to commit the biggest, irrevocable sin?

The carpet cutter in the shoebox underneath the kitchen sink would make a deep cut! How long would it take to lose consciousness when he slashed his wrists? Would he finally feel relieved? What would his parents do when they found out? Would they stand together? Or would they blame each other? Either way, it did not matter to him anymore. He was determined to get the carpet cutter.

All of a sudden, however, a sense of warmth bloomed in his chest and suffesed his entire body—as if someone was there and

---

72   Born May 27, 1975, in Venezuela: composer

had embraced him; as if this someone knew his every thought and felt his inmost pain; as if this someone bled with him without complaint; as if this someone waited patiently; as if this someone asked him whether he was truly ready to give up the chances of life; as if this someone promised that life had something good waiting for him. Would he stand up one more time?

Pictures ran through his mind like flashes: dropping bombs, a burning city, machine gun fire, dead people on the street, his father left behind at the gate, injured asylum seekers, his mother beating him, his neighbors shouting at him, a skinhead persecuting him, mass brawls at school, Marcus turning away from him, his mother turning away from him, his father dead-still on a hospital bed, cutting himself, his brothers-in-law turning away from him, Ceylin turning away from him, his KO loss, his sister burning her arms, his parents fighting, his grandmother dead on a hospital bed, Dr. Hoffmann staring at him. What should he do with his cursed life? He wanted to throw it away.

But then, other pictures came to his mind: his mother looking after him while he seesawed in the garden, his father carrying him on his shoulders in the swimming pool, his family coming together around the Christmas tree, Oma Erika hugging him, his siblings kissing him on his birthday, Marcus and Dominik laughing with him, marching with the Kasteler band while people clapped their hands, Mr. Siegert putting his hand on his shoulder and encouraging him, watching Martin Luther King Jr. speaking about his dream, Piero giving him his hand, Ceylin kissing and holding him, winning a comeback fight, Tom smiling and putting his hand on his shoulder, driving along the Pacific coast, singing and dancing with people from all around the world.

Tears streamed down his face. He was trembling. Could he throw away these precious people? Could he throw away himself? What was the good thing that waited for him? Could he possibly not feel lonely and worthless in the future? If there was the slightest chance for togetherness and happiness, would he seize it? If there was the slightest chance to be himself and develop himself, would he seize it? If there was the slightest chance for freedom and peace, would he seize it? Would he seize the chance of life? Would he look and work for his dreams with all his heart and with his entire mind, every day, without excuses? Could he keep the faith despite the struggles? Could he live a meaningful life?

Suddenly, the idea evolved in his mind. The first thing he would have to do, not only to survive, but to heal, was write everything down. Maybe he would understand himself better by putting it all on paper. Maybe he would grasp the thoughts and emotions that had driven him through his life. Maybe he would triumph over his fears and develop the courage to fully love himself. Maybe he would forgive himself for his destructive behaviors. Maybe he would develop a deeper understanding for other people. Maybe he would develop the courage to fully love all people. Maybe he would forgive others for their destructive behaviors.

Maybe he could even use his story and help create something good for the world. Maybe his story could help others deal with their fears and despairs. Maybe it could encourage people to love themselves and those around them. Maybe it could help people forgive themselves and others. Maybe it could make people turn to each other. Maybe it could help people build deep connections with each other. Maybe it could tear down some old walls and help build something new, something good. Maybe it could somehow help unite East and West, old and young, men and women—humanity.

This was the only way his life made sense to him: it had never been about Junis Sultan, but about sharing and encouraging our human experiences—the needs for bonding and freedom, the struggles for happiness and peace, and the connecting and liberating powers of love.

# AFTERWORD

*Status quo ante bellum*

*November 2018*

In the summer of 2012, I completed my studies at Goethe University, Frankfurt, and earned my boxing coach certificate. I was able to realize my larger goal of giving back to other people—a fulfilling journey which can take many forms, and which I entrust to everyone who seeks a positive change in their own and other people's lives. In the fall of 2012, I started a two-year teacher traineeship at a Frankfurter gymnasium. During that time, I taught children and teenagers both at school and in the boxing gym in Hochheim, and wrote the first draft of the book you are now holding in your hands. Since fall 2014, I've taught Politics and Economics and English in a full time position, lately even at the FEG, the school I once never wanted to visit again. But people can change if they choose to do so, and there is hope! The diversity at German high schools has increased in the last ten years, since more systematic German language support has been made available at the early stages of education. Accordingly, students with a migrant background now perform better in middle school, which can be seen in the latest PISA studies.

There are, however, still significant differences in performances, graduation certificates, and rates of school dropouts between ethnic German students and non-ethnic German students—to the detriment of the latter, and to society as a whole. The continuing segregation of children at the age of ten, largely based on their German language skills, still impedes the integration of non-ethnic German children and often leads to lifelong struggles, as well as high costs for society. Germans need to finally enforce new laws to stop systematic discrimination against non-ethnic German, especially non-European children, and institutionalize more equal opportunities in school. This political task is also necessary for other nations: we need to stop the consequent socio-economic, psycho-emotional, and biological damages of every unjust education system, not only because it is morally right, but because we have to adapt to the social reality of increasing globalization and migration. The well-being of nations—of people—will depend on how well integration is handled.

If foreigners, migrants, and refugees are to be better integrated, major changes in the education system are necessary because education is the key to integration. For Germany, one major step in the right direction would be to acknowledge students with a non-ethnic German, non-European background, offer heritage language courses that count equally on report cards, and provide more equal opportunities to students of different ethnicities. To this day, non-European languages are only rarely taught at German schools, and do not count on report cards. This practice is problematic for many reasons. One in ten children in Germany is a foreigner. At least one in three children has a migrant background, with an upward tendency. Most of these children have a non-European background. An education system that is not built on nationalistic and Eurocentric identity politics, but on human rights and democratic multilingualism, offers these children valid heritage language courses. Imagine how many students could be promoted; how successful they could be at school, and later in their work life; what bonds they could build with their relatives and their homelands just because they can speak the language; how many international businesses they could create; how much their often poor home countries—and their people—could prosper from decentralized cooperation. Imagine a better world!

There is a lot of work to be done these days. I therefore encourage my students to openly talk about problematic experiences, even when it feels uncomfortable. It is our responsibility to ourselves, and to generations to come, to have those uncomfortable talks, no matter what the context, to develop approaches to build a more just, more ethical, more functional society, and then act upon them.

Following the public discourse about the challenges of our increasingly globalized society—such as climate change, poverty, war, terrorism, mass migration, populism, and strained relations between Christians and Muslims—and developing with my committed students ideas for how people can come together and solve these problems, have continually enriched my perspectives on the subjects of this book. I'm happy to see how the new generation at my school promotes diversity as natural, and in most cases positively enriching, provided that there is mutual respect, reason, and goodwill on each side.

As regards my parents, no compromise could be reached after the fall of 2011, unfortunately. After innumerable talks and multiple cycles of their on-again/off-again relationship, it once again seems as if a solution can only be found through legal means. An alternative, presumably more challenging but also more rewarding, would be to seek professional help, considering that one parent has since been diagnosed with a dependent personality disorder and chronic depression, neither of which were ever treated, and the other parent—as usual in these toxic relationships[73]—has at least some strong narcissistic personality traits. After having experienced how mentally devastating these disorders can be for everyone involved, I can only recommend to those who are in such a relationship to seek professional help as soon as possible, or, if affected in other ways, to maintain strong, self-protecting boundaries. For my part, I clearly name my limits. I do not tolerate discrimination, constant guilt trips and shaming, or emotional manipulation. If any of these happen, I use direct language and allow myself to walk away, and to protect myself as long as I need. Keeping my parents' dysfunctional relationship in mind, it becomes even more evident that alleged "insurmountable religious and cultural differences" are only a pretext for our human failure to meet our own *and* other people's needs for bonding and freedom in a healthy way.

In the course of the revisions of this book, I studied the impacts of discrimination and childhood adversity, which helped me understand and reframe my experiences and relationships. The

---

73 Rosenberg, Ross. *The Human Magnet Syndrome: Why We Love People who Hurt Us.* Premier Publishing and Media, 2013.

recurrent social injustices we experienced in Kastel at the beginning of the 1990s caused sadness and anger to permeate my family's life. Soon, these recurrent negative emotions imploded on us. They could also have led to violent reactions against our environment if Gabriela had not treated other people politely and taught us to do likewise. Instead, they manifested themselves in emotional neglect, verbal assaults, and physical violence within our home. The abuse I experienced didn't only show in bruises or a bloody nose; it came close to a "biological attack." The unregulated, persistent doses of toxic stress led to chronic health problems and life-long risks[74]. As a young child, I (as the only one among my siblings) developed allergies, asthma, and cardiac arrhythmias, which prompted my pediatrician to send me to a specialist children's clinic. While the physical health problems faded away after a decade of medical treatment and regular exercise, the psychological and emotional wounds were more difficult to detect and treat. The prolonged abuse instilled in me a deep feeling of worthlessness and shame[75], which put my psycho-emotional stability at life-long risk. It requires me to pause again and again, face my relentless inner critic, and nurture a caring inner self. Self-love is the key to psycho-emotional stability.

Writing this book, my intention was not only to portray the struggles of people in our increasingly globalized society—such as identity crises, errors in reasoning ("us versus them"), pseudo-justified violence against "the others," or simple misunderstandings—but

---

74  Harris, Nadine Burke. *The Deepest Well: Healing the Long-Term Effects of Childhood Adversity.* Mariner Books, 2018.

75  Walker, Pete. *Complex PTSD: From Surviving to Thriving: A Guide and Map for Recovering from Childhood Trauma.* Azure Coyote Publishing, 2013.

also to show some ways in which we may grow toward positive change. My experiences, both negative and positive, and especially my goal to live a meaningful life have driven me to keep striving for bonding and freedom. We do well as social individuals to connect deeply with others; it makes us happy. And we do well to protect and cherish personal freedoms; it allows us to coexist in peace. Although that happiness and peace are often hard to reach and do not last forever, I keep envisioning their presence in my life. It inspires me. It's like a dream—a dream many people have shared and pursued for their families, friends, communities, countries, and for themselves to not just exist but live a life with purpose and passion.

Some people may disagree with my words, which is their good right. Some people may build their walls even higher, which I do not hope. I hope that I have not offended anyone with this book. Rather, I hope I have raised awareness and inspired readers to connect deeply with "other" people and stand up for freedom. I also do hope that the good of our common humanity will endure and prevail; that it does not surrender to the struggles of our time, or any time. That it does not give in to fear, resentment, or hate. That it does not disappear. That it is always there, proactively striving to overcome our weaknesses.

If we stay true to ourselves, with a positive attitude and continuing efforts, we will see the good of our humanity. We will flourish in our bonds as brothers and sisters, and in our freedom as individuals; we will taste the lush fruits of happy times together and of our reached personal goals; we will listen to the symphonies of reconciliation and human achievements—united and free at last.

*It is up to us.* Every day matters. Every person we meet matters. Every kind, compassionate, and supportive gesture matters. Every connection we build with another human soul matters. This is how we can tear down those old, inhumane, and false walls between people; though love for one another and through self-love, we can change from strangers into brothers, from status quo to status quo ante bellum.[76]

---

76 Latin: "From the existing state of affairs (social, political) to the state before the war"

# ABOUT THE AUTHOR

Junis Sultan teaches politics, economics, and English near Frankfurt, Germany. He studied as a Horizonte and Fulbright scholarship holder at Goethe University, Frankfurt, and California State University, Fullerton. Parts of his debut memoir were put on stage in the German National Library, Frankfurt. His memoir was also a finalist of the 2019 Restless Books contest for New Immigrant Writing. Junis is currently studying to receive his doctorate in modern political theory at the University of Heidelberg.

# WORKS CITED AND FURTHER READINGS

1. Arendt, Johanna. *The Origins of Totalitarianism.* Mariner Books, 1951.

2. Bourdieu, Pierre. *Reproduction in Education, Society and Culture.* SAGE Publications Ltd, 1990.

3. Clark, Ramsey. *The Impact of Sanctions on Iraq: The Children Are Dying.* World View Forum Pub, 1996.

4. Cohen, Hillel. "A Weapon That Keeps Killing." *Challenge to Genocide,* edited by Ramsey Clark. Intl Action Center, 1998.

5. Committee of Privy Counsellors. *The Iraq Inquiry.* Accessed January 1, 2019. www.gov.uk/government/publications/the-report-of-the-iraq-inquiry.

6. Foucault, Paul-Michel. *Discipline and Punish: The Birth of the Prison.* Vintage Books, 1995.

7. Harris, Nadine Burke. *The Deepest Well: Healing the Long-Term Effects of Childhood Adversity.* Mariner Books, 2018.

8. Hilfiker, David. "Biologische Kriegsführer." *IPPNW forum 79,* 2003.

9. Hoeffel, Joseph M. *The Iraq Lie. How the White House Sold the War.* Progressive Press, 2014.

10. Kant, Immanuel. *Groundwork of the Metaphysics of Morals.* Translated and edited by Gregor, Mary and Timmerman, Jens. 2nd edition. Cambridge University Press, 2012.

11. Melby, Eric D.K. "Iraq." *Economic Sanctions and American Diplomacy,* edited by Haass, Richard N. Council on Foreign Relations Book, 1998.

12. Mellody, Pia. *Facing Codependence. What It Is, Where It Comes From, How It Sabotages Our Lives.* Harper One, 1989.

13. Rasche, Uta. "Einwanderungsland wider Willen." www.faz. net/aktuell/feuilleton/sarrazin/analyse-deutschland-ein-ein-wanderungs-land-wider-willen-1580276.html.

14. Raimann, Anna. "30 Years Lost." www.spiegel.de/politik/deutschland/gescheiterte-integrationspolitik-30-verlorene-jahre-a-452367.html.

15. Rosenberg, Ross. *The Human Magnet Syndrome: Why We Love People who Hurt Us.* Premier Publishing and Media, 2013.

16. Said, Edward Wadie. *Orientalism.* Vintage Books, 1978.

17. "Prejudices." Information on Political Education. (Number 271). Federal Central Office for Political Education. SKN Print and Publishers. Reprint: 2009.

18. Walker, Pete. *Complex PTSD: From Surviving to Thriving: A Guide and Map for Recovering from Childhood Trauma.* Azure Coyote Publishing, 2013.